To Colma
With the
and best
Work Jo

M000313389

Battlebabble: Tom lee

Selling War in America

A Dictionary of Deception

Thomas Lee

Common Courage Press   Monroe, Maine

Copyright 2005 © by Thomas Lee

Library of Congress Cataloging-in-Publication Data is available from publisher on request.
ISBN 1-56751-286-0 paper
ISBN 1-56751-287-9 hardcover

ISBN 13 paper: 9781567512861
ISBN 13 hardcover: 9781567512878

Common Courage Press
121 Red Barn Road
Monroe, ME 04951

207-525-0900
fax: 207-525-3068

www.commoncouragepress.com
info@commoncouragepress.com

First printing
Printed in Canada

CONTENTS

PREFACE

Wars demand deception. I am not referring to the technical complexities of military strategy, in which deception has always played a fundamental role. I leave that study to the professional scholars as well as to the amateur enthusiasts who enjoy poring over the minutiae of battle tactics.

Some become "war buffs," re-enacting what appears to spectators as entertaining, colorful scenes—typically from the Civil War. There are no living veterans of that savage era to recall the screams of the wounded and dying. No one remains to protest genteel representations of what were scenes of unspeakable horror, as young men slaughtered each other—sometimes by the thousands—on a few acres of green grass.

Few would contemplate dressing in World War II uniforms, and acting out the carnage of Iwo Jima, or Guadalcanal. There are many aging veterans still with us, some of whose bodies and all of whose minds bear the scars of those bloody days. Even less likely would be representations of the icy horrors of Chosin Reservoir, from 1950 during the Korean "Conflict," or the My Lai massacre of hundreds of innocents—including women and children—in Vietnam in 1968. But despite what might seem like a logical progression of increased sensitivity towards the human suffering exacted by war, exactly the opposite has happened.

The United States, under Presidents Bill Clinton, George H.W. Bush, and his son George W. Bush, has waged war on Iraq and Afghanistan in a merciless mix of bombings, invasions, and deadly sanctions. Why? In order to gain secure access to Iraq's abundant oil—perhaps one-quarter of total world reserves—and, more recently, to establish a dominant, permanent military presence in the Middle East, a key step in the younger Bush and his advisors' published plans for American world domination.

Such blatant, destructive, and lethal imperialism could only have been carried out with an orchestrated, elaborate, and relentless campaign of deception on the part of the U.S. government. Beginning with "Operation Desert Storm," the fanciful pseudonym for the first Gulf War against Iraq in 1991, and extending to the passing of "full sovereignty" to Iraq's interim government—whose leaders were carefully screened by the U.S.—a tidal wave of deceptive rhetoric poured from the White House, aimed at drowning reason and protest.

To make matters worse, advances in communications technology during that same period—spurred in part by the commercial possibilities of bringing exciting scenes of sanitized high-tech warfare into the living room of entertainment-hungry citizens—served as willing and effective channels for the flood. Well before the U.S.-led attack on Iraq in 2003, major news outlets vied for attention in breathless anticipation of what was to be a self-fulfilling prophecy referred to as "Countdown: Iraq," "Target Iraq," or "Showdown Iraq." During the war, the televised news in particular was a daily drama extolling the technical superiority of the "coalition of the willing" war machine.

The reports came complete with stirring music and "talking-heads," mostly retired military officers. Using maps, pointers, and advanced graphics, they blithely moved "assets," "columns," and "ordnance" about the desert, pausing now and then to mention how "we" were "cleaning up pockets of resistance," or "attriting the enemy."

Fox News, which was the top-rated cable news station throughout the 2003 war, boasted of its "fair and balanced" coverage. In reality it was, and remained, a daily show of deference to the Bush White House and an unquestioning pro-war outlet. The White House returned the tribute, making Fox its favored TV channel. According to United Press International (UPI), "Researchers from the Program on International Policy at the University of Maryland find that those who relied on Fox for their news were more likely to have what the study called 'significant misperceptions' about the war in Iraq."

* * *

I did not write this book out of paranoia or partisan bias. I wrote it out of regard for truth. My awareness of the deceptive language used to encourage support for war and the campaign to identify that approval with patriotism evolved gradually as I watched, listened, and read—and became appalled.

The campaign began in 1991. Those were heady days for CNN—then a fledgling cable network—as it featured streaking Patriot missiles blasting the evil Iraqi SCUDS out of the sky. Meanwhile the "smart bombs" with nose-mounted TV cameras took us along on their deadly trip into buildings, vehicles, or bridges, all seemingly devoid of living human beings. (Much later, the Patriot missiles, despite the hype, would turn out to be almost useless.) The bombs, "smart" and "dumb," went on with their business of killing and wounding uncounted thousands of soldiers and civilians—anonymous to us but not to their families—whose sufferings were scarcely noted.

I watched, read, and listened, as did a growing number of deeply concerned like-minded people, while economic sanctions imposed by the UN virtually shut off the Iraqi people from the outside world. Throughout the nineties the restrictions took their cruel toll, triggering disease and death—especially among young Iraqi children—whose deaths numbered in the hundreds of thousands. Enforcement of "no-fly" zones delivered a steady rain of bombs and missiles that compounded the suffering. Organizations such as Human Rights Watch, and the American Friends Service Committee, along with many other groups concerned with peace and justice, spoke out against this little-reported war of attrition, to little avail.

After the tragedy of 9/11 the George W. Bush administration

seized the opportunity and accelerated towards a full-scale attack on an already devastated Iraq—an invasion long desired by many of those who had become the President's advisors and Pentagon appointees. Worldwide protests erupted as millions of people took to the streets in a futile effort to thwart the impending slaughter. None of the foreign demonstrators were American voters, however, and were dismissed, many of them as an out-of-step "Old Europe." At home, thousands of concerned American citizens rallied against settling this dispute with violence, as the overwhelming might of the U.S. and the UK gathered, preparing to roll over the vulnerable Iraqi troops, who lacked even a credible air force.

By that time, however, the rhetoric of war had won the battle for the "hearts and minds" of mainstream America. Protestors were labeled as "unpatriotic" at best, and at worst, "traitors." President Bush shrugged off their appeals for a nonviolent solution as the unimportant complaints of "focus groups." According to Bush there were only two categories of people and nations—those that were "with us" or "against us." There was only one choice once the war was underway. We were to "support the troops." To do otherwise was to encourage the "enemy."

* * *

George Orwell most effectively highlighted the use of deceptive political language as a tyrant's tool in his mid-twentieth century book *Animal Farm*, *1984*, and his famous essay "Politics and the English Language." In the latter Orwell wrote, " Political language...is designed to make lies sound truthful and murder respectable, and to give an appearance of solidity to pure wind." He invented terms such as "newspeak" and "doublethink" for this attempt at thought control.

"Newspeak," according to Orwell, described words

"deliberately constructed for political purposes: words, that is to say, which not only had in every case a political implication, but were intended to impose a desirable mental attitude upon the person using them."

Orwell's writings—scathing criticisms of totalitarian societies that strip all freedoms from individual citizens, a nightmarish scenario controlled by "Big Brother" and the "Thought Police"—may seem a bit outdated. A contemporary scholar, Rutgers University professor William Lutz, has written a series of books that merge some of Orwell's principles with more modern misuses of language.

Lutz uses the term "doublespeak," an amalgam of two Orwellian expressions, "doublethink" and "newspeak." Lutz defines doublespeak as "language that evades responsibility, [that] tries to make something unpleasant seem pleasant...It's language that's designed to mislead while pretending to lead you someplace." He encompasses a wide range of usage under the category of doublespeak, from harmless expressions to deceptive manipulation.

For example, "passed away" is a benign euphemism often used out of sensitivity to another's grief. On the other hand, there is the example cited in the first annual "Doublespeak Award" given by the *Quarterly Review of Doublespeak* to a U.S. Air Force Colonel in Phnom Penh, Cambodia. He had complained to American reporters, "You always write it's bombing, bombing, bombing. It's not bombing, it's air support."

Lutz dissects the use of doublespeak in almost all walks of life, including its use by the government and the military. His category of doublespeak is broad enough to cover ordinary jargon, such as CO (commanding officer) or AWOL (absent without leave) or to "service the target" (to bomb). Lutz's observations go beyond mere interesting analyses of rhetorical devices. They come with this warning: " You must appreciate just how powerful language is...how words and labels come to define and create our world for us, how words influence and direct our thoughts and feelings, and how words thus influence our behavior...the corruption of public discourse can have consequences that reach far beyond anything we imagine."

* * *

The language used by U.S. political leaders, military officials, and by the mainstream media—from the marketing of the first Gulf War in 1991, through the years of cruel sanctions and the 2001 attack on Afghanistan to the 2003 Iraq invasion—reached new depths of perversion of public discourse.

The U.S. had allied itself with Saddam Hussein, even then a murderous dictator, in the 1980s, in support of Iraq's war against Iran, a bitter eight-year struggle that killed 1.5 million people. The White House demonized Saddam after his 1990 invasion of Kuwait to the extent that his cruelty, seemingly unnoticed earlier, was said to require a massive U.S.-led coalition to expel his troops.

Hill & Knowlton, at that time the world's largest public relations firm, ably assisted in the task of garnering U.S. public support for the invasion. Their $11.9 million PR blitz—which included sponsoring public rallies, and a blizzard of news releases and "information kits"—highlighted the impressive tale of "hundreds" of Kuwaiti babies torn from their incubators by invading Iraqis and left to die. The account was fictional.

By 2001, ten years of sanctions had inflicted bitter suffering on the Iraq people, but had left Saddam in power. Then, in 2001, the shocking attack on the Pentagon and the destruction of the World Trade Center on 9/11 killed over 3,000 people. Suddenly, there was a new enemy—terrorists—and the Bush administration identified this unprecedented attack on American soil with Iraq and Afghanistan. American and the world community deserved to grieve over the murders on 9/11, but this grief was manipulated and converted into a cry for revenge on those whom the administration identified as aiding and abetting the perpetrators.

In the build-up to the second Gulf War, which was cloaked in the heroic phrase "Operation Iraqi Freedom," the U.S. defied the UN's calls for restraint, and cobbled together a "coalition of the willing." The only ally of consequence was the United Kingdom (the majority of whose citizens objected), which offered extensive experience in subjugating and occupying foreign countries— including long, bloody stints in Iraq during the 1920s and 1940s.

Simple reason would suggest that the Bush administration campaign to justify Operation Iraqi Freedom should have been seen by most observers as a blatant ploy to gain access finally to Iraq's lands and oil. Tragically, it was a surprisingly successful effort that skillfully portrayed Sadddam Hussein's Iraq as an imminent, deadly threat to the safety of all Americans. Selling the subjugation of Afghanistan was even easier. After all, there were some known terrorist sites there, which the administration soon used as justification to raze the country into even deeper poverty and misery.

The language used to stoke American passions such that a majority of U.S. citizens approved of their government's actions during these years of destruction and death requires another category of rhetoric. I have chosen to call it "battlebabble."

* * *

Battlebabble is not the often-bizarre terminology of Orwell's imagination in *1984*, nor is it limited to the many euphemisms encompassed by William Lutz's "doublespeak." It is language that includes those now familiar euphemisms of war—"collateral damage," "friendly fire," or "air campaign," as well as newer inventions such as "depleted uranium," and "detainees."

However, it also utilizes terms long assumed to be simply neutral, or benevolent, or even inspiring. Terms such as "hero," "glory," "bravery," "liberation," and "humanitarian," "Committee for the Liberation of Iraq," and "Coalition Provisional Authority," come within the category of battlebabble. Many of these words paint a picture of a courageous people sending their own sons and daughters into "harm's way" to free the oppressed in a selfless act of mercy. Nothing could be more useful to a government intent on conquest and domination than to create that perception in their citizens.

The history of the twentieth century shows a remarkable evolution in the recognition of respect for the human individual. The civil rights movement, the struggle for equal rights for women, the insistence on greater access for the disabled—although still far from achieving their ultimate goals—nevertheless reflect a society increasingly sensitive to these and other vital social issues. And yet, that century featured war on a scale unimaginable to earlier generations. An estimated 52 million humans were killed in the Second World War alone.

In the 1940s human creativity reduced the technology of war to absurdity—fashioning nuclear weapons that, in a full-scale battle, could destroy not merely the "enemy" but the attackers themselves—and all life on the Earth. Only the U.S. has used those weapons—an act that will forever blight our history.

Even though a nuclear "exchange" between nations has so far been forestalled, even "conventional" (non-nuclear) weapons are now so devastating that warfare has become increasingly lethal to civilians as well as soldiers. How do we reconcile the gathering momentum of social progress with governments' unending insistence on war as the final arbiter of disputes?

I have no easy answer to that challenge. I do know, however, that in order to go to war, governments need to convince their people that their cause is just, noble, and vital to the nation's interests, despite any evidence to the contrary. That does not infer that citizens are simply dupes of the establishment. It does mean that the enormously complex web of biological instincts, learned behaviors, and psychological undercurrents that make up a human being have allowed a kind of conditioning to take place, convincing us to battle to the death and call it a noble act.

But this acquiescence, although certainly not universal, is itself subject to the same kind of social evolution that has seen the eradication of, for example, slavery (almost), torture (usually), and wholesale neglect of our physical environment (in part). There is a growing realization that our mutual survival is based on global cooperation—the antithesis of warfare. As Jonathan Schell expresses it in *The Unconquerable World: Power, Nonviolence, and the Will of the People*— his fascinating analysis of the practicality of peaceful means of global conflict resolution—"violence...has become dysfunctional as a political instrument."

There must, then, be a "third way"—a nonviolent middle path between mere passive submission to the whims of despotic leaders and choosing to unleash the horrors of warfare. To hold this conviction, as I and many others do, is not to deny the reality of terrible injustices carried out by unscrupulous individuals and governments. Saddam Hussein, for example, was brutal and murderous. So too is the government of Sudan, which, as I write, is launching a genocidal slaughter of its black African population in western Sudan's Darfur region.

The U.S. government, professing repulsion at Saddam's cruelty—which was ignored when he was our ally—chose to launch a massive military invasion propelled by propaganda. Meanwhile, the U.S. has dutifully begun to send some assistance to the suffering victims in Sudan, without the same sense of urgency. After all, Sudan—where a civil war has raged for two decades at a cost of at least 2 million human lives—has little that the U.S. needs or wants.

* * *

How are we to respond to these and to similar crises in an effective yet nonviolent way? Mairead Maguire, recipient of the 1976 Nobel Peace Prize urges, "We need to pursue Gandhi's dream of unarmed, international peacemaking teams which resolve international conflict not through military solutions but nonviolent means. The world's governments need not only to reject military solutions, but to create and finance international nonviolent conflict resolution programs." The 1998 Nobel Peace Prize laureate John Hume agrees, saying, "Instead of sending armies to areas of conflict, we should send a philosophy of peace, accompanied by a large delegation of facilitators who would promote dialogue among conflicting factions."

The conviction that war is not the final resort, but a totally unacceptable alternative, is worlds away from the usual assumptions of our society. However, the often-misunderstood practice of nonviolence, which goes beyond the principle of refusing to kill—simple pacifism—has a long history in this country, beginning in the early nineteenth century with the Quakers "speaking truth to power." In the 1960s Martin Luther King Jr.— inspired by Gandhi's concept of the "shanti sena," an army of nonviolence—embraced this approach to propel the civil rights struggle. That courageous and effective movement exemplified well the War Resisters League's David McReynolds' definition of nonviolent action as "a practical, workable way to change society, not an abstract set of theories."

There are a number of small-scale but encouraging efforts currently underway which offer another choice for confronting serious international conflicts. They are practiced, organized responses that reject the stereotypical call for violence and seek another way through mediation, support, and attention to the root causes of the confrontation. For example, Peace Brigades

International (www.peacebrigades.org) teams have worked in Guatemala, El Salvador, Colombia, and elsewhere to provide moral support and assistance to local peace activists. Another organization, the Nonviolent Peaceforce (NP) is a project being developed to "mobilize and train an international nonviolent, standing intervention force." NP (www.nonviolentpeaceforce. org) already is active in Sri Lanka.

These and other so-called "peace" groups—a term often used as a pejorative by those who scorn such idealism—continue to proliferate. All are propelled by the conviction that we need to wage peace instead of war, for the sake of suffering humanity. In this country the many peace activists offer the logical proposition that their government should put at least as much effort into working towards the elimination of war as an acceptable alternative to settling international disputes as it puts into creating a mighty military machine that threatens the survival of civilization.

This seemingly modest proposal is the basis for Congressman Dennis Kucinich's campaign to call for the establishment of "a cabinet-level department in the executive branch of the Federal Government dedicated to peacemaking and the study of conditions that are conducive to both domestic and international peace." This "Department of Peace," according to the Ohio democrat would be "headed by a Secretary of Peace, appointed by the President with the advice and consent of the Senate."

The Department of Peace would aim to develop policies "that promote national and international conflict prevention, nonviolent intervention, mediation, peaceful resolution of conflict and structured mediation of conflict."

The response by much of the mainstream media to these ideas, and to Kucinich's campaign for the 2004 Democratic presidential nomination, was reminiscent of the conclusion to Mark Twain's riveting *War Prayer*. Twain wrote this antiwar parable during the Philippine-American War in the first decade of the twentieth century. It was published, according to his wishes, only after his death, and features a sermon delivered by a stranger who enters a patriotic church service blessing young men going to war. He points out to the congregation that they are praying unwittingly that God will help these soldiers to destroy human lives. Twain ends by writing, "It was believed afterward that the man was a lunatic, because there was no sense in what he said."

* * *

I have written this book out of step with the constant drumbeat of war, and out of synchrony with the rhythms of governmental and media rhetoric that equate heroism and courage with dispensing death and destruction.

Each of us can lead loving, compassionate, nonviolent lives ruled by reason—or we can kill each other if we give in to our human drives towards aggression and fear, particularly when those inclinations are aided and abetted by governments and individuals who persuade us that we are not really a global human family but a collection of armed camps.

I have no pretensions that this book can make a totally compelling case for universal peace and nonviolence. However, I do want to make a contribution towards that vital goal by clarifying some of the language of persuasion that impels us towards war—the battlebabble that pollutes our air and stifles our better instincts. I hope that this dictionary—presented not necessarily in order of importance but in alphabetical order for convenience—will help to alert the reader to the facts rather than the fictions behind the words.

* * *

Finally, this is not an anti-soldier book, a diatribe against the young men and women who are asked to risk their lives at their government's bidding. As former West Point instructor Lt. Col. Dave Grossman explains in chilling detail in his book *On Killing*, armies are made up of young people who are trained in methods honed over the centuries to kill on command, motivated almost solely to defend their own lives and the lives of their close comrades.

It would be unfair to condemn young soldiers for acting out what their training has conditioned them to do—to kill and maim whomever their government and superiors identify as the enemy. All of us, soldiers and civilians alike, have been threatened with drowning in a sea of rhetoric—a battlebabble used to soften and hide the grim realities of the new American colonialism in the Persian Gulf and elsewhere.

A

"Then Abram bound the youth with belts and strops,
And builded parapets and trenches there,
And stretched forth the knife to slay his son.
When lo! an angel called him out of heaven,
Saying, Lay not thy hand upon the lad.
Neither do anything to him. Behold,
A ram, caught in a thicket by its horns;
Offer the Ram of Pride instead of him. "
But the old man would not so, but slew his son,
And half the seed of Europe, one by one.

Wilfred Owen—World War I

Abrams tank: The M1 Abrams, officially commissioned by the U.S. military in 1980, has become the core of the U.S. armored forces. It also serves as a model for a popular child's toy.

Redesigned over the years, the Abrams evolved into a rugged, speedy and deadly machine. According to (www.army-technology.com) the Abrams M1A1 version is sheathed in "steel encased depleted uranium armor." Abrams tanks have enormous firepower, including toxic *depleted uranium* shells. They also have thermal sights, which means that they could "see," for example, through the thick black smoke from the burning Kuwaiti oil fields, and locate men and machines in blinding dust storms.

Many of the Iraqi tanks were older Soviet models. They lacked long-range guns and night vision. A political cartoon in a Sunday *London Times* portrayed an Iraqi tank on maneuvers. On the tank was a sign seen frequently on American cars: "Baby on Board." That was in sharp contrast to a hand-painted sign displayed on an American tank during the *Gulf War* which read: "Killing is our business, and business is good."

War buffs can purchase a 1/35 scale replica of the newest

Abrams tanks from the Japanese model manufacturer Tamiya, Inc. with "all you need to replicate (the) U.S. main battle tank during Operation Iraqi Freedom." Accessories such as an "M2 machine gun" and "Combat identification Panels" are included. If that seems too complicated, Hobbytech sells a 1:16 scale model M1A1 Abrams tank. It is "an impressive model for a child...it is fully functional and includes all the gear to get rolling." One's child presumably can look forward to hours of fun, simulating killing Iraqis (see *action figures, glory, military games, military training, military recruitment).*

Academies: Elite academic institutions, under the jurisdiction of the U.S. Department of Defense, where carefully selected, intelligent young men and women are taught to become military officers, willing and able to lead and inspire others to kill and *defeat* whoever the U.S. government decides is an *enemy.*

Admission to West Point, the Air Force Academy, and the Naval Academy is highly competitive. Those selected are considered to be privileged to enter these institutions, which offer rigorous programs in academic, military and moral education. For example, the United States Naval Academy's Character Development Program states that one of its goals is "to develop midshipmen who possess a clearer sense of their own moral beliefs and the ability to articulate them." Their Honor Concept is "based on the moral values of respect for human dignity, respect for honesty and respect for the property of others."

The graduates of the Academies are skilled, competent and disciplined men and women, dedicated to fulfilling what they see is their duty to their country with honor, courage and efficiency (see *bravery).* The nature of that duty was well described by Malham M. Wakin, Air Force Brigadier General (Ret.), professor emeritus at the United States Air Force Academy, in the Spring 2001 Notre Dame Magazine. He had been asked to comment on the unsuccessful attempt by a Catholic pacifist group to remove the ROTC program from campus.

Wakin, stressing the need for a professional military, wrote "The American concept of 'total war' has had to yield to the model of war as an instrument of politics. The primary mission of the profession of arms is to contain violence at the lowest level consistent with the achievement of limited political aims...The decision to commit military forces and the size of those commitments [are] made by civilian leaders elected by our civilians and so authorized to make those decisions. In a democracy, military professionals do not decide when or where the military instrument is to be deployed."

Only in recent years have women been admitted to the military academies. Given the purpose of those institutions, some object to the practice. Captain John F. Luddy, USMCR, a defense policy analyst with The Heritage Foundation, writing in the December, 1995 Marine Corps Gazette maintained that "They [women] are entirely incompatible with the military's main purpose: to transform a group of individuals into an efficient unit for the purpose of inflicting extreme and deliberate violence—in the words of one Army major, 'to kill people and break things.'" Luddy concludes "The presence of women in their midst requires men training for war to be sensitive, even as women are expected to join them in becoming insensitive enough to bayonet people."

In 1849 Henry David Thoreau wrote "The mass of men serve the state thus, not as men mainly, but as machines, with their bodies...they put themselves on a level with wood and earth and stones; and wooden men can perhaps be manufactured that will serve the purpose as well."

One and one half centuries later, the paradox of showering accolades on the bright, sincere, and idealistic young men and women who prepare studiously for leadership roles in the savageries of war at the behest of their political superiors continues unabated.

action figure: Any of a wide variety of dolls, which the manufacturers prefer to call "figures." Many of these are dressed in military garb and are sold by the millions to children and adults. In 1964, as the U.S. was sending "advisors" to Vietnam, Hasbro— the second-largest U.S. toy retailer —introduced "G.I. JOE." This classic military action figure made his debut as an 11-1/2 inch doll "with 21 moving parts." Paul Wolfowitz, Deputy Secretary of Defense under George W. Bush, served on the Hasbro board before he accepted the Pentagon position (see *military games, Project for the New American Century*).

As the years and wars ensued, JOE's horizons expanded to many other expressions, such as the bionic warrior "Atomic Man" in 1975,and in 2000, the "Bomb Disposal" JOE, with a bomb that detonates if disarmed incorrectly. By 2004 one could even purchase, for $11.99, the "G.I. JOE Military Basic: Armament Specialist (Hispanic)." According to Hasbro, he "depends on his M2.50 caliber machine gun, also known as 'Ma Deuce'...ages 5 & up."

Other manufacturers have entered this lucrative market. For example, Cotswold Collectibles offers "Gil: F-18 Enduring Freedom Pilot." Gil, at $43.99, is "stationed aboard the U.S.S. Enterprise" and carries "a great set of tiny accessories, including... survival drinking water and a map of Afghanistan...Gil has a concerned expression, pinkish skin tone, and very blond hair." The Cotswold collection also features "Stanley: Sniper, Baghdad." At $39.99, Stanley is "kitted out as a sniper trolling for targets around the city." He wears "extra cool sunglasses."

Hero Builders, Danbury, CT offers a 12-inch talking action figure of "Dual-Headed Uday" for a mere $39.95. Uday, Saddam Hussein's son, was killed along with his brother Qusay by U.S. troops in July, 2003. Uday's dual head can be turned to show "one side, Uday alive" and the "other side, Uday blowed-up." Uday says, in a faux-Arab voice "Someone must help me. I...I am still alive only I am very badly burned. Anyone! Can someone please call my father? I am in a lot of pain, I am very badly burned so if you could just (gunshot), you shot me! Why did you (3 gun shots)."

The "Talking Presidents" company in Irvine, CA now offers the "TOP GUN George W. Bush Action Figure" for $29.99 (see *mission accomplished*). The President is "dressed in a full flight suit...identical to the (one) George Bush wore when he landed on the flight deck of the U.S.S. Abraham Lincoln...The figure captures the good ol' boy essence of the original George, from his rugged Texas back country good looks to his characteristic placid political face."

"Talking Presidents" also sells the "Ann Coulter Talking Action Figure" for the same price. The Ms. Coulter figure, modeled after the well-known conservative syndicated columnist and frequent T.V. commentator will repeat any of 14 short phrases "when you press her button." The phrases do not include her comment offered several days after the 9/11 tragedy: " This is no time to be precious about locating the exact individuals directly involved in this particular terrorist attack...We should invade their countries, kill their leaders, and convert them to Christianity. We weren't punctilious about locating and punishing only Hitler and his top officers. We carpet-bombed German cities; we killed civilians, that's war. And this is war."

Advanced Unitary Penetrator (AUP): This powerful weapon is a fine example of the military's fondness for Freudian imagery. GlobalSecurity.org (www.globalsecurity.org) describes the AUP, equipped with the "Hard Target Smart Fuze (HTSF)" as having an "elongated narrow case...The 1,700 pound warhead is tucked inside a lightweight...'outer skin.'" It can penetrate "eleven feet of reinforced concrete." The HTSF allows the bomb to wait until it penetrates deep inside the target, such as a bunker or other facility, before it explodes.

This ability of the AUP—which can be adapted to many of the Air Force's large bombs (see *bunker buster*)—to penetrate deeply is usually described as being enhanced by having "heavy metals" in its warhead. Common Dreams (www.commondreams. org) notes that "there is a high probability that... (depleted uranium) is the main component of the advanced unitary penetrator used in guided bomb systems."

Boeing and Lockheed-Martin make the AUP. Both companies, along with Northrop Grumman, Raytheon, and Alliant Techsystems are listed on The Perpetual War Portfolio website (www.rationalenquirer.org), which tracks "five stocks poised to succeed in the age of perpetual war. The stocks were selected on the basis of popular product lines, strong political connections and lobbying efforts, and paid-for access to key Congressional decision-makers" (see *endless war*).

In 1999, during Operation Allied Force in Kosovo, some *soldiers* decided to give some advice to the *enemy* in the form of messages scrawled on the AUPs. They wrote, "You can run, but why die tired?"

aerial ordnance: *bombs* and missiles dropped from military airplanes in order to destroy inanimate targets and/or kill people. In *Operation Desert Storm*, coalition forces dropped 256,000 bombs, mostly of the "unguided," *dumb* type. *Operation Iraqi Freedom* used 27,000, most of which were computer-or satellite-guided (see *collateral damage, precision-guided munitions, smart bombs*).

These included *Hellfire missiles* fired from unmanned aerial vehicles such as the Predator UAV. These aircraft were used, according to the U.S. Air Force, for "delivering ordnance with pinpoint accuracy in combat zones deemed too 'hot' for manned aircraft." They are part of the emerging *high-tech battlefield* equipment planned by the Pentagon, with emphasis on killing efficiently from a safe distance.

aerial sorties: military airplanes taking off from airfields or aircraft carriers, often for the purpose of releasing *bombs* and missiles in order to destroy buildings and war machinery, and/ or to kill people. For example, the book *War and Health*, co-published in 2000 by the American Public Health Association and Oxford University Press reported that the "more than 80,000 tons of explosives dropped by coalition forces led by the U.S. killed between 50,000 and 100,000 Iraqi soldiers...Between 2,500 and 3,500 innocent civilians were killed during the air campaign"(see *casualties*). During *Operation Desert Storm* there were over 120,000 air sorties, while in *Operation Iraqi Freedom* there were more than 41,000.

airburst: the explosion of a *bomb* or other explosive device above the surface, raining death and destruction below. Various forms of such weapons were used against Iraq very effectively in 1991 and in 2003. Prominent among them were *cluster bombs*, such as the CBU-87 cluster bomb. This bursts in the air, releasing over 200 smaller *bomblets* which in turn fragment into hundreds of steel splinters over an area the size of four football fields. These are particularly damaging to *soft targets,* i.e. humans.

Artillery shells, used to kill people at a distance—which tends to make the act more palatable—can be set to explode above the surface as well. In addition, another fine example of an airburst is the one that occurs upon the detonation of *fuel-air explosives.* These weapons consist of containers of fuel and explosive charges. First, the fuel container bursts open, spreading the fuel into an enormous mist, which then ignites, creating a ferocious blast wave, incinerating anyone or anything in its vicinity.

At many public gatherings in the U.S., especially sporting events, or even church services, hearts swell with pride as the group sings the national anthem, including the lines, "...the bombs bursting in air, gave proof thro' the night that our flag was still there." This national hymn was written in 1814 during the Revolutionary War—one more war that could have been avoided through nonviolent means of dissent.

air campaign: concerted attacks on the *enemy* from the air. For example, in 1998 President Clinton canceled a planned air campaign against Iraq after Saddam Hussein pledged to cooperate with UN weapons inspectors. Charles Krauthammer, writing in the *Washington Post* noted that "the military's estimate of casualties from [this] initial strike" had been "10,000 Iraqi dead." Regardless, he complained that Clinton had "flinched." Krauthammer bemoaned the missed chance of launching a "relentless air campaign." Richard Cohen's column in the same issue noted "the Clinton administration waited too long. It needed to punch out Iraq's lights, and it did not do so." The *New York Post* accused President Clinton of not being able to "act like a man."

air support: attacks from the air, usually ordered by *soldiers* on the ground, in order to kill the *enemy* that they are encountering. William Lutz, author of *The New Doublespeak* and other books on the world of euphemisms, declared a U.S. Air Force Colonel the first recipient of a "Doublespeak Award." In 1974, the colonel complained to reporters in Phnom Penh, Cambodia," You always write it's bombing, bombing, bombing. It's not bombing, it's air support."

During *Operation Iraqi Freedom* most of the devastating air support was supplied by A-10s, attack planes that carry a 30mm Gatling gun capable of firing 3,900 rounds per minute and dropping up to 16,000 pounds of *bombs*.

air supremacy: achieved when one side in a war takes control of the skies over and surrounding the battle area by destroying most of the *enemy* planes and air defenses and killing their pilots and the people in their ground crews. By 1987, near the end of the *Iran-Iraq war*, a war during which the U.S. had supported Iraq, the Iraqi Air Force had nearly 750 aircraft, including Soviet MiGs and French Mirage fighters. In 1991, during the brief *Gulf War*, the far better equipped and trained U.S. Air Force quickly destroyed whichever of these Iraqi aircraft was not able to flee.

By 2003, after years of UN *sanctions* had, among other hardships, forced the cannibalization of their planes for spare parts, the Iraqis had only about 100 planes left in service. They played no part in *Operation Iraqi Freedom*. In the words of a March 31, 2003 report for *The Center for Strategic and International Studies,* "Iraq's air force and army aviation are definitely the dogs that didn't bark."

Air supremacy held by the U.S. and its *allies* allowed virtually unmolested access to the skies. This prompted many observers to describe those *Operations* as "slaughters" rather than as wars (see *turkey shoot).*

allies: countries which the U.S. coerced, cajoled or convinced in order to add their military forces and funds to those of the U.S. to support the attacks on Iraq. In the *Gulf War*, the allied coalition consisted of 34 countries, including France, Germany, and Canada. The non-U.S. troops numbered 295,000 compared to 430,000 from the U.S.. During *Operation Iraqi Freedom* approximately 49 countries, which included some of the above-mentioned (but not Germany, France, or Canada) joined the U.S. in a *coalition of the willing.* More than 300,000 coalition troops were sent to the Gulf region in 2003. Those included 250,000 U.S. soldiers, with the rest from Britain, Australia— and 200 from Poland.

American Enterprise Institute (AEI): One of America's most influential think tanks whose members, when deliberating on questions of international relations, usually think of tanks.

The AEI, founded in 1943, originally was considered a rather even-handed forum, until it assumed a marked conservative flavor in the 1980s. In fact, on the eve of the U.S.-led invasion of Iraq in March, 2003 President Bush remarked at AEI's annual dinner: "We meet here during a crucial period in the history of the [United States] and of the civilized world. Part of that history was written by others; the rest will be written by us." The president complimented AEI for having "some of the finest minds in our nation" and added, "You do such good work that my administration has borrowed 20 such minds."

Some of those "minds" borrowed by the White House included John Bolton, an AEI vice president who became undersecretary of state for arms control and international security affairs, and Richard Perle, who joined the *Defense Policy Board*. Jeane J. Kirkpatrick led the U.S. delegation to the UN Human Rights Commission, while James K. Glassman would serve as a member of the State Department's Advisory Group on Public Diplomacy in the Arab and Muslim World. While she perhaps does not qualify as a "borrowed mind" the wife of U.S. Vice President Dick Cheney, Lynne Cheney, is an AEI senior fellow.

The AEI is by no means the only conservative think tank with a conservative influence in Washington, D.C. Along with the AEI, the Hudson Institute, the Hoover Institute, and The Heritage Foundation all are funded by "a select but loyal group of like-minded foundations and corporate sponsors" according to a 2002 report by Jill Junnola on the Campus Watch website (www.campus-watch.org). These backers include, in part, the Lynde and Harry Bradley, the Smith Richardson, and the John M.

Olin Foundations. AEI's board includes Lee Raymond, chair and CEO of Exxon Mobil, and William Stavropoulos, chair of Dow Chemical Co.

There is a complex network of relationships among those affiliated with the AEI. It includes members of the *Project for the New American Century* (PNAC)—the authors of *Rebuilding America's Defenses*: *Strategy, Forces and Resources for a New Century* (RAD)—as well the *Committee for the Liberation of Iraq* (CLI) and the *Committee for Peace and Security in the Gulf* (CPSG). All of these had a hand in fostering the 2003 invasion of Iraq. The website of the Interhemispheric Resource Center (IRC), (www.rightweb.irc-online.org), reveals "the many ties that link the right-wing movement's main players, corporate supporters, educational institutions, and government representatives to each other in a new architecture of power."

American peace: according to President George W. Bush—and the people behind his throne who supply him with ideas—a vision of the entire world at "peace" under the military and economic domination of the United States. This happy state will come about without interference from the United Nations and without concern for international law. The world will be at the service of America's *national interests* (see *Pax Americana*).

Amiriya bunker: In the early morning of February 13, 1991, a U.S. Stealth fighter released two powerful laser-guided *bombs.* They quickly sought out and pierced the concrete and steel roof of a large *bomb* shelter, built in the middle-class Amiriya section of Baghdad in order to protect civilians during the *Iran-Iraq War*. The bombs exploded inside the shelter, tearing apart and incinerating most of the approximately 400 people hiding there from U.S. raids.

Even the sanitized video footage televised by the BBC and

ITN appalled viewers, who had been to that point impressed with the military's boasts of *smart bombs* which avoided civilian *casualties* (see *collateral damage*).

The U.S. and its allies immediately claimed that the bunker had been a "military facility," housing a "command and control center." If in fact, civilians had been in the facility, they insisted, had not Saddam Hussein put them there for propaganda purposes? According to the February 14, 1991 *Washington Post Foreign Service*, on the day after the carnage, Army Lt. Gen. Thomas Kelly, operations director for the Joint Chiefs of Staff told reporters: "We are chagrined if (civilian) people were hurt..."

Among other issues raised by this slaughter was the question as to how the media should report the horrors of war. John Taylor, in his detailed analysis of this question in *Body Horror: Photojournalism, Catastrophe and War (The Critical Image)* reports the following attitude. Ron Spark, chief lead writer for the *Sun* wrote, "A newspaper that tells only part of the truth is a million times preferable to one that tells the truth to harm its country."

antemortem identification media: according to the U.S. Department of Defense, these are "Records, samples and photographs taken prior to death...These pre-death records would be compared against records completed after death to help establish a positive identification of a remains."

Many instances of widespread DNA sampling have caused public controversy. For example, in 1994 the U.S. military began to require all military personnel and many employees of civilian contractors to give DNA samples. These could be used as "genetic dog tags" in case, as so often happens in this era of powerful weapons, only fragments remained of a person's body after he/she was killed in combat.

In 1996, two Marines stationed in Hawaii refused to donate

such samples. They cited the well documented potential for abuses which could result from the U.S. Government keeping these samples in storage for many years, including, for example, the use of DNA analysis to "weed out" those with "high-risk" genes who were applying for medical insurance.

Both men were court-martialed and found guilty. The Marine Corps prosecutor had requested a sentence of six months confinement and a dishonorable discharge. However, they were given a written reprimand and confined for only eight days. The publicity from this trial led to Congress passing a law in 1996, which limits the use of the DNA databank to casualty and criminal identification.

Now, although the military retains the DNA samples for 50 years, individuals may request that, upon their discharge, their samples be destroyed.

antipersonnel devices: "personnel" are people. "Devices" are anything that is constructed to kill, injure, wound, and mutilate people. "Devices" do not distinguish between soldiers and civilians, or among men, women and children. The only limits to the form that such devices can take is the range of human ingenuity. Over the centuries, antipersonnel devices have moved from the primitive though effective club or spear to the more highly technical contemporary tools such as *biological and chemical weapons*, *fuel-air explosives, landmines, cluster munitions*, and *nuclear* weapons.

The techniques of modern warfare, evolving throughout the twentieth century, became remarkably efficient. Over 8 million soldiers and as many civilians were killed in World War I. During the Second World War, just a few decades later, 17 million soldiers and 35 million civilians were killed.

A new century brings new opportunities to expand techniques to bring suffering and death to the *enemy.* For example, military affairs analyst William Arkin detailed a good example of such creativity in the *Los Angeles Times* (December 8, 2002). He describes a "microwave weapon...designed to inflict intense pain on human skin...as antipersonnel weapons, [they] send a narrow beam of energy that penetrates the skin...heating [it] to 122 degrees Fahrenheit...the microwaves inflict intense pain; often, the reaction they produce is panic." Arkin describes an "enormous effort" to move this weapon to "combat readiness."

There are some scruples about some antipersonnel devices. The microwave weapon, for example, in order to be approved under "existing treaties and international law" must "inflict pain" while avoiding "burning, eye damage or other prolonged effects that could be 'unnecessary suffering.'"

There are antipersonnel methods that lie outside the strict definition of "devices" but which may be at least as effective in causing "unnecessary suffering." John Pilger, looking back in the *Sydney Morning Herald* (June 22, 2000) on the effects of the American-led invasion of Iraq in 1991 wrote: "In evidence before the House of Commons Foreign Affairs Select Committee, the major international relief agencies reported that 1.8 million people had been made homeless, and Iraq's water, sewerage, communications, health, agriculture and industrial infrastructure had been 'substantially destroyed', producing 'conditions for famine and epidemics.'"

Apache helicopter: The U.S. military is fond of naming some of its powerful weapons after former victims. For example, the Apaches, still a proud people—though much diminished in numbers—are honored by the AH-64 Apache helicopter. This is the primary attack helicopter in the U.S. arsenal, and is favored as well by the UK, Israel and Saudi Arabia. Each costs $18 million. It is a *gunship/anti-tank* helicopter, carrying a variety of lethal weapons, including a chain gun, which can fire up to 650 rounds per minute, and as many as 16 *Hellfire missiles.*

The chain gun is a highly modified version of the infamous Gatling gun. This was patented in 1862 by Richard Gatling, an American medical doctor who imagined that the destructive power of this machine gun would terrify people into making war a thing of the past. However, the weapon and its improved versions would be used to terrifying effect in almost every conflict of the following half century. It proved to be very effective against Native Americans. The British used it as well against Indians during the occupation of that country.

The Apache-64 is portrayed by (www.science.howstuffworks.com) as "the most lethal helicopter ever created...a terrifying machine to ground forces. (It's) chief function is to take out heavily armored ground targets, such as tanks and bunker*s*" (see *take out*).

The U.S. Army also destroys tanks, vehicles, and people with the more advanced Apache Longbow, the Kiowa warrior, and the Blackhawk.

area denial munitions: Landmines. The International Committee of the Red Cross (ICRC) regards landmines as "the greatest violators of international humanitarian law."

Landmines are relatively simple, small weapons. Fashioned of wood, metal or plastic, they contain explosives that detonate from slight direct pressure, or by tripwires, tilt rods, or by remote control. Blast mines are the most common. They are plastic cylinders often scattered by the thousands over wide areas from airplanes. Fragmentation mines are mounted on stakes. When someone touches the tripwire, the mine bursts into metal fragments, which mutilate and kill. Bounding mines are buried, with protruding spikes, which when touched cause the mines to burst up through the ground several feet. They then explode, scattering fragments up to 300 feet.

Adults may survive, though mutilated, although they may often lose a limb. Children, being smaller and more vulnerable, often lose one or more limbs, and may suffer severe injuries to the genitals and abdomen, blindness and disfigurement.

Worldwide, over 100 million landmines have been planted in 70 countries since World War II. Since 1975, landmines have killed and/or mutilated more than 1 million people. Some landmines—the so-called "dumb" variety—may remain active for as long as 50 years. Newer "smart" versions self-destruct after a predetermined time. According to the Human Rights Watch (HRW) *Landmine Monitor Report* of 2003, the U.S. apparently did not use landmines banned by international treaties during *Operation Iraqi Freedom.*

However, they did use Claymore mines. A Claymore is detonated on command, sending out a fan-shaped hail of hundreds of small steel spheres that can injure and kill people within a hundred yard radius. A recent text on alternatives to landmines, referring to Claymores, says " On the positive side, from the humanitarian perspective, the Claymore may enable a soldier to discriminate between combatants and noncombatants before detonating a mine."

HRW (www.hrw.org) reports, "The Pentagon refused to rule out landmine use in Iraq...at least 90,000 antipersonnel mines were stockpiled in the region prior to the conflict." In 1991, the U.S. and their allies scattered 117,634 landmines, mostly from the air, while Iraq forces deployed many more. The Iraqi mines were purchased from China, former Soviet nations, and Italy.

Since 1997, 150 countries have signed the "Convention on the Prohibition of the Use, Stockpiling, Production and Transfer of Antipersonnel Mines and on Their Destruction," usually referred to as the Ottawa Treaty, or Mine Ban Treaty. The United States, along with over 60 other countries—including most countries in the Middle East—has not. President Clinton committed the U.S. to adhering to the Treaty by 2006 "if alternatives have been identified and fielded." One rationale offered for noncompliance has been that our country has "unique responsibilities for international security"(see *Rebuilding America's Defenses)*.

In late February 2004, President Bush unveiled a new landmine policy. It renounced Clinton's earlier goal of broad compliance. While Bush did agree to eliminate 1.2 million landmines of the "dumb" variety (see *conventional weapons*) he decided not to destroy the more than 9 million of the "smart" variety in U.S. stockpiles. The 2004 "Fact Sheet on New United States Policy on Landmines" states that while the U.S. "is committed to eliminating the humanitarian risks posed by landmines...the military capabilities provided by landmines remain necessary for the United States military to protect our forces and save lives." Also, the U.S. will continue to produce "smart" landmines. The executive director of Human Rights Watch (www.hrw.org), Stephen Goose, called this decision " a shocking reversal of U.S. policy...[it] completely undermines any claim the U.S. has to be a leader on this issue."

The *New Scientist* reported in 2003 that the U.S. is interested in developing a theoretically "non-lethal" landmine. The prototype Taser Area Denial Device (TADD), when triggered, fires darts attached by lightweight electrical cables. These transmit high-voltage electrical pulses of up to 50,000 volts, incapacitating the victim.

armed humanitarian intervention: the launching of a military assault on another country or region, without its permission, in order to prevent or end widespread grave human rights violations occurring there. There have been interventions that have been authorized by the United Nations, such as in Bosnia in 1993. Others, like NATO's attack on Kosovo in 1999, were carried out without asking for UN permission for fear that the Security Council might withhold it.

The international debate on the possible justification of armed humanitarian intervention was complicated by the U.S.-led coalition's massive attack on Iraq in 2003, done without UN authorization. Humanitarian reasons were invoked, but were overshadowed, at least initially, by rationales for a *pre-emptive strike* to prevent the use of alleged *weapons of mass destruction*, and an opportunity to strike a blow at an alleged center of terrorism.

In the 2000 document *Humanitarian Intervention: Crafting a Workable Doctrine—Three Options Presented as Memoranda to the President*, prepared by the U.S. Council on Foreign Relations, the authors ask," Faced with massive violence against innocent human beings by their governments or by their neighbors, what are other governments to do? Stand by? Or act forcefully, if necessary, to halt the killing and establish order?"

Neither choice speaks to the essential question of the underlying causes for the crisis, nor do they offer any sense that there could ever be a large-scale, co-operative nonviolent response. John Tirman asks in the December 2003/January 2004 *Boston Review,*" If obligations exist to ameliorate calamities underway, are there obligations to prevent calamities? Are not the origins of a crisis useful in sorting out remedies?...It is as if to say, 'we will tolerate brutal regimes and deprivation unless and until conditions are so severe that only the military can rescue the victims.'"

arms control: a largely unrealized ideal of limiting or even halting the manufacture and trade in arms ranging from handguns to *nuclear weapons*. There are no binding international laws controlling the export of *conventional weapons*. In the mid-1970s President Jimmy Carter tried to restrain U.S. military arms sales, especially to underdeveloped nations. These efforts failed as a result of the increasing use of arms sales as a tool of "diplomacy."

As the U.S. Commission on Integrated Long-Term Strategy stated in 1988, "Where American intervention seems necessary, it will generally require far more cooperation with Third World countries than has been required in the past."

This philosophy continues to drive arms sales and inhibit meaningful control. In the 1980s the U.S. and the Soviet Union were the source of three-fifths of all arms sales to the Third World, while France, Great Britain, West Germany, Italy and China supplied 22 percent. President Ronald Reagan's undersecretary of state held that "This Administration believes that arms transfers...(can) serve as a vital and constructive instrument of our foreign policy."

Michael Klare pointed out in a report in the January/February 1991 *Bulletin of the Atomic Scientists*, " The Reagan Administration raised no objection to French sales of advanced missiles to Iraq, or to Brazilian sales of multiple-launch rocket systems...Reagan (and later Bush) authorized the sale to Iraq of $1.5 billion worth of sophisticated U.S. scientific and technical equipment—much of which has apparently been used in the development of conventional, nuclear, and chemical weapons. Indeed...Reagan and Bush continued to allow deliveries...long after Iraq had used chemical weapons in attacks on Iran and its own Kurds."

William Lutz, in *The New Doublespeak,* recalls the then President Bush's 1991 speech at the United States Air Force Academy in which he warned "Nowhere are the dangers of weapons of proliferation more urgent than in the Middle East." He announced, "I am today proposing a Middle East arms control initiative." Several days later, Secretary of Defense Dick Cheney explained "We simply cannot fall into the trap of...[saying] that arms control means we don't provide any arms to the Middle East." As Lutz points out, "the arms race in the Middle East continues unabated...actively aided by massive sales of arms."

The *Center For Defense Information* (CDI)(www.cdi.org) in its January 23, 2004 report *U.S. Post-Sept.11 Arms Trade Policy* warned of an emerging trend: "The United States is more willing than ever to sell or give away high technology weapons to countries that have pledged assistance in the global war on terror, regardless of past behavior or current status...countries that in the past have been criticized for human rights violations (and) lack of democracy...Arms transferred by the United States too often end up in the hands of terrorists...American weapons have also been used by Al Qaeda, insurgent groups in Sri Lanka and the Philippines, and misused by such governments as Colombia, Uganda, and Iraq."

The CDI, an important resource for details on the international arms trade, calculates that in 2003 "The value of global authorized arms exports (was) $29 billion per year...The United States was the leader in total worldwide arms sales in 2002, with about $13.3 billion, or 45 percent of global conventional weapons deals." The permanent members of the UN Security Council—France, Russia, China, the UK and the U.S. together are responsible for 88 percent of the world's arms trade.

A global network of non-governmental organizations is seeking greater controls on the international arms trade. Their October 9, 2003 report, *Shattered Lives: The Case for Tough International Arms Controls*, and a petition for its support, is available at www.controlarms.org.

artillery: large, crew-operated weapons such as howitzers and missile launchers, capable of killing at great distances. According to GlobalSecurity.org. "The Field Artillery mission is to destroy, neutralize, or suppress the enemy by cannon, rocket and missile fires..." (see *neutralize*).

Artillery killed the majority of people in the wars of the twentieth century. In the U.S.-led coalition attacks on Iraq in 1991 and 2003, "improved" *high-tech* artillery proved to be devastating, particularly those that launched *cluster munitions*. These include Multiple Launch Rocket Systems. Each contains 644 smaller *bomblets*. An estimated 5-20 percent of these bomblets fail to explode in the air. They lie, waiting, scattered across the ground. According to Human Rights Watch (www.hrw.org), these lethal leftovers, when stepped on or handled, killed and injured more than 4,000 civilians, many of them children, after *Operation Desert Storm*.

An October 31, 2003 article by Fred W. Baker III for the TRADOC News Service details some of the activity of the 2nd Battalion, 4th Field Artillery, Multiple Launch Rocket System Unit during *Operation Desert Storm*. He reports," For the first time in combat, it fired the Army Tactical Missile System Quick Reactionary Unitary missile (ATACM), capable of striking targets 300 kilometers away..." They fired 240 of these, as well as 168 M-26 tactical rockets. Both of these use cluster munitions.

Lt. Col. Dave Grossman, in his book *On Killing*, a detailed account of how men are taught to kill in combat, maintains, "There has never been any difficulty in getting artillerymen, bomber crews, or naval personnel to kill." He quotes from Gwynne Dyer's *War*; "On the whole however, distance is a sufficient buffer: gunners fire at grid references they cannot see." They can, says Dyer, "pretend they are not killing human beings."

assassination: Typically refers to killing a politically prominent person, such as a head of state, suddenly and secretively. In the year after September 11, 2001, according to investigative reporter Seymour M. Hersh in his book *Chain of Command: The Road from 9/11 to Abu Ghraib*, "The targeting and killing of individual Al Qaeda members without juridical process came to be seen within the Bush administration as justifiable military action in a new kind of war." Hersh quotes a July 22, 2002 directive from Secretary of Defense Donald Rumsfeld to Air Force General Charles Holland. The message included "The objective is to capture terrorists for interrogation, or, if necessary, to kill them, not simply to arrest them in a law-enforcement exercise."

The U.S. Army Field Manual 27-10, *The Law of Land Warfare* (1956) states: "This article [from the Hague Convention of 1907] is construed as prohibiting assassination...or putting a price on an enemy's head, as well as offering a reward for an enemy 'dead or alive.'" However, the interpretation and application of both U.S. and international law as it applies to assassination is the subject of much debate.

Professor Sebastian Jodoin, in a detailed analysis on Quid Novi Online (www.law.mcgill.ca) concerning the legality of an assassination of Saddam Hussein admits that the question is "a complex one." He cites the executive order issued by President Gerald Ford in 1975 that prohibited "political assassinations." President Jimmy Carter later removed the word "political," a move also reaffirmed by President Ronald Reagan. In February 2001 Senator Bob Barr (R-Georgia) introduced House Resolution 19, which proved to be an unsuccessful attempt to overturn the ban. According to Barr "The president of the United States...ought always to have the whole range of options."

Jodoin's opinion is that it is unclear whether the presidential executive order currently in force would apply in the case of *Operation Iraqi Freedom*, because it is also not clear if that war even conforms to U.S. Constitutional law.

Professor Jodoin adds as well, "the rules on [international] assassination are vague and unclear." Scholarly distinctions aside, the Bush administration made no secret of its intention to assassinate Saddam Hussein during *Operation Iraqi Freedom* in 2003. They assumed, incorrectly, that part of the *Shock and Awe* bombing would kill Saddam. Later, on April 9th, a CIA informant reported that the Iraqi leader and his two sons, Uday and Qusay, were meeting with top aides in a building in a residential area in Baghdad.

Within minutes, a B-1 bomber dropped four 2,000-pound *bombs* (see *bunker busters*), ripping apart the building, along with a nearby restaurant, and at least three homes. The dead numbered at least 18 civilians. An extensive analysis of their body fragments using DNA analysis (see *antemortem identification media*) failed to identify Saddam or others of the *enemy*.

In the aftermath of the war, which ended officially on May 1, 2003 (see *bring 'em on*), there was no shortage of blatant calls for Saddam's head. *New York Times* foreign affairs columnist Thomas Friedman wrote (November 6, 2003): "Saddam Hussein is the reason God created cruise missiles...So if and when Saddam pushes beyond the brink, and we get that one good shot, let's make sure it's a head shot." Former Clinton adviser George Stephanopoulos concluded on ABC's "This Week" (November 9, 2003): This is probably one of those rare cases where assassination is the more moral course...we should kill him."

Back in 1993, several years after the conclusion of *Operation Desert Storm*, U.S. and Kuwaiti intelligence services reported a plan to explode a powerful car *bomb* in an attempt to assassinate the then president George Bush during his visit to Kuwait. After analyzing the bomb, the C.I.A. and the F.B.I. concluded that Saddam's intelligence was behind the plot.

In retaliation, President Bill Clinton had the U.S. Navy launch 23 Tomahawk cruise missiles against the Iraqi intelligence headquarters in June 1993. In the November 1993 *New Yorker* investigative reporter Seymour M. Hersh wrote " The former F.B.I. chemist [Frederic Whitehurst] who tested the explosive recovered in Kuwait says he told superiors that it did not match known Iraqi explosives...When he later saw an official F.B.I. document misstating his findings, he filed an official protest. The inspector general's report eventually confirmed that Whitehurst's findings had been distorted, but said government officials assured investigators that they had other evidence linking the plot to Iraq."

assertive disarmament: a term coined by Dr. William Van Cleave when he was the chief strategic weapons advisor to America's Strategic Arms Limitation I (SALT I) delegation (1969-1972). He advocated destroying China's developing nuclear facilities in order to safeguard world peace. He referred to this as "assertive disarmament."

Such an attack, unprovoked except by the perception of a threat to the attacker and/or the wider community is more often termed "preemptive." An example of such a strike is the 1981 Israeli destruction of the Osirak nuclear reactor, which was being built with French assistance. On a larger scale, such actions are generally known as a *preemptive war,* such as *Operation Desert Storm.*

An associate of Van Cleave—Robert Lawrence, Department of Political Science, Colorado State University—champions the application of assertive disarmament to preempt nuclear terrorism. A summary of his remarks at a 2001 Toronto foreign policy conference asserts that "The potential devastation of (nuclear terrorism) warrants assertive disarmament...while the cooperation of other countries...would be preferable, the U.S. may have to proceed...unilaterally."

In June, 2002, President George W. Bush declared at the West Point commencement, "If we wait for threats to fully materialize, we will have waited too long." He told the cheering young officers, "We must take the battle to the enemy." Bush's challenge echoed that of Defense Secretary Donald Rumsfeld in 2001, when he remarked, "...the only way to deal with the terrorist network is to take the battle to them...That is, in effect, self-defense of a preemptive nature." Widening the net, the Bush administration's

2002 *National Security Strategy* states, "We make no distinction between terrorists and those who knowingly harbor or provide aid to them."

The Center for Defense Information (CDI)(www.cdi.org) labels this approach as a blueprint for *preventive war*, rather than preemptive. This is a war initiated by the fear that the presumed enemy may one day acquire a potent means of aggression. This rationale for initiating a preventive war, considered highly likely to create fearful and aggressive states, is widely judged to fall short of even the requirements of the *just war* criteria.

Richard K. Betts, Director of the Institute for War and Peace Studies, Columbia University, writing in the Spring, 2003 *Ethics and International Affairs* states, "...a preemptive-preventive doctrine moves us closer to a state of nature than a state of international law...the stress of living in fear should be assuaged by true prevention—arms control, disarmament, negotiations, confidence-building measures, and the development of international law" (see *arms control*).

People who warn against assertive disarmament are often dismissed by its protagonists as "anti-interventionists."

assets: anything that the *enemy* has—buildings, equipment, people—that are deemed worthy of destroying or killing. As John Taylor notes in *Body Horror: Photojournalism, Catastrophe and War (The Critical Image)*, during the *Gulf War* "Enemy soldiers were referred to as 'units' and 'assets' represented by green rectangles. General Schwarzkopf stood in front of maps on which these abstract signs for armies were first placed and then removed once they had been sufficiently 'pounded' or 'attrited.' Schwarzkopf was able to believe he killed armies and not individuals 'largely because of the power of a system of representations which marginalizes the presence of the body in war, fetishizes machines, and personalizes international conflicts while depersonalizing the people who die in them.'"

While the colorful graphics and special effects were far superior during the televised reporting of *Operation Iraqi Freedom* as compared to *Operation Desert Storm*, both featured a wide variety of "talking-heads,"—usually retired military officers—who referred dispassionately to "assets," often human, as being *suppressed, degraded, neutralized, attrited, hammered, pounded, reduced,* or *taken out.*

asymmetric warfare: the kind of warfare that often takes place when the *enemy*, faced with a vastly superior force, refuses to act like real men and stand still so that they can be killed. Robert Allen, in a 1997 lecture at the Army Management Staff College, said that it is "in essence ...a means for usually inferior militaries to gain advantage over mightier opponents." Because the United States is the world's only superpower, it follows that the U.S. military must constantly face the threat that the enemy will use "non-traditional" methods generally considered to be cowardly acts. These would include all aspects of terrorism, with *conventional* or even *nuclear, chemical,* or *biological weapons*. Also, they may employ *information warfare*, and disrupt the military's, or the country's computer/communications capabilities.

The Army's response, according to Allen, ought to be as follows: "We should consider letting the Reserve Component fight the bulk of future symmetrical, conventional wars. We could lighten the active forces and give them increased lethality. With information dominance and precision, high-tech weapons at the heart of the force ...(we) could respond...quickly to ever-changing, fast-moving asymmetric threats...Will the Army be ready? Yes we will!" This appears to come under the *bring 'em on* category brought to prominence by George W. Bush in 2003, and would seem to invite a state of *perpetual war.*

The purpose of the Army Management Staff College is "to

prepare...military and civilian leaders who aid our nation's soldiers to meet their mission in times of conflict and peace." A blueprint for a systematic approach to the search for nonviolent resolutions of differences was not included in the above lecture.

Students of the subject of asymmetric warfare often expand its definition to include a wide spectrum of unequal warfare. For example, some maintain that there can be an opposite type of asymmetry. The U.S. slaughter in 1945 of at least 200,000 civilians by dropping two atomic bombs on Hiroshima and Nagasaki was a terrible asymmetry of force applied by a superior military might. One could add the series of bombing raids on Tokyo and on over 60 other Japanese cities in that same year, killing 80-100,000 civilians. The raids were led by General Curtis LeMay. They featured *napalm* incendiary bombs which, in the words of the highly-decorated LeMay "scorched and boiled and baked (them) to death."

atrocity: appalling, monstrous, cruel behavior—such as 9/11, the murder of 4 U.S. civilian contractors and the desecration of their corpses in Fallujah, Iraq on March 31, 2004, or the use of *firebombs* and *cluster bombs* by the U.S. forces in Iraq.

The now all-too-familiar 9/11 massacre needs no recounting. In Fallujah, a city about 30 miles west of Baghdad 4 civilian contractors were shot and killed. Their bodies were burned and dragged through the streets. In March, 2003, U.S. warplanes dropped dozens of *firebombs* filled with kerosene-based jet fuel on Iraqi *soldiers* near bridges leading to Bagdhad, burning them alive. Col. James Alles, commander of the Marine Air Group 11 told reporters "The generals love napalm. It has a big psychological effect."

Technically firebombs are not *napalm*—used extensively in Vietnam and also in the *Gulf War*—but now in disrepute (see *firebomb, conventional weapons*). The *San Diego Union-Tribune*,

August 5, 2003 quotes military officials as defending the use of firebombs as opposed to napalm. They maintained a firebomb, which burns as fiercely as napalm, "has significantly less impact on the environment."

In the strange logic of war, acts which by their nature are atrocious, such as incinerating people, or leaving explosives scattered across populated areas—knowing that unsuspecting children would frequently detonate them accidentally—are regarded as regrettable necessities. They are simply part of the *job* the military is sent to do. When acts of killing, injuring and burning are done outside the context of the battlefield, the world reacts with justified horror.

Perhaps that explains why viewers of Fox News, on April 1, 2004 saw Henry Kissinger explaining—with a straight face—that during his career he never was forced to deal with such an atrocity as the Iraqi Fallujah incident, in which charred bodies were dragged through the streets. He advised that the perpetrators be found and dealt with severely. It is possible that Kissinger, one of the chief architects of the Vietnam War, never regarded the *carpet-bombing* of thousands of innocent Vietnamese and Cambodians as anything more than an effective military tactic. It is also possible that Christopher Hitchens, in *The Trial of Henry Kissinger,* is correct when he concludes that Kissinger is a mass murderer who should be tried for war crimes.

attrited: the wearing away of an *enemy's* equipment and human *forces*, i.e. by destroying the former and killing and/or wounding the latter. The U.S. Department of Defense official definition of "attrited" is this: "The reduction of the effectiveness of a force caused by loss of personnel and materiel." This attrition often may be relentless and gradual, or may be sudden and catastrophic.

The media were fond of the term, especially during *Operation*

Iraqi Freedom. For example, CNN correspondent Walter Rodgers, *embedded* with the 3rd Squadron, 7th Cavalry of the U.S. Army 3rd Infantry Division reported on April 2, 2003 that he was traveling with a "mighty army rolling in the direction of Baghdad...heavy Air Force bombing day after day appears to have, to use the army's word, attrited, that is to say, badly degraded the units which are supposed to be defending Baghdad. What we're seeing here is essentially pockets of resistance, but nothing overly serious" (see *degrade, pockets, units*).

axis of evil: In his State of the Union address in January 2002, President Bush used this phrase to label countries that he said, "were arming to threaten the peace of the world." He identified those as Iran, Iraq, and North Korea. White House speechwriter David Frum, who has revealed that his assignment for contributing to the State of the Union address was to link the September 11 attacks on the World Trade Center to a rationale for "going after Iraq" saw Iraq as closely resembling one of the Axis powers of World War II.

Frum decided that conjuring up the memories of the feared former alliance among Germany, Japan and Italy might serve as a powerfully evocative catchphrase. One does not ordinarily think of one country as constituting an "axis, "so Frum's original designation was an "axis of hatred" between Iraq and two other countries suspected of developing nuclear weapons, Iran and North Korea. According to Joseph Montville, Director of the Preventive Diplomacy program at the Center for Strategic and International Studies in Washington, D.C., adding North Korea to the list appears to have been an afterthought "to avoid intensifying the suspicion of Muslim countries that the war on terrorism was a war on Islam." Chief speechwriter Michael Gerson changed the phrase to "axis of evil" to mesh with the religious tone of the President's rhetoric after September 11.

In order to nourish a fear of terrorist threat, the phrase created a fictional relationship among those countries. It appears to have undermined the effectiveness of Iran's moderate leaders, and forced a dangerous confrontation with North Korea. It was heard with dismay by much of the world community, particularly Europe.

David Frum departed his White House position not long after the State of the Union speech. In his 2003 book *The Right Man* Frum writes that, with a few exceptions, "Conspicuous intelligence seemed actively unwelcome in the Bush White House." He describes the President as "often uncurious and as a result ill informed" but goes on to say that Bush is "nothing short of superb as a wartime leader."

Frum concludes "An American-led overthrow of Saddam Hussein...would put America more wholly in charge of the region than any power since the Ottomans, or maybe the Romans."

B

> *"I saw high explosives fired from huge distances in the Gulf War reduce battalions of Iraqis to scattered corpses. Iraqi soldiers were nothing more on the screens of sophisticated artillery pieces than little dots scurrying around like ants—that is, until they were blasted away. Bombers dumped tons of iron fragmentation bombs on them...Helicopters hovered above units like angels of death in the sky. Here there was no pillage, no warlords, no collapse of unit discipline, but the cold and brutal efficiency of industrial warfare by well-trained and highly organized professional soldiers...We equip and train the most efficient killers on the planet."*

Chris Hedges, *War is a Force That Gives us Meaning*

barracks: a large building in which many soldiers sleep, dream, and keep pictures of their loved ones. On December 9, 2003 a car filled with explosives blew up near a barracks of the U.S. 101st Airborne Division. Fox News reported that, even though 63 people were injured, "incredibly no one was killed...it could have been much worse, a near cataclysmic loss of life."

On December 18, 1998, CNN.com explained, "The United States and Britain plan to continue military attacks on Iraq as the Iraqi people prepare to enter the holy month of Ramadan."

General Henry (Hugh) Shelton, Chairman of the Joint Chiefs of Staff, showing aerial photographs at the Pentagon briefing on these air strikes said, "Here are their barracks shown in this area, Area One, before the strike, along with the headquarters up in this area. If you go from these barracks, the pre-strike to the post-strike, you'll see out of the five barracks, four of the five were destroyed... In terms of the two targets, the first one, the barracks area, that belongs to the Special Republican Guards. These are the units that in fact guard the WMD, to help transport it...We have no way of knowing whether or not the barracks were occupied at the time. We hit the barracks ...sometime between 1:00 and 4:30 in the morning, a.m., Baghdad time. You would assume that with the advance notice they got, probably some of the troops had left their barracks. There may have been others inside."

biological weapons: lethal microbes, or their toxins, usually intended to be dispersed over wide areas, for which there is little defense—in which case they are *weapons of mass destruction.* These agents of death and disease include bacteria (e.g. anthrax, plague), viruses (e.g. smallpox, Ebola), and toxins (e.g. Ricin, botulism). Biological warfare has a long history. For example, in 1763, Lord General Jeffrey Amherst, British Commander-in-Chief of America, approved the distribution of smallpox-infected blankets to Native Americans during Pontiac's Rebellion. The Japanese used biological agents in China during World War II.

There has actually been little documented wide-scale use of biological weapons. However, after World War II, a few countries—including the UK and the U.S.—developed major biological weapons programs for production and dispersal. According to GlobalSecurity.org (www.globalsecurity.org), major U.S. cities were used as laboratories—unknown to the inhabitants—to test "aerosolization and dispersal methods."

In 1969, President Nixon shut down the unpopular and divisive biological warfare program by executive order, curtailing multi-million dollar projects that had developed an arsenal of bacteria, fungi and toxins. Biological weapons were considered unpredictable, hazardous, and not considered essential for national defense—and as some thought, Nixon may have been trying to deflect attention from his disastrous Vietnam policy. The U.S. Army Medical Research Institute of Infectious Diseases (USAMRIID) was then founded to continue to develop defenses for the military against biological attacks.

The Biological and Toxic Weapons Convention (BTWC) was

created in 1972, in an international effort to stop the acquisition and/or production of biological weapons. As of 2002 there were 146 signatories, including the U.S.. The *Stanford Journal of International Relations*, September 7, 2001 reports "In July 2001, this Ad Hoc group [formed to strengthen the effectiveness of the Convention] met in Geneva to negotiate a draft protocol... The United States withdrew from these negotiations, citing the ineffectiveness of the enforcement mechanisms, as well as the risks posed to U.S. national security and private industry by the release of proprietary information during on-site inspections."

According to the Monterey Institute of International Studies (www.miis.edu) in 2004 there were at least 12 countries still thought to have programs for producing biological as well as *chemical weapons,* including China, Israel, North Korea, and Iran. In the wake of 9/11 Congress appropriated $6 billion for biodefense. Some of those funds were soon put to work building laboratories for handling, modifying and experimenting with dangerous biological agents, giving rise to suspicions that this research will inevitably move towards developing capabilities for offensive biological weapons.

Before the *Gulf War,* Iraq had a major biological and chemical weapons program. Steven Aftergood and Joyce Battle, writing in *Secrecy News*, a newsletter published by the Federation of American Scientists (FAS)(www.fas.org), cite evidence from the National Security Archive collection "documenting U.S. partnership with Iraq in its 1980-1988 war against Iran." They point out that during this period of renewed U.S. support Saddam "had invaded Iran...had long-range nuclear aspirations...abused the human rights of its citizens...and possessed and used chemical weapons on Iranians and his own people. The U.S. response was to renew ties, to provide intelligence and aid and to ensure Iraq would not be defeated by Iran, and to send a high-level presidential envoy named Donald Rumsfeld to shake hands with Saddam."

The newsletter (quoting Senator Robert Byrd) cites a 1995 letter by former CDC [Center for Disease Control] Director David Satcher. Byrd says Satcher "points out that the U.S. Government provided nearly two dozen viral and bacterial samples to Iraqi scientists in 1985—samples that included the plague, botulism, and anthrax." The U.S. Senate Committee on Banking, Housing, and Urban Affairs with Respect to Export Administration reveals in its May 25 and October 7, 1994 reports that from 1985 to 1989 numerous samples of potentially dangerous biological materials were sold to Iraq, with the approval of the U.S. Department of Commerce. The Committee revealed that "...these microorganisms exported by the United States were identical to those the United Nations Inspectors found and removed from the Iraqi biological warfare program."

One of the justifications for the then impending war against Iraq was—according to Secretary of State Colin Powell, in his address to the United Nations Security Council, February 5, 2003—"There can be no doubt that Saddam Hussein has biological weapons and has the capacity to rapidly produce more, many more." Iraq claimed to have destroyed its considerable stocks of biological weapons after the Gulf War. Coalition forces, unconvinced of this, searched in vain after the 2003 *Operation Iraqi Freedom* for evidence of stockpiles of biological agents and delivery systems.

The U.S. has not forgotten the potential of biological weapons as an effective tool of warfare. The 2000 document *Rebuilding America's Defenses: Strategy, Forces and Resources for a New Century*, widely regarded as the blueprint for the George W. Bush administration's 2002 *National Security Strategy* contains this advice: " The U.S. must seek to transform the "art of warfare" by developing, among other space-age weapons, "advanced forms of biological warfare that can target 'specific' genotypes [which] may transform biological warfare from the realm of terror to a politically useful tool."

blowback: A U.S. Central Intelligence Agency (CIA) term for "unintended consequences" of secret intelligence or military operations. For example, the U.S. covertly transferred billions of dollars through Pakistan during the 1980s to the Islamists fighting the Soviet Union. This was followed by the U.S.-led invasions of Iraq in 1991 and 2003, and the intervening years of punishing sanctions.

In his review of Chalmers Johnson's 2000 book *Blowback: The Costs and Consequences of American Empire,* Regis T. Sobol points out how Chalmers, a respected economist, president of the Japan Policy Research Institute, and professor emeritus at the University of California explains the current chaos, particularly in the Middle East, as a reaction to that history. Johnson argues that the violent reactions, in the form of "rogue states" or acts of "terrorists" are [blowback] reactions to the U.S. objective of creating a "global American empire held together by military and financial domination of other countries and their markets. In short, we want to own the world" (see *globalization, hegemony, National Security Strategy, Pax Americana).*

In *Blowback*, Johnson maintains that the U.S. "props up its power with cruise missiles, aircraft carriers, and financial manipulations instead of resorting to diplomacy, development aid, and international law."

body bags: When the remains of the 58,000 American soldiers killed during the Vietnam War were sent home, they were encased in a simple sack—the body bag. During *Operation Desert Storm* in 1991, the Pentagon began referring to body bags as "human remains pouches." As of December 2002, the Defense Supply Center had 34,000 of these black vinyl pouches in its warehouses.

In 2003 the Pentagon began to add to its supply of "human remains pouch type II"—nylon bags coated with rubber and used to evacuate human remains (dead people and parts of dead people) from rugged terrain.

When the remains are ready for shipment home, they are placed in a pouch. The pouch is put into an aluminum transfer case, which can be packed with ice. They are flown to the air force base in Dover, Delaware. There, families may choose a casket or an urn. In the November 2, 2003, *Toronto Star*, Lt. Col. Jon Anderson described business at the Dover mortuary as "steady." It has remained so ever since.

body count: a running total of the number of combatants killed during a war. The number of *enemy* dead is considered a yardstick of success. The unwitting civilian victims are not part of the official tally. Body counts were a regular feature of the evening news during the Vietnam War. Eventually, the mounting toll of the dead had a depressing effect on the American public, contributing to their loss of enthusiasm for the war.

Body counts of the enemy were not favored during the *Gulf War* and *Operation Iraqi Freedom.* There were some practical reasons. In the *New York Times*, April 10, 2003, Mark Burgess, a researcher at the Washington, D.C-based Center for Defense Information (CDI)(www.cdi.org) commented on the difficulties of obtaining accurate counts. "It's an unanswerable question...We don't know the exact number who stood and fought. There really wasn't much in the way of conventional battles." Columnist John Broder added, "The powerful munitions used by American and British air forces probably left hundreds or thousands of battlefield victims pulverized, burned or buried in rubble."

U.S. General Tommy Franks, in the initial stages of Operation Iraqi Freedom, said, "We do not do body counts." Much earlier, General Colin Powell had been asked by a reporter how many

Iraqis had been killed in the Gulf War. He replied, "That is really not a matter I am terribly interested in."

Interest in body counts was revived in December 2003. The coalition began to report on the number of Iraqi soldiers killed, but only in specific battles. It was widely regarded as a political decision, based on the American public's growing unease over the numbers of their soldiers killed every day. As of February 2, 2005, the day on which President George W. Bush delivered his State of the Union address, 1436 U.S. soldiers had been killed since May 1, 2003, when President Bush had declared "*mission accomplished*"—most of them after Bush had challenged the Iraqis to "*bring 'em on.*"

Some reactions were more prosaic. Ralph Kinney Bennet, writing on Tech Central Station (www.techcentralstation.com), March 26, 2003: "We are seeing amazingly light casualties...[after all] The North and the South each lost over 11,000 killed and wounded in one day at Antietam..."

The U.S. has not published any estimates of the number of Iraqis killed in the Gulf War, neither combatants nor civilians (see *casualties, collateral damage*).

bomb: a weapon consisting of powerful explosives packed into a casing that is designed to burst upon impact, shattering and/or incinerating structures and people. A bomb may be a crude, though deadly, homemade device detonated from contact, remotely, or by a desperate individual, as in the case of a suicide bomber.

Typically, in wartime, larger, much more powerful bombs are dropped from the air. The airplane, soon after its invention, graduated quickly from a novel means of transportation and a convenient way to deliver mail into an instrument that could deliver death and destruction. The *enemy* could be targeted from above, and the nature of warfare changed dramatically. As aircraft grew faster and flew higher, bombs were "perfected" as well, growing into increasingly more devastating weapons. Bombs do not "fall," as in "Bombs fell last night in Baghdad..." Bombs are dropped by people onto people, and onto vehicles or buildings containing people.

The major categories of bombs (which come under the weapons category of *dropped ordnance*) are the general-purpose (GP), fragmentation, penetration and cluster bombs. GP bombs, weighing between 500 to 2,000 pounds were the bombs most frequently used of the 256,000 dropped during the *Gulf War*. Much of their effect is due to the blast pressures, as well as the fragments. The fragmentation bomb, such as Big Blue (BLU-82), a 15,000-pound behemoth that explodes just above the ground, consists of 10 to 20 percent explosive, the rest being casings that are scored to break into thousands of high-speed lethal shards. It is quite effective in *preparing the battlefield*. According to the Federation of American Scientists (FAS), "fragmentation is effective against troops, vehicles, aircraft, and other soft targets" (see *soft targets*).

Penetration bombs, such as the *advanced unitary penetrator*, have specially hardened casings, sometimes containing *depleted uranium*, to allow them to penetrate deep into hardened targets such as bunkers, before they explode (see *bunker busters*). Cluster bombs are specialized fragmentation bombs. They are canisters filled with *bomblets,* small bombs which fragment into a massive cloud of steel splinters (see *airburst).*

During *Operation Iraqi Freedom* in 2003, most of the reported 27,000 bombs that were dropped were of the *smart* or *precision-guided* variety. These are self-guiding bombs; directed originally by television cameras, then laser beams, and more recently, by satellite navigation systems. Although much more accurate than dumb bombs (the military now prefers the more polite "gravity bombs"), a system failure can send a smart bomb far from its intended target, and cause tragic *collateral damage.*

The largest gravity bomb in the U.S. arsenal is the 21,000-pound Massive Ordnance Air Blast (MOAB), dubbed "the Mother of all Bombs." Touted for its "psychological effects" it was not used against the Iraqis, but it was tested successfully and with great fanfare during *Operation Iraqi Freedom.*

Newer types of bombs under development will add even more insidious weaponry to the already powerful U.S. arsenal. For example, the e-bomb will generate concentrated beams of microwave energy. These could destroy the innards of anything that uses electricity—putting out of business an entire city, or frying the equipment on a *high-tech battlefield.* A new generation of *nuclear weapons* is also on the drawing boards.

The future seems bright for death-by-bomb. As space weapons continue to develop we have the following scenario to look forward to, as described by Paul Hirst, professor of social theory at Birbeck College, London University at a 2003 conference on the future of weaponry. Concerning the as yet theoretical notion of creating war machines of molecular size, Hirst said; "Imagine: micro aircraft that fly by their own sensors and carry many deadly submunitions; intelligent jumping mines that shower selected targets with small guided bomblets...the result would be... deadly bio-machines of finite life that could be released by [the] submunitions, showering opponents in millions of nanobots...that could literally eat humans alive."

bomblet: little bombs—particularly effective in maiming and killing little children—although not designed specifically for that purpose. In the "steel rain" that follows the explosion of a cluster bomb dropped from an airplane, or a *cluster munition* which soars to its target propelled by *artillery*, hundreds of these bomblets—each about the size of a soda can, tennis ball or flashlight battery—burst into the air.

The deadly "rain" descends, scattering hundreds or thousands of the small containers across the landscape. Most explode, creating a shower of high-speed, white-hot metal splinters. These do terrible damage to whatever they strike. Merely a single fragment can shred human organs. Those containers that fail to explode (estimates range from 5-20 percent in some cases) are "duds"—potential killers that can lie in wait for many years until something or someone disturbs them.

Over a million such duds still wait in Indochina, Afghanistan, Angola, Chechnya, Bosnia, Kuwait, and Iraq and elsewhere. For example, in Kuwait, duds are still being found and destroyed at the rate of about 200 per month. Human Rights Watch (www.hrw.org) reports that, by 1993, exploding duds had killed 1,600 Kuwaiti and Iraqi citizens. Twenty-five hundred had been injured—sixty percent of the victims were children under the age of fifteen.

Many of the bomblets are bright yellow and attract children's attention. A popular cluster bomb, the BLU-97, delivers 202 yellow bomblets, each of which shears into 300 metal shards. Each bomblet also releases a highly flammable powder that can ignite anything within range. The BLU-97 bomblets were the same color as the wrapping on the humanitarian food packets handed out by U.S. and British in Iraq during *Operation Iraqi Freedom.* A similar problem had developed earlier in Afghanistan, where the U.S. eventually changed the wrapping color.

According to a 2003 report prepared for the Traprock Peace Center (www.traprockpeace.org) there are approximately 1.2-1.5 million unexploded bomblets scattered across Iraq from the 1991 Gulf War, and another 32,500 left from Operation Iraqi Freedom in 2003. At least 372 Iraqis have been killed by these bomblets since the latter war according to Iraq Body Count (IBC) (www. iraqbodycount.org). The number of wounded and disfigured may never be accurately determined.

In a 2003 *Field Artillery* article, Army Col. Thomas

Torrance, commander of the 3rd Infantry Division artillery, and Lt. Col. Noel Nicolle, while deploring the dud rate, maintain that bomblets delivered by artillery are "The munition of choice for killing tanks and personnel in the open." The British Defence Secretary Geoff Hoon defended the use of bomblets to the *Daily Telegraph* on April 5 2003 as "perfectly legal" and as having a "highly legitimate role." Cluster munitions, which disperse the deadly bomblets, are not covered under the Ottawa Treaty—to which Britain is a signatory—banning the use of landmines (see *area denial munitions*) even though duds are, in effect, small landmines. The U.S. has not signed the treaty.

bravery: showing courage in the face of great difficulties and dangers, for example, declaring oneself to be a conscientious objector (CO). This may be done by a person who is facing compulsory military duty, or by someone who is already in *uniform* and realizes that he or she cannot in good conscience kill.

To take such a position is to incur the wrath of the state, particularly during a war, when there is an urgent need for *soldiers* who will follow the government's demands to kill despite one's personal convictions or objections. About 5,000 COs who could not show that they were members of pacifistic religious groups were imprisoned in the U.S. during World War II. Approximately 40,000 who objected to fighting were allowed to perform public service as an alternative, often under conditions of extreme harassment. Their story is featured in the award-winning documentary *The Good War and Those Who Refused to Fight it.*

In 1971 the Supreme Court disallowed objection to a particular war. One would now have to prove conclusively that one objected to participating in any combat, either on religious grounds or personal conviction. As a result, between 50,000-100,000 young men left the U.S. during the Vietnam War to avoid being drafted (see *desertion*).

According to the Center on Conscience and War (CCW)(www.nisbco.org), in 1991, during the *Gulf War*, 111 COs were officially recognized before the military refused to approve any more applications. This resulted in the imprisonment of 2,500, who were sometimes "beaten, harassed, and treated horribly." The CCW, which offers counseling on CO rights, report that they had "several hundred" requests for advice from enlisted soldiers as *Operation Iraqi Freedom* appeared imminent. Only a small percentage of those who actually apply for CO status meet the strict requirements, and decisions on their status take from six months to one year.

The first widely publicized CO during *Operation Iraqi Freedom* was Marine Lance Cpl. Stephen Funk. He refused to answer his unit's call to report on February 9, 2003. In an interview in *The Guardian*, April 2, 2003, he said he believed that the war was "immoral because of the deception involved by our leaders...I would rather take my punishment now than live with what I would have to do for the rest of my life." During his training, Funk said recruits who were not being sent to Iraq encouraged him and his fellow soldiers to "Kill a raghead for me—[we're] so jealous" (see *raghead*). He said that his *chaplain* had advised him," It's a lot easier if you just give in and don't question authority...Jesus says to carry a sword." Funk concluded, "War is about destruction and violence and death. It is young men fighting old men's wars. It is not the answer."

He was found guilty of "unauthorized absence" and sentenced to six months in the military prison at Camp Lejeune in North Carolina, after which he was to receive a bad conduct discharge (see *desertion)*. According to the *San Francisco Chronicle,* September 7, 2003, "The Marine prosecutor, Maj. Mike Sayegh, told the jury that the case was about 'a kid who thought he could beat the system...All of this conscientious objector stuff is nothing but a made-up bedtime story.'"

About half of the 60 soldiers who applied for CO status in 2004 were approved. They chose not to enter combat in Iraq. The case of Staff Sergeant Camilio Mejia was unique, however. After fighting in Iraq he was sent home on leave and refused to return. Mejia said he had gone to Iraq as "an instrument of violence, and now I have decided to become an instrument of peace." On March 15, 2004, standing near a statue of Gandhi on the grounds of the Peace Abbey in Sherborn, MA—founded by a Vietnam War conscientious objector—he announced his intention to seek CO status. That is a lengthy process. According to attorney Eugene Fidell, a lawyer experienced in the hassles over CO status, Mejia would have to prove that he is opposed to all war, and not just to combat in Iraq. If he restricts his objections to Operation Iraqi Freedom, said Fidell, "that is the kiss of death." In June 2004 Meija was sentenced to one year in prison, losing all rank and most pay, and will receive a bad conduct discharge.

There are many other examples of bravery in the military. Many of the young men and women who are recruited (see *military recruitment*) and trained to kill, under conditions of great psychological stress (see *military training*), perform acts of great courage when they are faced with threat of injury and death in battle. Those who send them off to face those dangers deserve reproach, and not the *soldiers*, who are in a real sense, also victims.

CNN.com described the U.S. Army's 288th birthday celebration held in June 2003 at the Pentagon. Vice-President Dick Cheney told the assembly "Many brave Americans have laid down their lives so that liberty could triumph." Deputy Secretary of Defense Paul Wolfowitz commended retiring Army General Tommy Franks, who commanded the wars in Afghanistan and Iraq. Wolfowitz said his [Franks'] war *victories* were "*brilliant*." CNN.com noted that "[The] ceremony at the Pentagon...included a large cake."

brilliant: an Irish expression used to remark favorably on anything from a good pint to a well-executed football play. It is also a favored descriptive for military officers and maneuvers. For example, as noted above, Deputy Secretary of Defense Paul Wolfowitz described as "brilliant" Army General Tommy Frank's *victories* in Afghanistan and Iraq. Media reports hail Defense Secretary Donald Rumsfeld as having a "brilliant war plan," and even a "daringly brilliant...plan." The campaign to topple Saddam is noted for its "brilliance." General Wesley Clark is hailed as a "brilliant analyst." Not to be outdone, columnist Mona Charon lauded Robert Reilly, named manager of media in Iraq in 2003, as a "brilliant star in the Pantheon of the Unconfused."

Even the elaborate and expensive plan hatched during the development of President Ronald Reagan's Strategic Defense Initiative ("Star Wars") program had a use for the versatile term. Rather than house missiles in giant "garages" orbiting the planet, defense officials proposed the plan "Brilliant Pebbles". The "pebbles" were to be thousands of small missile interceptors orbiting in space, waiting for a Soviet missile attack. The pebbles would sense, intercept and destroy the incoming missiles. The idea has since been shelved, in favor of other kinds of controversial interceptors.

According to the U.S. Naval Institute Military Database (www.periscope1.com), "the major criticism of Brilliant Pebbles [was] the political feasibility of orbiting thousands of military satellites." However, Edward Teller, known as "father of the hydrogen bomb" was an uncritical and vocal supporter of Brilliant Pebbles. Columnist Gary Gilson wrote after Teller's death in 2003, "His scientific brilliance helped change the world."

bring 'em on: a challenge issued by President George W. Bush on July 2, 2003, in response to growing concerns about the chaos in Iraq since the "official" end of the war two months earlier. In that period at least 64 Americans had died, most as a result of being killed by attacks, by landmines, or in accidents. Only the day before Bush's remarks a Marine was killed and three others injured while clearing mines (see *area denial munitions)* and another *soldier* died from wounds suffered earlier.

The president, when asked about the growing number of these postwar deaths answered: "There are some who feel that conditions are such that they can attack us there. My answer is: Bring 'em on! We've got the force necessary to deal with the security situation."

The numerous replies to what were widely regarded as, at the least, intemperate remarks included those of Senator Frank Lautenberg (D-NJ). Lautenberg said "I am shaking my head in disbelief. When I served in the Army in World War II I never heard any military commander—never mind the commander-in-chief—invite enemies to attack U.S. troops." He added that Bush's words were "tantamount to inciting and inviting more attacks against U.S. forces."

Bush's challenge also provoked a prompt rise in the membership rolls of Military Families Speak Out (MFSO)(www. mfso.org), an organization of over 800 military families established to call for an end to the occupation of Iraq and the return of all U.S. troops to their home bases. Jeffrey McKenzie of Gasport, NY, a co-founder of MFSO had this retort: "Bush said 'bring 'em on.' We say bring 'em home."

There was no official verbal or written answer on the part of the Iraqis to the President's public challenge. However, two days after the President issued his challenge, Lt. Gen. Ricardo S. Sanchez, the commander of the allied forces in Iraq, acknowledged, "we're still at war." And only two months later—in late August, after the 138th soldier had died in Iraq since May 1—as many Americans had lost their lives as had been killed during the 43-

day war.

President Bush assumed a more subdued tone. On July 10, 2003 he admitted that it would take some time for the situation to improve. According to *The Houston Chronicle* (July 11, 2003) Bush told reporters "We haven't been there long," he said. "I mean, relatively speaking, we've been there 90 to 100 days—I don't have the exact number...We're making steady progress."

broad and concerted campaign: phrase used by President George W. Bush on the evening of March 19, 2003, to describe the savage assault about to be launched against Iraq. The attack would be widespread, bringing death and destruction across Iraq, a small country already ravaged by twelve years of *sanctions*. It would be intense, with 300,000 U.S. and British forces, backed by more than 600 warplanes, poised to terrify the *enemy* with a ferocious initial bombardment that would create *shock and awe.*

The President announced the onset of *Operation Iraqi Freedom* seated safely behind the "Resolute" desk, fashioned from timbers of a 19th century warship. Looking appropriately grim and determined, Bush reassured his television audience that "this will not be a campaign of half-measures." After promising that the full might of America's superior power would overcome the "dangers to our country and to the world" he ended his address by offering his geographically specific blessings—"May God bless our country and all who defend her."

Surely some in the audience were reminded of Mark Twain's brief book *The War Prayer.* It was published—at his request—posthumously, because " I have told the whole truth in that, and only dead men can tell the truth in this world." The prayer says, in part, " O Lord our God, help us to cover their smiling fields with the pale forms of their patriot dead; help us to drown the thunder of the guns with the shrieks of their wounded, writhing in pain... We ask it, in the spirit of love, of Him Who is the Source of Love...

Amen."

West Virginian Democrat Senator Robert Byrd responded to the President's call to war by remarking, "Today I weep for my country...No more is the image of America one of a strong, yet benevolent, peacekeeper. Around the globe, our friends mistrust us, our word is disputed, our intentions questioned."

bunker buster: a powerful *bomb* designed to penetrate through earth and concrete in order to destroy deep, hardened bunkers. Most of the bunker busters now in the U.S. arsenal are fashioned from ordinary explosives. Those in the planning stages are enormously more powerful and dangerous *nuclear weapons.*

During the *Gulf War* in 1991, the U.S. used many relatively small laser-guided bunker busters to destroy shallow concrete bunkers. Black and white videos, showing a bombs-eye view of the approach to the targets, gave birth to the video-game aura of that war. Years later that technology would be far exceeded by the colorful graphics used to entertain the television audience during *Operation Iraqi Freedom.*

The Air Force demanded even bigger bombs for more protected bunkers. U.S. government laboratories quickly created the GBU-28B—a 5,000 lb laser-guided bomb. Over 19 feet long, and packing 630 lbs of explosives, the GBU-28B can penetrate 20 feet of concrete and 100 feet of rock and dirt before exploding. Many experts assume that the outer casing is strengthened by *depleted uranium.* During the second phase of the "*Shock and Awe*" bombardment of Baghdad in March 2003, two GBU-28Bs were dropped on a suspected communications building. The *New York Post* (March 29, 2003) reported, "People [were believed to be] buried beneath the rubble." It was not clear why these massive bombs were used on an above ground target.

In April 2002, the Bush administration ordered the Department of Energy to study the feasibility of using nuclear weapons to demolish deeply buried targets. Earlier in 2002 the White House had released, with little publicity, the 2002 *Nuclear Posture Review* (NPR), a Congressionally mandated reexamination of U.S. nuclear policy. According to the Union of Concerned Scientists (www. ucsusa.org) the NPR "calls for new types of nuclear weapons, proposes new roles for their use, and emphasizes a strengthened commitment to building new nuclear weapons...this undermines what must be the preeminent U.S. security goal: preventing the proliferation of nuclear weapons."

The NPR specifically calls for "improved earth penetrating weapons (EPWs) to counter the increased use by potential adversaries of hardened and deeply buried facilities." The document makes it clear that "nuclear weapons will remain the cornerstone of U.S. military power for the next fifty years."

Enter the Robust Nuclear Earth Penetrator (RNEP). The U.S. already has a stockpile of EPWs. The planned RNEP will be based on the B61-11. This a nuclear bunker buster which, according to the Los Alamos Study Group, writing in the February 10,1997 *Global Politics* (The Brookings Institution) "was developed and deployed in secret, without public and congressional debate, contrary to domestic and international assurances that no new nuclear weapons were being developed." The atomic bomb dropped on Hiroshima—that act that has permanently stained the history of our country—had a yield of about 12 kilotons—an explosive force equal to that of 12,000 tons of TNT. The proposed RNEP theoretically could equal twenty Hiroshima bombs.

The Council for a Livable World (www.clw.org) warned: "According to Princeton University physicist Robert Nelson... the B61-11 can achieve a depth of only 20 feet in dry earth... eject(ing) a massive cloud of radioactive dust and debris into the atmosphere...Larger nuclear yields necessary to destroy targets deep underground would create considerably more fallout."

On March 20, 2003, the International Physicians for the

Prevention of Nuclear War (IPPNW)(www.ippnw.org) published a study which warned "Even a very low-yield nuclear EPW exploded in or near an urban environment would inevitably disperse radioactive dirt and debris over several square kilometers and could result in fatal doses of radiation to tens of thousands of victims."

Moreover, as Senator Diane Feinstein (D-CA) cautioned during an unsuccessful attempt in 2003 by the U.S. Senate to block funding for the RNEP, "By seeking to develop new nuclear weapons ourselves we send a message that nuclear weapons have a future battlefield role and utility." The Bush administration, in its request to Congress for fiscal year 2005, asked for $27.6 million to work on a nuclear bunker buster, and $9 million to develop small nuclear weapons for battlefield use—so-called "mini-nukes." Senators Kennedy and Feinstein proposed an amendment that would cut those funds. The Senate rejected the amendment in June 2004. However, on November 20, 2004 Congress passed an appropriations bill with no funding for new nuclear weapons. The *Chicago Tribune* (November 23, 2004) said the decision "was hailed...by arms control advocates as the biggest success in more than a decade." The Defense Department urged restoration of the funds, claiming, "We have to adapt capabilities that we have to meet the threats."

William D. Hartung of the World Policy Institute, and military adviser to Foreign Policy in Focus (www.fpip.org) calls the U.S. nuclear weapons policy "nuclear unilateralism—a disaster waiting to happen." Hartung warns that the "premise of this emerging nuclear doctrine is a desire to make U.S. nuclear weapons more usable. This dubious proposition is grounded in the notion that a low-yield weapon could more readily be used as a threat, or actually dropped on a target, without sparking nuclear retaliation."

Proponents of the renewed research on new nukes, such as

Senator Pete Domenici (R-NM)—known to some as the "patron saint" of the nuclear industry—says that such research is needed to give the U.S. new weapons in the war against terrorists—"Let [nuclear scientists] think, let those people design...Don't put mental blinkers and blinders on their brains."

According to the Charleston.net *Post and Courier* (April 24, 2003) the "renewed interest in battlefield nuclear weapons comes primarily from civilian Pentagon officials such as...Donald Rumsfeld and Paul Wolfowitz." They cite the reaction of Robert Peurifoy, retired vice president of Sandia National Laboratory, a government operated National Security facility: "If you can find somebody in a uniform in the Defense Department who can talk about a new need [for nuclear bunker busters] without laughing, I'll buy him a cup of coffee."

C

"True, there has been some discussion of American casualties resulting from a land invasion of Iraq. But, as always when the strategists discuss this, the question is not about the wounded and dead as human beings, but about what number of American casualties would result in public withdrawal of support for the war, and what effect this would have on the upcoming elections for Congress and the Presidency."

Howard Zinn

cakewalk: A term based on a 19th century dance invented by African-Americans in the antebellum South, meaning, "something easily accomplished." In a February 13, 2002 op-ed piece in the *Washington Post*, Kenneth Adelman, longtime advisor to Defense Secretary Donald Rumsfeld, wrote, "I believe demolishing Hussein's military power and liberating Iraq would be a cakewalk. Let me give simple, responsible reasons: (1) It was a cakewalk last time (2) They've become much weaker (3) we've become much stronger; and (4) now we're playing for keeps." He did not include an explanation of why killing perhaps more than 100,000 Iraqis in *Operation Desert Storm* was not "playing for keeps."

Adelman, a member of the Defense Policy Board—a source of neoconservative influence on the Pentagon and the White House— scoffed at the idea that up to 200,000 ground troops would be necessary. In a later *Washington Post* article on April 10, 2003, after *Operation Iraqi Freedom* employed over 300,000 troops, and the combined casualties were in the thousands, Adelman wrote: "Predicting that the next war in Iraq would be a 'cw'—for my sake, now think 'crushing win'—my early 2002 article established the baseline."

camp: a site where soldiers live. When a "camp" is bombed or otherwise attacked, many of the people there are killed, injured and mutilated (see *barracks, garrisons, elements, enemy positions, units*). For example:

"The camp was the target of frequent missile attacks by the resistance fighters." (*The Hindu,* May 2, 2004)

"The attack on Camp Anaconda came as a Russian was killed and two others kidnapped while they were driving near Baghdad." (*Star/* Manila, May 13, 2004)

carpet bombing: massive, indiscriminate bombing raids, also known as "area," "saturation," "blanket," or "terror" bombing. The British invented the technique in Iraq early in the twentieth century. Under the Treaty of San Remo, the British took control over Iraq in 1920, mandated by the League of Nations. The unwelcome occupiers preferred a stable Iraq over one fragmented by competing ethnic and religious factions. Under the leadership of Winston Churchill, then Secretary of State for War, Wing-Commander Arthur Harris ordered relentless, overwhelming aerial bombardment of Iraqi and Kurdish villages.

Harris concluded, "The Arab and Kurd now know what real bombing means in casualties and damage. Within forty-five minutes a full-size village can be practically wiped out and a third of its inhabitants killed or injured."

Hugh Trenchard, then the RAF Chief of Staff, wrote that Churchill had initiated widespread bombing as a means of finding "a cheaper means of control." Churchill had even written to Trenchard inquiring about the possibility of using "asphyxiating bombs...I am strongly in favor of using poison gas against uncivilized tribes." Gas never was used in the bombs, but the practice of saturating a hostile area with bombs became a feature in most succeeding wars. Sir Arthur Harris went on to fame and fortune as Chief of Bombing Command in the Second World War. His finest hour was in the incendiary air raids on civilians in Germany, culminating in the firebombing of Dresden (see *firebombs*). The U.S. almost outdid Harris in the number of slaughtered civilians they tallied in Hiroshima and Nagasaki.

Trenchard predicted, quite presciently, "Air power is of vital concern to the Empire and in Iraq...further evidence is accumulating of its great potentialities." During the *Gulf War* in 1991 the U.S.-led coalition unleashed an unrelenting torrent of over one-quarter million bombs, of which 6-7 percent were of the *smart bomb* variety. Incendiary bombs, *fuel-air explosives,* and *daisy cutters* were part of the witch's brew that rained down. Air Force General Merrill (Tony) McPeak proclaimed that it was "Probably the first time in history that a field army has been defeated by air power."

Twelve years later, groaning under the weight of Saddam Hussein's tyrannical rule compounded by the merciless UN *sanctions*, and having been repeatedly bombed since the Gulf War, the Iraqis once again were attacked on a massive scale from the air. This time, despite the avowed intention of inspiring *"Shock and Awe"* by the intensity of the bombing, the coalition took care to insist that *precision-guided munitions* were avoiding intentional injuries to civilians (see *collateral damage*).

Much of the bombing in *Operation Iraqi Freedom* escaped the strict definition of "carpet bombing," because it was not entirely indiscriminate. However, as documented in the report *Continuing Collateral Damage: The Health and Environmental Costs of War in Iraq 2003* (www.medact.org) the effects of the widespread air assault led to "limited access to clean water and sanitation... disruption of social services and public services, including health services, and social breakdown...The death toll and disease burden could be numbered in the tens of thousands."

In any case, both the 1991 and 2003 aerial assaults on Iraq, continuing the decades-old tradition of bringing death, disease and mutilation to uncounted thousands, would presumably have pleased the British RAF command of the 1920s, who urged " a free and vigorous use of...aerial resources."

casualties: according to Pentagon spokesperson Jim Turner, a military casualty is "any person who is lost to the organization by having been declared dead, duty status whereabouts unknown, missing, ill, or injured." This baldly utilitarian definition may be augmented enormously. One need only consider the extent to which such casualties extend far beyond those individuals who can no longer play a useful role in the military's task of inflicting similar casualties on the *enemy.*

The dead leave behind their loved ones who will never fully recover from their loss. The injured—who include many amputees, those who have been blinded, unable to walk, or otherwise disabled and disfigured—return in sorrow to their devastated families. The *psychiatric casualties* may return to those waiting at home whole in body, but with ravaged minds (see *cowardice*).

The Pentagon refuses even to estimate the number of Iraqi casualties, both military and civilian (see *body count*). The Iraqi casualty figures are vastly greater, their wounds as grievous, and their access to modern medical care minimal. Both of the invasions of Iraq by the U.S. and their *allies,* carried out by a military force of overwhelming superiority, combined with the murderous *sanctions* between the wars, left an incalculable legacy of millions of deaths and blighted lives.

For example, during the *air campaign* in the 1991 *Gulf War* 50,000 to 100,000 Iraqi soldiers were killed, according to estimates by the International Physicians for the Prevention of Nuclear War (www.ippnw.org). The civilian death toll in 1991—after the bombing had stopped—rose to 110,000 due to the destruction of Iraq's infrastructure. Seventy thousand of those were children under 15 years of age.

On October 29, 2004 the noted British medical journal *The*

Lancet published a study by a research team at the renowned Johns Hopkins University in Baltimore. They concluded, after extensive interviews across Iraq, that at least 100,000 Iraqi civilians had died as a consequence of the 2003 U.S.-led attack on Iraq—mostly from bombing or rocket attacks.

Iraq Body Count (www.iraqbodycount.org), in a detailed August 7, 2003 study derived from over 300 press reports stated that "To our knowledge, no U.S. or UK government-directed program is specifically targeted towards the injured citizens of Iraq...It has been left to a few charities and aid-agencies which have struggled against U.S. obstruction to gain a foothold for their work with the sick and injured. The United Nations has remained ineffectual, firmly kept in the background by U.S. diktat."

On February 2, 2005 President George W. Bush delivered his State of the Union address. He hailed the "newly elected leaders of Afghanistan" (see *Operation Enduring Freedom*) and "a free and sovereign Iraq" (see *democratization, occupation*). On that same date the Pentagon (www.defenselink.mil) reported that U.S. military casualties in Iraq had reached 1436 killed and 10,770 wounded.

The December 9, 2004 *Boston Globe* reported that despite the fact that 1 in 10 *coalition* soldiers wounded in combat had died, that was a major improvement compared to past wars. However "Those who survive have much more grievous wounds...more than half of those injured sustain wounds so serious they cannot return to duty." They note that the wounded "have required limb amputations at twice the rate of past wars, and as many as 20 percent have suffered head and neck injuries that may require a lifetime of care."

Earlier, in the August 30, 2003 *Boston Globe,* Major General Kenneth L. Farmer Jr., U.S. Army deputy surgeon general remarked, "Patterns of injury (are) very different in Iraqi versus U.S. soldiers...Iraqi soldiers (experience) the whole spectrum of injuries: upper and lower extremities, chest, abdomen and back."

Even the general term "injured" rather than "wounded" hides bitter realities. As author Stan Goff, a retired Special Forces master sergeant, and a member of Bring Them Home Now (bringthemhomenow.org) Coordinating Committee observes," Tearing and cavitation of tissue, the shattering of bone, not to mention the absolute septic filth of these insults to the human body...(are) not the image the Department of Defense and the U.S. Press wants us to carry around inside our heads. We might lose our stomach for war."

In the midst of the carnage, there were some light moments. On CNN, July 16, 2003, Jamie McIntyre, CNN senior correspondent was asked by host Aaron Brown, "...a battle where 150 to 200 enemy soldiers are killed is what? Big, medium, little? McIntyre replied: "Militarily, it's not very significant. It's a very small battle. But psychologically, especially coming after a day when the U.S. suffered some casualties, it's a big boost for morale."

The Center for American Progress (www.americanprogress. org) published a March 24, 2004 memo from Fox News director John Moody to Fox correspondents. Moody complained, "The real news in Iraq is being obscured by temporary tragedy." A few weeks later, he cautions them to "not fall into the easy trap of mourning the loss of U.S. lives."

catastrophic success: an oxymoron which Peter Cochrane, chief technologist for British Telecommunications claims to have coined. Cochrane uses the term to refer to a scenario in which one builds a business so rapidly that "Systems are falling apart; customers are complaining; and in one very short step, you'll be in an almost terminal situation."

Various U.S. officials began to employ the term with a somewhat more positive spin. U.S. Defense Secretary Donald Rumsfeld, speaking with Jim Lehrer on the February 20, 2003

News Hour said of the impending invasion of Iraq: "...We expect... that it's our job to be ready for any conceivable contingency. And therefore all the way from that unhappy thought —and dangerous thought [chemical and biological weapons)—all the way over to catastrophic success where so many people surrender so fast that the task becomes very quickly humanitarian assistance and medical assistance and water and those types of things—so they [the Pentagon] have developed contingency plans for the full spectrum of contingencies."

On April 11, 2003, several weeks into the war, Rumsfeld said in a press briefing, "We did recognize there was at least a chance of catastrophic success...and that we needed to be ready for that... and, we have been." Asked about the widespread looting including the theft of many museum treasures, Rumsfeld responded: " Let me say one thing. The images you are seeing on television you are seeing over, and over, and over, and it's the same picture of some person walking out of some building with a vase, and you see it twenty times and you think, 'My goodness, were there that many vases? Is it possible that there were that many vases in the country?"

On that same day the *San Francisco Chronicle* reported: "The medical system in the capital has 'virtually collapsed'...of the 40 hospitals in the city, 39 have been looted or closed." Ten months later, on February 14, 2004, the *New York Times* reported "Iraqi doctors say the war has pushed them closer to disaster." Eman Asim, the Ministry of Health official the overseer of Iraq's 185 public hospitals said, "It's definitely worse now than before the war...Even at the height of sanctions, when things were miserable, it wasn't as bad as this."

Lawrence Di Rita, a special assistant to Rumsfeld, in remarks cited by the *Los Angeles Times* (July 18, 2003) offered these reassuring words: "We're going to get better over time... We've always thought of post-hostilities as a phase" distinct from combat...The future of war is that these things are going to be much more of a continuum. This is the future for the world we're in at the moment...We'll get better as we do it more often."

chaplain: a member of the clergy from any of 200 religions and denominations who is hired by the United States government to serve as a military officer assigned to provide spiritual guidance and comfort to the armed forces. The Continental Congress instituted the military chaplaincy in 1775.

According to Chaplain (Lt. Col.) Michael A. Brown, a United Methodist Church chaplain for the Air Force's 5th Bomb Wing, "Our most important mission is to spiritually and morally prepare airmen, soldiers, sailors and Marines to take life and die... the combatant must believe the enemy combatant is indeed a threat to the peace and security of the United States...when you kill over a personal issue, it's murder. When you kill as a designated representative of your government to remove a threat to your nation—that is war." According to Brown (without elaboration), "Piety continues to be a tradition in American military ranks."

Most chaplains represent various factions of Christianity. Although the early Christian church members were pacifists, under Emperor Constantine the Great in the 4th century the Christian religion became the state church. Generally, Christian denominations have dutifully served in whatever wars their respective state has declared. Mahatma Gandhi once said, "The only people who do not think Jesus was a pacifist are Christians." On the other hand, the highly influential Catholic Saint Augustine (354-430 AD) described a *just war* as "benevolent severity."

Chaplains have a dangerous and difficult task. They may be called to offer comfort and spiritual enrichment at the risk of their own lives. Of course, those whom our government considers the *enemy* are often supplied with their own chaplains, who likewise beseech the Almighty to bless and protect the troops under their care. Is it difficult for God, presumably the same Deity invoked under different names, to decide who shall be killed or mutilated in a particular battle?

Meanwhile our chaplains carry out their challenging and contradictory role, including blessing weapons of enormous destructive power such as the nuclear submarine "U.S.S. City of Corpus Christi." That city's name means "the Body of Christ."

chemical weapons: highly toxic forms of certain gases, liquids, or solids that will disable and/or kill when spread by a variety of means including *artillery, bombs* and spray tanks. Except for Russia, the United States has the world's largest chemical weapons stockpile. Iraq, despite the fact that a U.S.-led *coalition* attacked Iraq in 2003 in part because the U.S. claimed that Saddam Hussein was hiding vast quantities of such weapons, apparently has none.

It is true that at one time Iraq possessed and used these cruel weapons against its own people, as well as against Iran. As detailed in the *New York Times* (Dec.23, 2003) Donald Rumsfeld—-later the secretary of defense under George W. Bush—traveled to Iraq in 1984 as a special envoy for the Reagan administration. There, he reassured officials that, according to the *Times,* "The United States was eager to improve ties with President Saddam Hussein despite his use of chemical weapons, newly declassified documents show."

Iraq frequently used mustard gas and the nerve agent Tabun against Iranian soldiers, killing at least ten thousand. At least 100,000 suffered lingering, often serious effects, according to a March 2, 2003 National Public Radio report. Although the U.S. condemned the attacks, Mr. Rumsfeld was told to convey the message to Iraq that the condemnation was "strictly in principle and that America's priority was to prevent an Iranian victory in the Iran-Iraq war [1980-1988] and to improve bilateral ties."

According to a detailed analysis by journalist Jeremy Scahill (Aug.2, 2002) for Common Dreams News Center (www.commondreams.org), "In 1988, Saddam's forces attacked Kurdish civilians with poisonous gas from Iraqi helicopters and planes. U.S. intelligence sources told the *L.A. Times* in 1991, they 'believe that the American-built helicopters were among those dropping the deadly bombs.'" Five thousand men, women, and children were killed in that assault. Later, "senior officials" revealed that they did not want to see Iraq punished because "they wanted to shore up Iraq's ability to pursue the war with Iran." During that war, more than one million humans were killed.

The *Sunday Herald* (Scotland)(September 8, 2002) discusses a U.S. Senate committee report revealing that the U.S., under Presidents Ronald Reagan and George Bush, Sr. "sold materials including anthrax (and) nerve gas...to Iraq right up until March 1992." The *Herald* also notes that U.S. Defense Department documents "show that Britain sold Iraq the drug pralidoxine, an antidote to nerve gas, in March, 1992, after the end of the Gulf War. Pralidoxine can be reverse engineered to create nerve gas."

The Germans used chemicals with deadly effect in World War I, during which chlorine, phosgene, and mustard gas killed 92,000 and injured over one million more. After the war, the Geneva Protocol of 1925 prohibited such horrendous weapons. However, although none were used in World War II, Germany and later many other nations, including the U.S., mounted large-scale chemical weapons research programs. The U.S. used massive amounts of chemical defoliants during the Vietnam War, such as Agent Orange, resulting in many human *casualties*. Exposure to chemical weapons during the *Gulf war* is now widely regarded as a cause of the *Gulf War Syndrome*.

Finally, in 1997, an international Chemical Weapons Convention (CWC) went into effect. Signed by the United States in 1993, it "bans the production, acquisition, stockpiling, transfer and use of chemical weapons." However, the United States already had accumulated the world's second largest stockpile weapons of those weapons. In September 2003 the U.S. asked for an extension of its pledge to destroy 45 percent of its chemical weapons by 2004. Millions of decaying rockets, mortars, and other devices filled with these deadly materials are stored at eight depots across the country. The U.S. is gradually destroying these by incineration or the less controversial neutralization, but it seems unlikely that the multi-billion dollar task will be done by the new 2012 deadline.

The eagerness of the George W. Bush administration to gather public support for a long-planned attack on Iraq in 2003 led the President to sell the notion that Saddam Hussein, our former ally, was once again prepared to unleash the scourge of chemical weapons. The President declared on September 26, 2002 "The Iraqis possesses biological and chemical weapons." In his Address on Iraq, October 7, 2002, he stated boldly, "We know that the regime has produced thousands of tons of chemical agents, including mustard gas, sarin nerve gas, and VX nerve gas."

By February 5, 2003, Secretary of State Colin Powell was telling the United Nations Security Council "Our conservative estimate is that Iraq today has a stockpile of between 100 and 500 tons of chemical weapons agent. That is enough to fill 16,000 battlefield rockets." The day after Powell's presentation, President Bush maintained "Iraq has also provided Al Qaeda with chemical and biological weapons training." Just before the war began, President Bush, in a March 6, 2003 press conference flatly declared, "Iraqi operatives continue to hide biological and chemical agents to avoid detection by inspectors."

Intense searching for chemical weapons and other *weapons of mass destruction* after the "official" end of the war found nothing. On February 24, 2004, the Associated Press reported Hans Blix, the former chief UN weapons inspector from 2000 to mid-2003 as concluding "The justification for the war—the existence of weapons of mass destruction—was without foundation...Saddam was dangerous to his own people but not a great, and certainly not an immediate, danger to his neighbors and to the world."

By early 2004 the Bush administration was scrambling to defend their having gone to war based on their grandiose assertions about Iraq's supposed stockpiles of *nuclear,* chemical, and *biological* weapons. In January 2004, the widely respected Carnegie Endowment for International Peace (www.ceip.org) published a point-by-point rebuttal of those assertions.

As evidence mounted for the suspicion that the war had been waged for motives other then those offered publicly by the Bush White House, a curious incident that had occurred back in April 2002 began to assume more relevance. In The Hague, 48 of 49 member states of the Chemical Weapons Convention—financially dependent on the U.S and under heavy pressure from the Americans —voted to dismiss Jose Bustani, the Head of the Organization for the Prohibition of Chemical Weapons (OPCW).

On April 23, 2002 the *New Scientist* reported " The move followed a two-month campaign against Bustani by the U.S... The U.S...alleged that Bustani wanted the OPCW to take over the search for chemical weapons in Iraq...This led to suggestions that the U.S. was trying to remove Bustani because, if Iraq accepted, this would remove one justification for a U.S. attack on Iraq."

civilization: Historians,   anthropologists,   sociologists, theologians, and other assorted scholars are divided over a common definition of "civilization." In its widest sense it is generally understood as, according to the American Heritage Dictionary: "The type of culture or society developed by a particular nation or region or in a particular epoch."

As the administration of George W. Bush began to beat the drums of war in its march towards the invasion of Iraq for the second time in only twelve years, a particular notion of civilization began to emerge as a tool to foster support. In May 2002, in the first stop of his European tour, Bush told the German Bundestag, "Our generation faces new and grave threats to liberty, to the safety of our people and to civilization itself."

On September 4 of that same year the President addressed a letter to certain Congress members that warned, "The months ahead will be important ones and the civilized world must come together to deal with the threat posed by the Iraqi regime." By January 30, 2003, Vice President Dick Cheney was exhorting an enthusiastic audience at the 30th annual Conservative Political Action Conference "We are defending both ourselves and the safety and survival of civilization itself."

The result of choosing any other path but war to deal with the regime of Saddam Hussein was now clear. It would be the loss of the progress made by humanity over the thousands of years since civilizations as cultural entities had emerged. Ironically, these had evolved in a few distinct population centers such as China, India, Africa—and one from the very region now known as Iraq.

This was now a "war of civilizations." Mahdi Elmandjra, in his 1991 *The First Civilizational War*, had denounced the *Gulf War* as hinging on a Euro-centric point of view of civilizations. He urged increased recognition of the world's cultural diversity. On the other hand, the Harvard political scientist Samuel Huntington, in his popular 1996 *The Clash of Civilizations and the Remaking of World Order* maintained that the wars of the future would pit against each other civilizations defined by common language and (especially) religious beliefs. It was to be, as he said, "The West against the rest"—the latter being most especially the Chinese and the Muslims. Huntington urged that the West maintain their technological and military superiority.

Peter Berkowitz, in his observations on Huntington's thesis (*Boston Globe*, Feb.15, 2004) concludes that "[Huntington's] bedrock claim that the sources of conflict in international affairs are permanent, that religion is primary, and that the dream of a democratic and multicultural international order is a dangerous delusion are congruent with abiding conservative convictions."

Now that the Cold War had disappeared, it appeared that the Bush administration had filled the void by invoking Huntington's philosophy. They sponsored a clash of good versus *evil*—the U.S. and whatever *allies* it could gather (see *coalition of the willing*) against Islam, as represented by Iraq.

Retired Army Lt. Gen. Jay Garner, who served (briefly) as the first civil administrator (see *viceroy*) in charge of *reconstruction* and humanitarian aid after the "official" end of *Operation Iraqi Freedom* maintained a positive approach as Iraq lay in ruins. He told reporters that Iraq "was the jewel of the Middle East at one time and it can be the jewel of the Middle East again...And as we all know, not to offend you any, but a lot of civilization began here also, and law began here. And so we're returning all that."

cluster munitions: remarkably cruel weapons typically delivered as *bombs* or *artillery* shells. Both are deadly containers that explode above the surface (see *airburst*), spewing out clusters of up to several hundred smaller *bomblets* over a wide area. The newest cluster bomb, the CBU-107, first used in Iraq in 2003, spews out a volley of 3000 metal "arrows".

Bomblets fragment into a vicious hail of hot, jagged metal shards that can pierce whatever humans are in the vicinity, shattering their bones and internal organs, and tearing off their limbs. About 30 percent of those who are not killed immediately die from their injuries, even if good medical care is available.

Cluster munitions do double duty as killers. In many cases from 5-20 percent of the bomblets fail to explode. These live "duds" can lie in wait for years until an unsuspecting person—often a child—touches and detonates them. According to a 2003 report prepared for the Traprock Peace Center (www.traprockpeace.org) at least 372 Iraqis were killed after *Operation Iraqi Freedom* from accidental contact with some of the thousands of duds left over from that war. There are no precise figures for those killed and maimed over the last 13 years from the 1.2-1.5 million unexploded bomblets remaining from the 1991 *Gulf War*, during which the U.S and UK dropped up to 80,000 cluster bombs containing as many as 30 million bomblets. In the 2003 Operation Iraqi Freedom, *coalition* forces dropped 1,276 cluster bombs, delivering 247,836 bomblets.

According to a companion paper to MedAct's detailed and informative report, *Continuing Collateral Damage: the Health and Environmental Costs of War on Iraq 2003*, cluster munitions should not be tolerated as legal weapons of war. MedAct (www. medact.org), an organization of health professionals dedicated to publicizing the health consequences of war, poverty and environmental degradation, is the UK affiliate of the International Physicians for the Prevention of Nuclear War (www.ippnw.org), the recipient of the 1985 Nobel Peace Prize.

They emphasize that, while "cluster weapons are not illegal *per se*... because of their indiscriminate effect, the use of cluster munitions, especially in built-up areas" violates several principles of the *Geneva Conventions* concerning protection of civilians. They cite the *Landmine Monitor Report* of 2003, which documents the use of cluster munitions in many populated areas throughout Iraq during Operation Iraqi Freedom, including Baghdad, Basra, Hillah, Mosul and Nasiriyah. They conclude that there is a widespread belief that cluster munitions "should be made illegal on the basis of their long-term negative effects on health and reconstruction, which go well beyond the scope of the conflict's objectives."

International pressure has led to at least a first step in dealing with the "explosive remnants of war (ERW)," many of which are cluster munitions. In December 2003, after a year of negotiations,

92 countries including the U.S. agreed on establishing a new protocol to the 1980 Convention on Conventional Weapons. However, this protocol, still not ratified and legally binding, does not prohibit the use of any weapons. It speaks only to responsibilities for clearance of ERW and programs to warn and educate populations at risk. According the Human Rights Watch (www.hrw.org), the agreement is a "step forward, but it falls far short of what is needed."

The U.S. military recognizes that unexploded cluster munitions are hazardous to both civilians and its own forces. The UK uses *bomblets* in its *artillery* shells that self-destruct if they do not explode immediately. The U.S. has agreed that cluster munitions produced after 2005 will be 99 percent reliable. However, according to Human Rights Watch Briefing Paper, March 2003, this policy does not forbid using existing munitions, with a higher rate of dud production. They explain "The U.S. stockpiles more than one billion of these...there is a fundamental inconsistency in acknowledging the dangers of these...and the need to replace them, while still permitting their use."

coalition of the willing: an expression favored by the George W. Bush administration to refer to a group of nations patched together, principally through coercion, to give an appearance of international support for the coalition's invasion of Iraq in 2003.

That attack, known as *Operation Iraqi Freedom,* required every bit of public support it could muster. According to a distinguished panel of forty-four legal scholars (www.smh.com. au) "The initiation of a war against Iraq by the self-styled 'coalition of the willing' would be a fundamental violation of international law."

In late January 2003, Britain's Prime Minister Tony Blair arrived in Washington D.C. bearing a pledge of support from nine European leaders for President Bush's plans to disarm Saddam

Hussein's regime. That would mark the beginning of what Elmar Brok, a German Christian Democrat labeled "the race of the vassals." The major signatories were the United Kingdom, Italy and Spain. On March 18, 2003, U.S. Secretary of State Colin Powell released the names of 30 countries that had publicly signed on in support of the impending U.S.-led invasion. He referred to these as a "coalition of the willing." According to the *Washington Post* (March 19, 2003) one of those countries, Colombia, had been unaware that its name was included on the select list.

Powell revealed that were 15 other supporting nations who preferred to remain anonymous. On that same day, The Heritage Foundation (www.heritage.org), a Washington, D.C.-based conservative think tank, always eager to please, announced that " To date there are 54 countries that have joined the Coalition of the Willing—*not* including Canada, Germany, and France, which have recently offered conditional support...This does not include all of the 15 nations that have offered quiet support."

Two days later, on March 20, the Bush Administration added Micronesia and the Marshall Islands, along with a few other small nations, to swell the "official" total to 43. The next day, it became 45. Finally, the White House issued a press release on March 27 listing "forty-nine countries publicly committed to the Coalition." They added, "This number is still growing." The announcement stressed that the population of the Coalition countries numbers "1.23 billion people," the members have a "combined GDP of approximately $22 trillion," and number "every major race, religion (and) ethnicity."

Combat troops came from the U.S., Britain, Australia and Poland. Assistance from the rest of the coalition ranged from medical and decontamination teams to at least 13 written statements of "support." In September 2003, months after the "official" end of hostilities, and Iraq's people and infrastructure had been devastated, a new partner arrived. Almost 800 years after the Mongol general Hulegu—a grandson of Genghis Khan—had sacked Baghdad, killing 80,000 people, 180 Mongolian Army soldiers arrived in Iraq, offering their services.

In the final analysis, despite the boast by Secretary of Defense Donald Rumsfeld in a March 20, 2003 press conference that "The coalition in this activity is larger than the coalition that existed during the Gulf War in 1991" the hodgepodge of partners in 2003 turned out to be more dependents than allies. The 1991 *Gulf War*, another shameful invasion, had at least the veneer of international support because of its ratification by the United Nations.

The title "coalition of the willing" has been lampooned by critics variously as the "coalition of the coerced," "coalition of the billing," "coalition of the shilling," "coalition of the sullenly acquiescent," and "coalition of the bought off." Detailed analyses by the Institute for Policy Studies (IPS)(www.ips-dc.org)(May 12, March 24, 2003) discussed the leverage employed by the Bush Administration in assembling the coalition. The reports note that "some governments, including Spain, Italy, Austria, Denmark, Portugal and Japan, have accepted the U.S. position as their own, despite the massive opposition of their publics...Other governments simply fear repercussions from the world's sole superpower, whose President has openly threatened that after September 11, every country is either 'with us or with the terrorists.'"

Some may have recalled the experience of Yemen, described in the IPS reports. After that country voted against a resolution authorizing what was to be the Gulf War, a U.S. diplomat told the Yemeni ambassador, "That will be the most expensive 'no' vote you ever cast." A few days later, "The U.S. cut its entire aid budget to Yemen."

Eight Eastern European countries that had joined the coalition of the willing were eager for membership in NATO. On May 8, 2003 President Bush asked the U.S. Senate to approve the NATO membership of seven of those countries. Jordan garnered $1 billion from Congress in their April 2003 supplemental appropriations bill, and Egypt was given $300 million. Poland was awarded a special deal on 48 U.S.-made F-16 fighter jets. Australia was promised a free trade agreement.

Despite George W. Bush's claim that the U.S.-led coalition "includes nations from every part of the globe," the coalition nations numbered less than 20 percent of the world's population —a world in which the majority of the citizens, in unprecedented public demonstrations, opposed the war.

Moreover, the Institute for Policy Studies (www.ips-dc.org) points out that the coalition of the willing "included several countries with dismal human rights records." They added, "The U.S. State Department's annual human rights survey describes the overall human rights situation in 18 of the coalition countries as poor or extremely poor."

Every little bit helped, however. The wire service Agence France-Presse reported that in March 2003, Morocco had offered 2,000 monkeys to help detonate land mines. They noted, "An official at the Moroccan Embassy could not confirm the presence of monkeys in the coalition of the willing."

Coalition Provisional Authority (CPA): the organization given total authority over the affairs of Iraq after the official *end of hostilities* in *Operation Iraqi Freedom.* On May 22, 2003 the UN passed Security Council Resolution 1483, which gave the Coalition Provisional Authority its mandate to take over Iraq's governance. The CPA earlier had taken over the functions of the Office for Reconstruction and Humanitarian Assistance (ORHA). President George W. Bush appointed retired Army General Jay Garner on April 23, 2003 to head the ORHA as the Civilian Administrator of Iraq (see *Viceroy*).

Garner, who had helped develop the *Patriot missile* system and commanded missile batteries during the *Gulf War*, had most recently been president of SYColeman, a *defense contractor*. Garner's reign lasted about two weeks until it appeared that he was unable to handle the post-war chaos. He was replaced by L. Paul Bremer III. Bremer's qualifications for seeing to it that Iraq emerge from the brutal U.S.-led attack as a nation that would best serve U.S. interests included having been managing director at Kissinger Associates, a worldwide consulting firm founded by Henry Kissinger, a principal architect of the Vietnam War.

In an interview for The *Washington Post*, June 18, 2003, Bremer remarked "As long as we're here, we are the occupying power...It's a very ugly word, but it's true" (see *occupation*). In July 2003 Bremer established the *Iraqi Governing Council*, a 25-member organization of handpicked Iraqis who were given a veneer of authority, with Bremer having absolute veto power over their decisions.

The Coalition Provisional Authority finally disbanded when, on June 28, 2004, "full sovereignty" was handed to a 33-member Iraq interim government—selected through collaboration between the Iraqi Governing Council and the United States. Bremer left behind dozens of regulations limiting the new government's authority (see *occupation*).

collateral damage: generally understood as referring to the occasional, regrettable loss of civilian life during a war. However, even if one restricts its meaning to include harm done only to non-combatants—disregarding the inevitable deaths, injuries, and long-term physical and psychological damage to the *soldiers*—the full extent of the human cost of war is typically underestimated.

MedAct, an organization of health professionals dedicated to publicizing the health consequences of war, poverty and environmental degradation, is the UK affiliate of the International Physicians for the Prevention of Nuclear War (IPPNW), the recipient of the 1985 Nobel Peace Prize. In November 2002

MedAct published a detailed, objective analysis of the human suffering brought on by the 1991 *Gulf War*. This report, *Collateral Damage*—available at (www.medact.org) or (www.ippnw.org)—offers a graphic picture of the extent and ramifications of the first U.S.-led onslaught against Iraq.

According to MedAct, as many as 120,000 Iraqi soldiers as well as up to 15,000 civilians may have been killed during the Gulf War in 1991. Another 20,000 to 35,000 civilians died in the "uprisings and other postwar violence." There may have been 300,000 wounded Iraqi soldiers. Of the estimated 1.8 million refugees, disease and hunger killed between 15,000 and 30,000. Approximately 100,000 Iraqi civilians died within one year from the effects of the war on their health. Child and infant mortality increased enormously, and the environment in which the weakened survivors were trying to survive had suffered "unprecedented damage". The UN had placed Iraq under strict economic *sanctions* in 1990. Twelve years later, "... between 344,000 and 525,000" children under the age of five had died. "The health of the Iraqi people...suffered enormously from the combined impact of the war and sanctions, and has not returned to prewar levels."

This was the scene spread out far below the military aircraft in late March 2003, as they carried out their massive bombardment of Baghdad, a city of five million people. The coalition's plans were to instill *Shock and Awe* on an already suffering, battered people. The ensuing seven weeks of concentrated bombing, *artillery* strikes, cruise missiles, and other modern weaponry massed against a country that had already suffered so much, wreaked predictable havoc.

MedAct had hoped that a better understanding of the nature and extent of the human tragedy in Iraq during and after the Gulf War might influence war planners to at least reconsider another devastating attack on a population already profoundly weakened by the war ten years earlier, and by the brutal *sanctions* which followed. In MedAct's words, "This full cost must be counted, not only to help plan effective humanitarian intervention and reconstruction, but to insure informed debate about whether future conflicts will prove more harmful than the problems they purport to solve." Four months after the report was released, the U.S.-led *coalition of the willing* unleashed the terrors of *Operation Iraqi Freedom*.

Accurate data on collateral deaths and injuries as a result of *Operation Iraqi Freedom* are difficult to ascertain. However, on October 29, 2004 the noted British medical journal *The Lancet* published a study by a research team at the renowned Johns Hopkins University in Baltimore. They concluded, after extensive interviews across Iraq, that at least 100,000 Iraqi civilians died as a consequence of the 2003 U.S.-led attack on Iraq—mostly from bombing or rocket attacks. MedAct concurred with those results.

Compounding the immediate effects of deaths and injuries was the ravaging of Iraq's environment and physical infrastructure—water supplies, electrical power, sanitation systems, hospitals, and agricultural ecosystems. Caught between fearsome weapons and the destruction of their surroundings, over half of the Iraqi civilian deaths were among women and children.

The U.S. Air Force insists that it goes to great lengths to prevent civilian deaths. According to Air Force Master Sgt. Douglas Frickey, interviewed for the April 17, 2003 *Air Force Print News*; "Even though our top goal is to take out the desired target, our primary concern and bottom line is to lessen and, if, possible, avoid, at all costs, any type of civilian casualties"(see *take out*). The interviewer added, "Collateral damage estimation is not a true science, but it is a discipline that requires intense attention and precision, and one in which on-the-job training is the only schooling available, Frickey said."

According to the *Guardian* (April 3, 2003)"Pentagon experts estimate that human and mechanical errors send ten percent of precision weapons astray." These go astray from "targeted buildings and facilities in or near densely populated urban areas..." (see *precision-guided munitions*).

Air Force Link (May 28, 2003) passed on some of Defense Secretary Donald Rumsfeld's thoughts on the effects of war on the Iraqis. While admitting that Iraq's problems are real, he insisted that they shouldn't be blown out of proportion. Comparing Iraq to the United States at the end of the American Revolution, Rumsfeld mused "Those early years of our young republic were characterized by chaos and confusion...so too it will take time and patience, trial and error, and hard work for the Iraqi people to overcome the challenges they face today."

column: rows of *soldiers*, or rows of vehicles containing soldiers. Typical media accounts concerning military action involving columns are as follows:

"A column of about 20 Iraqi armored vehicles was destroyed Tuesday by British forces from the air..." (CNN.com, March 27, 2003)

"A column of Iraqi tanks that tried to attack coalition forces was destroyed in a lopsided battle..."(CNews, March 27, 2003)

"This was the third column of Iraqi troops that the British have pummeled in the last 24 hours." (foxnews.com, March 27, 2003)

"British aircraft have bombed a column of about 70 Iraqi armored vehicles..." (CNN.com, March 26, 2003)

When columns are "destroyed" or "pummeled" or "bombed," the people in those columns are often torn to pieces and incinerated. Sometimes soldiers will leave their damaged vehicles and become *dismounts*. Then the attacking forces will *engage* the dismounts— now even more vulnerable as *soft targets*— with whatever weapons they have at their disposal in order to kill and injure the fleeing survivors. This is considered a type of *victory.*

combat debut: Traditionally, in the upper echelons of society, young women have been officially enrolled into those elevated circles in the form of a "debut." The "debutantes," shy and graceful, appear dressed in their finest before an admiring gathering as a formal dinner and dance begin.

The military is fond of referring to the first entrance of almost anything into combat as a debut. Instead of young women appearing in quiet elegance, the combat debut may take the following form:

"The U.S. Navy's newest combat aircraft, the Boeing F/A-18E Super Hornet, made its combat debut on 6 November, when aircraft from the...U.S.S. Abraham Lincoln struck air defence sites in Southern Iraq."

"...A newly formed Stryker brigade combat team...intended as a model for the Army of the future... scheduled to make its first combat debut in Iraq."

"Six years before its scheduled deployment, the E-8A [aircraft] makes a spectacular combat debut."

"Sensor Fuzed Weapon combat debut forces troops to surrender."

And so the dance of death commences as soldiers, weapons, aircraft and ships are welcomed into the company of their peers.

Committee for Peace and Security in the Gulf (CPSG): a group of political insiders assembled in 1990, with the discreet blessing of the White House, to win support for attacking Iraq and removing Saddam Hussein.

Stephen Solarz—then a Democratic congressperson from New York—recruited former Reagan Department of Defense official Richard Perle as well as Ann Lewis, a former political director of the Democratic National Committee, to serve as the committee's directors. Perle, who in March 2003 would resign as chairperson of the *Defense Policy Board*—advisors to Secretary of Defense Donald Rumsfeld—amid allegations of a financial conflict of interest, became the principal fundraiser for the CPSG.

According to the *Washington Post* (June 23, 1991) Perle raised much of the money from *defense contractors* described as a "who's who of the defense industry" in order to pay for a national advertising campaign. The defense contractors reportedly "did not contribute out of hope of sales in the Mideast, but to 'encourage general support for the President.'" Jim Lobe of the Project Against the Present Danger (www.presentdanger.org) reported that CPSG received a considerable grant from the Lynde & Harry Bradley Foundation. This Wisconsin-based organization has also been a major donor to the *Project for the New American Century* and the *American Enterprise Institute.* Many of the members of the CPSG would become involved with both of those conservative organizations— and some would ultimately assume positions of influence in the George W. Bush administration. (For a guide to these Byzantine interconnections see rightweb.irc-online.org).

The newly formed CPSG urged the George Bush, Sr. administration to eliminate Iraq's military capability as "an explicit goal." They rejected the premise that a withdrawal by Saddam Hussein's forces from Kuwait would be sufficient—they insisted on a military solution (a.k.a. war) even though it would "regrettably result in casualties."

The first *Gulf War* stopped short of a full-scale military invasion of Iraq. In 1998, the CPSG, by then a 39-member group, appealed in a letter to President Clinton to "go beyond a military strike in Iraq and to help overthrow Iraqi President Saddam Hussein and replace his regime with a provisional government." The letter urges that the U.S. "recognize a provisional government of Iraq based on the principles and leaders of the Iraqi National Congress... that is representative of all the peoples of Iraq." Further, the President should "launch a systematic air campaign against the Republican Guard divisions...and position U.S. ground force equipment in that region..."(see *air campaign, Iraqi National Congress*).

Those signing the letter to Clinton included Richard Perle, Stephen Solarz, William Kristol, Donald Rumsfeld, and Paul Wolfowitz (for the latter three see *Committee for the Liberation of Iraq*). CNN.com (February 20, 1998), commenting on the letter, was of the opinion that "While it's no secret the Clinton administration would welcome the removal of Hussein from power, it is against federal law for the U.S. government to assassinate a head of state. In addition, the administration considers the proposal announced Friday as too expensive—in military commitment and overall cost—and too difficult to justify in international forums such as the United Nations" (see *assassination*).

When George W. Bush assumed the presidency, and appointed Donald Rumsfeld as his secretary of defense, and Paul Wolfowitz as deputy secretary of defense, those considerations would be put aside. The United Nations would be scorned, and assassination became *decapitation*.

During the 2003 full-scale attack on Iraq—desired for years by the CSPG and its adherents—the bombing of the *Amiriya bunker*, which killed hundreds of innocent Iraqi civilians, was eerily reminiscent of the 1991 bombing of a Baghdad building, which had also slaughtered hundreds. After the 1991 tragedy, the *New York Times* (February 14, 1991) quoted the reaction of Ann Lewis, a charter member of the CSPG. Lewis said, "War is not surgery, and even in surgery sometimes the wrong people die." At the time she was voicing her sentiments, the Committee for Peace and Security in the Gulf was answering its phone with the greeting "The Peace Committee."

Committee for the Liberation of Iraq (CLI): a group formed in late 2002, consisting of mostly neoconservatives and foreign policy hawks. Their aim was, in the words of their mission statement, "to promote regional peace, political freedom and international security by replacing the Saddam Hussein regime with a democratic government that respects the rights of the Iraqi people and ceases to threaten the community of nations... The regime of Saddam Hussein has...acquired weapons of mass destruction...it has supported international terrorism...the current government of Iraq poses a clear and present danger to its neighbors, to the United States and to free peoples throughout the world."

Basically, the role of the CLI was to unleash an unabashed lobbying effort to make a case for attacking Iraq. According to Committee Chairperson Bruce P. Jackson, the Iraqi government was "a tyranny that needs to be changed." Jackson, a director of the *Project for the New American Century* (PNAC) and former Lockheed Martin vice president (see *defense contractors*) earlier had successfully lobbied for NATO expansion. Jackson revealed, "People in the White House said, 'We need you to do for Iraq what you did for NATO.'"

As the CLI took shape, polls were showing that the American people were reluctant to support a war against Iraq, fearful of its many consequences. In early November 2002 a Gallup poll found that 60 percent of Americans wanted to give diplomacy more time, and only 25 percent favored an immediate war. According to Kurt Nimmo, writing on November 19, 2002 for the Global Policy Forum (www.globalpolicy.org), the CLI was determined "to convince the American people that bombing and terror in the name of democracy against...enemies is the 'moral' thing to do."

The CLI, although it began officially in 2002, had deep roots in earlier efforts to move U.S. foreign policy towards the establishment of a global American empire. The *Project for the New American Century* (PNAC), a Washington, D.C.-based conservative think tank, was created in 1997. Its goal was to work towards the establishment of a worldwide *American peace*, or *Pax Americana*—a "peace" marked by unilateral military aggression against any country that the U.S. government decides is not acting in America's *national interest*. The PNAC June 1997 "Statement of Principles" signers included Jeb Bush, Dick Cheney, Paul Wolfowitz, and Donald Rumsfeld.

The PNAC aims are amply spelled out in their September 2000 document entitled *Rebuilding America's Defenses: Strategy, Force, and Resources for a New Century* (RAD). The report opens by stating flatly that the U.S. is a superpower that "faces no global rival. America's grand strategy should aim to preserve and extend this advantageous position as far into the future as possible."

This aggressive philosophy was a rebirth of an earlier document encouraging *preemptive* unilateral military strikes. Paul Wolfowitz, then undersecretary of defense for policy, drafted the 1992 *Defense Planning Guidance*. The George Bush Sr. administration considered it too radical. By 1998 Wolfowitz, joined by, among others, Donald Rumsfeld, would write to President Clinton urging him to "turn your administration's attention to implementing a strategy for removing Saddam's regime from power."

When President George W. Bush named Dick Cheney as his vice president and put Cheney, a founding member of PNAC, in charge of the new administration's transition, the door to the White House suddenly was wide open. Donald Rumsfeld became secretary of defense, while Paul Wolfowitz would serve as deputy defense secretary. The latter's formerly rejected *Defense Planning Guidance* would morph into the Bush administration's September 2002 *National Security Strategy*.

Then came the terrible tragedy of September 11, 2001. Just nine days later, PNAC published an open letter to President Bush, arguing "even if evidence does not link Iraq directly to the attack, any strategy aiming at the eradication of terrorism and its sponsors must include a determined effort to remove Saddam Hussein from power in Iraq."

The CLI disbanded after the official *end of hostilities* in Iraq was declared in May 2003. The CLI had done its job well. By October 2003, a Pew Research Center poll found that two-thirds of the adult respondents were convinced that Saddam Hussein had assisted the September 11th terrorists. Iraq would be savagely attacked by the U.S.-led *coalition of the willing.* Following the principles of the PNAC and the RAD, "liberated" Iraq would no doubt house a major U.S. military presence indefinitely.

The Committee for the Liberation of Iraq had numbered among its members some of the same people who had been instrumental in this evolution of a radical re-orientation of American foreign policy. These included former House Speaker Newt Gingrich, Richard Perle, former assistant secretary of defense, and William Kristol, editor of the conservative *The Weekly Standard*, an architect of the RAD and co-founder of the PNAC. *The Weekly Standard* is owned by Rupert Murdoch. He also owns Fox News, one of *Operation Iraqi Freedom's* most ardent cheerleaders.

constabulary duties: a new assignment that the George W. Bush administration plans for the U.S. military so that its *soldiers* can become a roving police force, especially in those countries which the U.S. wants to control.

The American Heritage Dictionary defines a "constable" as "a peace officer with less authority and smaller jurisdiction than a sheriff, empowered to serve writs and warrants and make arrests." George W. Bush had far more grandiose plans for his military constables. On September 29, 2002—writing well before the onset of *Operation Iraqi Freedom*—Jay Bookman, deputy editorial page editor of the *Atlanta Journal-Constitution* predicted that " This war, should it come, is intended to mark the official emergence of the United States as a full-fledged global empire, seizing sole responsibility and authority as planetary policeman."

Bookman's misgivings were widely shared, and with good reason. They were based on several documents outlining the Bush administration's unique and menacing plan for global domination. This would seem like a paranoid analysis if it were not for the words of the documents themselves. In May 1992, the Pentagon revised a draft of its global strategy, "softening" the language. That earlier document was roundly criticized when disclosed in the *New York Times* in March 1992, and was reportedly repudiated by the first President Bush. It stated that "Our first objective is to prevent the re-emergence of a new rival...While the U.S. cannot become the world's policeman...we will retain the preeminent responsibility for addressing selectively those wrongs which threaten not only our interests, but those of our allies and friends..."

The later, "softer" draft read "While the United States cannot become the world's policeman, neither can we allow our critical interests to depend solely on international mechanisms that can be blocked by countries whose interests may be very different from our own...we maintain the capabilities for addressing selectively those security problems that threaten our own interests." So much for the United Nations. The revised Pentagon document—a partly classified, unpublished framework for Pentagon planning—is known as the *Defense Planning Guidance 1994-1999*. It is assumed to be the model for the September 2000 paper *Rebuilding America's Defenses: Strategy, Forces and Resources for a New Century.*

The latter document was created by the *Project for the New American Century*, a conservative think tank formed in 1997 by Dick Cheney, Donald Rumsfeld, and Paul Wolfowitz among others, many of whom would become central figures in planning U.S. Middle East policy. *Rebuilding America's Defenses* is an extraordinary manifesto that emphasizes "This report proceeds from the belief that America should seek to preserve and extend its position of global leadership by maintaining the preeminence of U.S. military forces." It points out "At present the United States faces no global rival. America's grand strategy should aim to preserve and extend this advantageous position as far into the future as possible."

In order to maintain this superpower status, one of the "core missions" for U.S. military forces must be to "perform the 'constabulary' duties associated with shaping the security environment in critical regions." The kinds of forces envisioned are not those of "major theater campaigns" (a.k.a. big battles with thousands of troops). Rather, they need to be "forces configured for combat, but capable of long-term, independent constabulary operations." As examples the report names "the continuing 'no-fly' zone and other missions in Southwest Asia, and other presence missions in vital regions of East Asia" (see *no-fly zones*).

These constabulary forces are "far more complex and likely to generate violence than traditional peacekeeping missions... They demand American political leadership rather than that of the United Nations." They are to "establish security, stability, and order. American troops, in particular, must be regarded as part of an overwhelmingly powerful force."

In order to maintain a military presence ready to send in the constables to any region that does not act within our national interests the report recommends a much more widespread military force, beyond the 130 nations where we already maintain troops. That would include permanent bases in the Middle East, in Southeast Europe, Latin America, and in Southeast Asia.

On September 20, 2002, the White House released its *National Security Strategy*, which reads in part like another draft of *Rebuilding America's Defenses.* It even goes beyond the latter document, pressing for a policy of "convincing or compelling states to accept their sovereign responsibilities."

Shortly before the March, 2003 invasion of Iraq by U.S.-led

coalition forces, the Center for Strategic and International Studies (www.csis.org) and the Massachusetts Institute of Technology published *A Wiser Peace: An Action Strategy for a Post-Conflict Iraq*. They recommended the immediate development of a "Transnational Security Force" that would be ready with detailed plans for "civil security," civil policing efforts," supporting the "security requirements of humanitarian and emergency relief efforts." They urged "The United States must immediately identify and train a core force of U.S. military troops to perform constabulary (i.e. joint military and law enforcement) duties in Iraq."

That planning was not done, and chaos followed the war. As coalition troops faced daily attacks, troops not trained for constabulary duties were expected to carry them out. Eventually, according to the *Washington Post* (Feb. 23, 2004) "the new Iraqi security forces are to be given greater responsibility for maintaining order in the cities." But Secretary of Defense Donald Rumsfeld cautioned in the same interview that this would be a slow process. He appeared pleased that Iraqis were still anxious to join the security forces despite continuing attacks against police and military recruiting stations. Rumsfeld said "Instead of responding by acquiescing, we see that volunteers are still in line to join the police, they're still in line to join the army...instead of retreating, they are leaning forward and taking losses, and God bless them for it."

containment: a policy designed to discipline the leaders of an *enemy* state but which also results in punishing its innocent civilians.

During the 1980s the U.S. was allied with Iraq in opposition to the Iranian regime. But within a few days after Iraq invaded Kuwait in 1990 containment replaced cooperation. Containment included *sanctions*, control of the skies over Iraq, and UN weapons inspections. UN Resolution 661 called for economic sanctions on Iraq, barring all exports and imports, except for "medical supplies, foodstuffs, and other items of humanitarian need." After the cease-fire following *Operation Desert Storm*, UN Resolution 687 kept the sanctions in place.

The U.S., Britain, and France unilaterally established two *no-fly zones* soon after the war, to tighten the noose around Iraq. (No UN resolutions supported that action.) Iraq was prohibited from using any aircraft in either the Northern or Southern zones. By 1996 the latter no-fly zone would be extended from the Kuwait border to the vicinity of Iraq. By 1998 the Clinton administration had moved to "enhanced containment" of Iraq by "aggressive enforcement" of the no-fly zones. Legitimate targets were now broadened to include "command and control sites, relay stations, and intelligence gathering sites."

Air attacks, common throughout the 1990s, now accelerated. The Iraqi people, subjected to the terror of years of bombing, and unable to obtain sufficient food, medicine, or other necessities despite the conditions of the UN and an inadequate *Oil for Food* program, were suffering a humanitarian crisis of enormous proportions. An August 7, 2002 study by 12 non-governmental organizations (NGOs) said that, while much blame must be placed on the Iraqi government, the UN Security Council had "failed to provide protection to children who have suffered disproportionately under sanctions."

The NGOs—including Save the Children UK, Global Policy Forum, and the Quaker UN Office—cited several independent studies including one by the UN Children's Fund (UNICEF) which "amply documented a substantial rise in mortality of children, five years of age and below, and credible estimates suggest that at least 400,000 of these young children have died due to the sanctions."

Despite the overwhelming evidence that the Iraqi people were suffering and dying due to over a decade of "containment"—

a tragedy that had provoked worldwide opposition—Secretary of State Colin Powell would say in 2001, "I think we ought to declare our containment policy a success. We have kept him [Saddam] contained; kept him in his box." Senator Carl Levin, chair of the Senate Armed Services Committee told reporters in August 2002, "Containment is working."

"Successful" containment, in the words of a 2002 report by the British Catholic aid agency CAFOD (www.cafod.org.uk), had "resulted in untold suffering for millions of people—physical, mental, and cultural...A once prosperous nation—home to the world's second largest oil reserves—is being systematically de-developed, de-skilled, and reduced to penury."

The report warned of the implications of what was the then threatened attack on Iraq—and would, a few months later become *Operation Iraqi Freedom.* "It would be difficult to imagine a single more effective way of wreaking further devastation on an already devastated country... A militaristic or purely security approach to the problem of international terrorism is unimaginative and doomed to failure. Only if the world is prepared to tackle the root causes of conflict, liberation struggles, [and] terrorism (including state terrorism) is there a chance of arriving at durable and sustained solutions."

conventional weapons: all weapons with the exception of those that are *nuclear*, *biological*, or *chemical*. In other words, they are your "ordinary" weapons—*bombs*, *artillery*, landmines (see *area denial munitions*), machine guns, grenades, etc. This rogues' gallery of weapons realistically can be considered as *weapons of mass destruction.* While they are unable to kill and injure as many people in as short a time as their deadlier counterparts, they have killed far more, though in smaller increments. During World War I, for example, conventional weapons killed almost nine million *soldiers.*

The Convention on Conventional Weapons (CCW), also known as The United Nations Convention on Inhumane Weapons, or the Inhumane Weapons Convention, was concluded in Geneva in October 1980. Over the next 23 years various protocols were added and amended in this attempt, according to the UN, to "prohibit the employment in armed conflicts...weapons, projectiles and material and methods of warfare of a nature to cause superfluous injury or unnecessary suffering."

The kinds of weapons that are banned by the CCW are fragmentation weapons that strike people with fragments that are not detectable by X-rays, and landmines that do not self-destruct and are not detectable. It also "prohibits attacking civilians with any weapon or device designed to burn people or set fire to objects, through flame, heat or both." (The U.S. did not agree to that protocol.) The Convention also "prohibits the use of laser weapons specifically designed to cause permanent blindness to the naked eye..." In December 2003, 92 countries including the U.S. agreed to establish a new protocol outlining responsibilities for clearing live explosives left over from warfare—excluding landmines, covered in another protocol.

The parties agreeing to the CCW affirm that "the civilian population and the combatants shall at all times remain under the protection and authority of the principles of international law derived from established custom, from the principles of humanity and from the dictates of public conscience."

Certainly the CCW has made progress in lessening some of the ravages of war. Still, the various protocols of the CCW might be interpreted as follows: Please refrain from employing the weapons restricted by this Convention. However, you may continue in good conscience to lacerate humans with fragments which can be detected by X-rays. Shells tipped with *depleted uranium* still may be used, although they do incinerate the inhabitants of whatever armored vehicle they enter. *Daisy cutters, firebombs*, and *fuel-air explosives* are acceptable as well. Litter the landscape with landmines, as long as you can find where you put them. And please, do not use lasers to blind the *enemy*, but any other weapons you may have at hand that may cause blindness are certainly within your rights to use. Kill, maim, and incinerate your enemy, but please, don't cause "unnecessary suffering"—we prefer that you inflict only that which is necessary.

Before the 1991 *Gulf War* the international trade in conventional weapons was brisk and proceeded, with few exceptions, with little concern for arming those regimes that might become security threats (see *arms control*). There has been some reduction in the arms trade since then, leaving six major sources of conventional weapons: The U.S., France, the United Kingdom, Russia, China, and Germany. The first five supply most of the world's arms, with the U.S. accounting for the largest percentage of sales. All five nations are permanent members of the UN Security Council, whose aim is to foster world peace and security.

Countdown Iraq: just one example of a variety of promotional themes emblazoned across TV screens well before and also during *Operation Iraqi Freedom*. The various major news outlets vied for attention in a show of breathless anticipation of what was to be a self-fulfilling prophecy (as "countdown" implies) of an attack against Iraq. During the war, the televised news was a daily drama extolling the technical superiority of the *coalition of the willing* war machine.

One could hear, for example, CNN correspondent Walter Rogers reporting "Imagine for a moment a giant wave of steel sweeping across the southern Iraq desert, and imagine that almost hourly that wave grows in strength and numbers." The reports came complete with stirring music and "talking-heads"— usually retired military officers. Using maps, pointers, and advanced graphics, they blithely moved *assets*, *columns*, and *artillery* about the desert, pausing now and then to mention how "we" were "cleaning up pockets of resistance," or "attriting the enemy" (see *attrited, enemy, pockets*).

The "news" program themes differed depending on the particular attitudes of the parent news companies. MSNBC used "Countdown: Iraq," while NBC countered with "Target: Iraq." CBS offered "America at War," and CNN, which had made its fortune as the folks who brought you the first *Gulf War* in 1991, used "Showdown Iraq." CNN International, mindful of a more discerning world audience went with "Standoff in Iraq". The Canadian CBC, running against the tide, chose "Attack on Iraq."

The soundtracks for much of this were chosen carefully. The April 4, 2003 *Pittsburgh Post-Gazette* concluded that "CBS's music [was] the most overtly warlike, a surging electronic wall of sound that seems to use the beating rotors of attack helicopters as its rhythmic inspiration." Composer Peter Fish explained that he was trying to convey a "climate of fear." Over at Fox News "Hard-rock instrumentals blare as fighter jets, one of which morphs into an audibly screeching eagle, cross the screen..." Richard O'Brien, vice president and creative director of Fox News remarked that its music is "rock-influenced, for sure. We try to keep the sound and look younger and hipper than what our competition is."

Fox News is part of media giant Rupert Murdoch's properties, which also include the *Weekly Standard* (see *Committee for the Liberation of Iraq*). Murdoch, who insisted that in attacking Iraq "Bush [was] acting very morally, very correctly" felt that "There is going to be collateral damage. And if you really want to be brutal about it, better we get it done now than spread it out over months" (see *collateral damage*).

Even Murdoch's blunt comments were outdone by several popular TV personalities. For example, commenting on anti-war protestors in Hollywood, Joe Scarborough remarked, "These leftist stooges for anti-American causes are always given a free pass," while colleague Michael Savage added "They are absolutely committing sedition, or treason." Neil Cavuto, when the first statue of Saddam Hussein was torn down addressed those "who opposed the *liberation* of Iraq" by concluding, "You were sickening then, you are sickening now."

What passed as news—but in reality was a daily show of deference to the Bush White House—led to Fox becoming the top-rated cable news station throughout the war. Fox became the White House TV news channel. President Bush, by his own admission, does not read the daily newspapers. According to United Press International (UPI) "Researchers from the Program on International Policy at the University of Maryland find that those who relied on Fox for their news were more likely to have what the study called 'significant misperceptions' about the war in Iraq."

There was little relief from the daily diet of jingoism. Colman McCarthy, a long-time dedicated peace activist, teacher, and director of the Center for Teaching Peace in Washington, D.C. offered this plea in the April 19, 2003 *Washington Post*. "The tube turned into a parade ground for military men—all well-groomed white males—saluting the ethic that war is rational, that bombing and shooting are the way to win peace..."

McCarthy added "Why no dissenting voices to say what millions of people around the world proclaimed in the streets: that this U.S. invasion was illegal, unjust and unnecessary?" George Bush lectured the world that you're either with us or against us. America's networks got the message. They're with."

cowardice: the refusal of a *soldier* to take part in combat due to his overwhelming fear in the face of possible death on the battlefield. Upon conviction in a military court, the most severe penalty for doing so is death by execution.

The Manual for Courts-Martial defines cowardice as "misbehavior motivated by fear." They do add that fear is "a natural fear of apprehension when going into battle." The Military Judges' Benchbook describes cowardly conduct as "the refusal or abandonment of a performance of duty" before or in the presence of the enemy as "the result of fear."

Because fear is certainly a common emotion under the extreme stress of battle, cowardice cases are difficult to prosecute. The last U.S. military cowardice conviction on record is that of Pvt. Michael Gross, who was found guilty of running away from his company in Vietnam in 1968. He was sentenced to two years in prison.

During the horrendous carnage of the First World War, more than 306 British and Commonwealth soldiers were executed for military offenses, including 245 for *desertion* and one for cowardice. The Germans reportedly executed 18 for similar offenses. However, in the Second World War, the British did not pass a single death sentence, while the Germans executed about 20,000. In the Battle of Moscow during that war, 8,000 Soviet citizens were executed on charges of cowardice.

The lone execution in the Second World War was that of Pvt. Eddie Slovik, who was convicted of desertion. He was unfortunate to have been put on trial during some of the bloodiest fighting of the war, including the Battle of the Bulge. Desertion had become a growing problem, and General Eisenhower refused pleas for clemency for Pvt. Slovik.

During *Operation Iraqi Freedom*, Staff Sgt. Georg-Andreas Pogany, assigned to a team of Green Berets, though not one himself, was in the U.S. compound near Sammara, north of Baghdad when he saw the mangled body of an Iraqi killed after the man was seen shooting a rocket-propelled grenade. Pogany later told CNN.com that "The initial reaction was just a horrible sight and just a disbelief of what I was seeing and the fact that—

or trying to comprehend that that was a human being." Pogany became physically ill, vomited repeatedly, and suffered a panic attack that night.

The next morning he went to his sergeant, told him about his reactions, and asked for help because he was not fit to continue. After being confined to his room and put on a suicide watch, he met with a psychologist who diagnosed his condition as "a normal combat stress reaction" and recommended a few days rest. Instead, Pogany was sent back to Fort Carson, Colorado and charged with "cowardly conduct as a result of fear."

Eventually a military court reduced the charge to dereliction of duty, and offered Pogany a hearing, which could result in a decrease in rank rather than a prison term. He refused the offer, claiming that he was innocent. As of early 2004, the military was considering its options. Pogany returned to regular duty. He told *The Denver Post* in late January 2004, "I'll probably have to go back to Iraq...and go into battle and show them I can do my job" (see *job*).

Meanwhile, an advocacy group, the Shot at Dawn Campaign (SAD)(www.shotatdawn.org.uk) lobbies for pardons for all the 306 British and Commonwealth soldiers executed during the First World War. Each of the soldiers was tied to a post, blindfolded and shot at sunrise. SDA has constructed a memorial to their memory in the English Midlands. In Canada, in the House of Commons, on December 11, 2001, the names of the 23 Canadians among the executed—22 for desertion, and one for cowardice—were read into the First World War Book of Remembrance. Veterans Affairs Minister Ronald J. Duhamel said," The hardships they endured prior to their offenses will be unrecorded and unremembered no more."

Lt. Col. Dave Grossman, in *On Killing: The Psychological Cost of Learning to Kill in War and Society* (1996) writes; "Faced with the soldier's encounters with horror, guilt, fear, exhaustion, and hate, each man draws steadily from his own private reservoir of inner strength and fortitude until finally the well runs dry...at least 98 percent of all soldiers in close combat will ultimately become psychiatric casualties"(see *psychiatric casualties*).

critical regions: areas throughout the world in which the George W. Bush administration felt free to order the U.S. military to intervene with all necessary force in order to safeguard American "interests," "values" and the "American way of life" (see *national interests*).

The *Project for the New American Century* (PNAC)—a Washington, D.C.-based private conservative organization assembled in 1997 to offer advice on America's global strategy—published a highly influential report in September 2000. *Rebuilding America's Defenses: Strategy, Forces and Resources for a New Century* (RAD) would become the blueprint for the Bush administration's foreign policy agenda—embodied in its September 2002 *National Security Strategy.*

Among the four "core missions" listed in RAD for a remodeled 21st century U.S. military is its role in "perform(ing) the constabulary duties associated with shaping the security environment in critical regions" (see *constabulary duties*). Where exactly are these regions and what specifically defines them as critical?

It doesn't matter. Neither of the above documents defines the regions with any specificity nor spells out the ways in which any particular population will incite our attacks beyond a few generalities. They include enough detail to conclude that the U.S. military will be deployed throughout the world—and in the words of the RAD—"...control of space will inevitably require the application of force both in space in from space." Neither do they define the causes for which people will die— which they cite as American "values," "principles," "moral interests," "national interests," and "the American way of life" (see *national interests*).

The RAD continues, "At present the United States faces no global rival. There are however, potentially powerful states dissatisfied with the current situation and eager to change it." The report goes on to explain that the task of the new military will be to "defend key regions of Europe, East Asia, and the Middle East..." They urge the maintenance of an "American peace" based on a "secure foundation [of] unquestioned U.S. military preeminence." This will be done "by deterring, or, when needed, by compelling regional foes to act in ways that protect American interests and principles."

These American forces stationed throughout the world must be "highly versatile and mobile with a broad range of capabilities; they are the cavalry on the new American frontier." A key requirement for the military who are faced with "constabulary missions," or "small-scale contingencies" in critical regions must be "configured for combat...the first order of business... is to establish security, stability, and order. American troops, in particular, must be regarded as part of an overwhelmingly powerful force." Additionally, the constabulary missions "demand American political leadership rather than that of the United Nations."

Writing for the Inter Press Service (June 11, 2003), Jim Lobe notes the pattern of ongoing or planned re-deployment of U.S. military forces and equipment around the world. He describes the aim of "establishing semi-permanent or permanent bases along a giant swath of global territory-increasingly referred to as 'the arc of instability'—from the Caribbean Basin through Africa to South and Central Asia and across to North Korea." Additionally, there are plans to set up "forward bases in Algeria, Morocco, and possibly Tunisia, and establish smaller facilities in Senegal, Ghana, and Mali that could be used to intervene in oil-rich West African countries, particularly Nigeria." He adds another list of small bases throughout the Far East and Central Asia. Lobo concludes that this unprecedented global U.S. military presence will "permit Washington to play 'GloboCop'" (see *forward-based forces*).

The tragic destruction of the Twin Towers and the attack on the Pentagon on 9/11 proved to be the impetus for conflating the Bush administration's established plans for global dominance (see *American peace, Pax Americana*) with a newly hatched *global war on terrorism* (*GWOT*). Now the ubiquitous presence of the U.S. military protecting America's "interests" and "values" could be seen as necessary to nip any hint of rebellion in the bud. "We will not hesitate to act alone," warns the *National Security Strategy*, "if necessary, to exercise our right of self defense by acting preemptively against such terrorists, to prevent them from doing harm against our people and our country." The U.S.-led coalition *victory* in *Operation Iraqi Freedom* was promoted as a success in the global war on terrorism.

What emerges from all this is described by *Empire* author Niall Ferguson. "The United States," says Ferguson "is the empire that dares not speak its name. It is an empire in denial, and U.S. denial of this poses a real danger to the world" (see *hegemony*).

crusade: the very last word one ought to use to describe a worldwide war against terrorism. Despite the fact that "crusade" has come to refer in general to a concerted effort for or against almost anything, the word retains a powerful emotional connection to the historical Crusades—that slaughter of Muslims and Jews carried out with the encouragement and blessings of the Christian Church.

At the Council of Clermont in 1095 Pope Urban II exhorted Christendom to "succor your brethren in the East, menaced by an accursed race, utterly alienated from God. The Holy Sepulcher of our Lord is polluted by the filthiness of an unclean nation." In

1096 the Christian armies, supported by the assurance that "God wills it" would take Jerusalem and slaughter 30,000 Muslims and 6,000 Jews. The Crusades, eight in all, continued over the next 200 years. As writer James Carroll warns (*Boston Globe*, Sept. 25, 2001), " The savagery of these wars remains unforgotten in vast stretches of the world today, but also the lines that they drew remain contested borders even now...Europe did not become 'Europe' until it defined itself against Islam, and that negation remains embedded in the West's self-understanding today."

A few days after the horrible events of September 11, 2001, President Bush declared that "This is a new kind of evil, and we understand, and the American people are beginning to understand, this crusade, this war on terrorism, is going to take awhile...(but) we will rid the world of the evildoers" (see *evil*). In an ominous show of *carte blanche* support, Congress, on September 14, 2003 granted President Bush the right to "use all necessary and appropriate force against those nations, organizations, or persons he determines planned, authorized, committed, or aided the terrorist attacks."

The *New York Times*, Sept.22, 2001 noted that "One of the President's close acquaintances outside the White House said Mr. Bush clearly feels he has encountered his reason for being, a conviction formed and shaped by the President's own strain of Christianity. 'I think, in his frame, this is what God asked him to do', the acquaintance said. 'It offers him enormous clarity.'"

God's promptings notwithstanding, the outcries of concern over his remarks led to the President, two days later, to say he "regretted" using the word crusade, considering its religious implications. White House Press Secretary Ari Fleischer, adept at repairing Bush's gaffes, said the President only meant to say that his is a "broad cause" to stamp out terrorism worldwide.

Only a few months later, in his January 2002 State of the Union speech, the President revealed his perception of the identity of the threat to the U.S. and to the world—the *axis of evil*—Iraq, Iran, and North Korea. The ongoing war would be between good and evil. The following year President Bush celebrated the "official" end to the hostilities in *Operation Iraqi Freedom* by announcing, *"mission accomplished."*

The President declared to his troops: "Wherever you go, you carry a message of hope—a message that is ancient and ever new. In the words of the Prophet Isaiah, to the captives, 'come out,' and to those in darkness, 'be free.'" As George Monbiot observed on AlterNet.org, July 30, 2003, "The United States is no longer just a nation. It is now a religion. Its soldiers have entered Iraq to liberate its people not only from their dictator, their oil and their sovereignty, but also from their darkness... American soldiers are no longer merely terrestrial combatants; they have become missionaries. They are no longer simply killing enemies; they are casting out demons."

Stephen Mansfield, in his book, *The Faith of George W. Bush* (2003), offers some insight into the President's religious convictions. Mansfield writes that Bush told Texan evangelist James Robinson, " I feel like God wants me to run for President. I can't explain it, but I sense my country is going to need me...God wants me to do it."

Certainly New York's Governor George Pataki agreed with that conclusion during his remarks to the September 2004 Republican National Convention. Speaking of Bush, Pataki announced, "Ladies and gentlemen, on this night and in this fight there is another who holds high that torch of freedom. He is one of those men God and fate somehow lead to the fore in times of challenge."

Earlier, back at the Pentagon, the conflation of war, national security, and missionary zeal had surfaced in the person of Army Lt. General William G. "Jerry" Boykin. In June 2003, Boykin—in dress uniform and polished jump boots—spoke from the pulpit of the Good Shepherd Community Church in Sandy, Oregon. "Why do they hate us?" he asked. "The answer to that is because we are a Christian nation. We are hated because we are a nation of believers...Our spiritual enemy will only be defeated if we come against them in the name of Jesus." This curious dismissal of the nature of American democracy might not have been so disturbing were it not for the fact that Boykin was the U.S. deputy undersecretary of defense for intelligence.

Earlier, to another congregation in Florida in January, while discussing a battle against a Muslim warlord in Somalia, Boykin declared, "I knew my God was bigger than his. I knew that my God was a real God and that his was an idol." In October 2003 Secretary of Defense Donald Rumsfeld, when pressed, declined to criticize Boykin, preferring instead to praise the General's "outstanding" military record. Soon, however, Boykin released a written statement apologizing to those who had been offended by his statements. In it he insisted, "I am neither a zealot nor an extremist...only a soldier who has an abiding faith."

At Boykin's request, an official investigation into his remarks began in October 2003. After 10 months, the Pentagon investigators concluded that Boykin had violated several military regulations. A prompt dismissal of this zealous high-ranking official might have helped in supporting the White House claim that the U.S. is not engaged in a religious war against Islam. However, the New York Times (December 27, 2004) reported that Pentagon officials were putting together a plan that would give the military "a more prominent role in intelligence gathering operations" and would utilize "combat operations." Part of the plan was being drafted "under the direction of Lt. Gen. William Boykin, a deputy undersecretary of defense who has already demonstrated that he should not be allowed anywhere near the most serious matters of national security."

D

"'What was the end of all of the show, Johnnie, Johnnie?'
Ask my Colonel, for I don't know,
Johnnie, my Johnnie, aha!
We broke a king and we built a road—
A courthouse stands where the Reg'ment goed.
And the river's clean where the raw blood flowed.
When the Widow give the party."

Rudyard Kipling

daisy cutter: the picturesque name now preferred by the military for this 15,000 pound *bomb* of enormous destructive power. Officially known as the BLU-82 (Bomb Live Unit), it was developed for use in Vietnam to blast clearings in the jungle. There are no daisies to cut down either in the jungles of Vietnam or in the deserts of Iraq, but the daisy cutter was used in 2001 against Taliban fighters in the Afghanistan *Operation Enduring Freedom*. The Air Force admits to using 11 of the huge bombs, also known as "Big Blue," in the *Gulf War*. U.S. aircraft dropped leaflets on Iraqi troops with the warning "Flee and Live, or Stay and Die" accompanied by a picture of the daisy cutter.

`Although officially denied, numerous media outlets, including the April 3, 2003 *Guardian*/UK reported that two daisy cutters had been dropped on the Iraqi Republican Guard troops defending the town of Kut and the southeast approaches to Baghdad. The huge bomb, which is dropped from a cargo plane, descends on a parachute. Three feet above the ground the 12,600 pounds of a mixture of ammonium nitrate and aluminum detonates, creating a massive firestorm.

CASI—the UK Cambridge University-based Campaign Against Sanctions in Iraq (www.casi.org.uk)—reported eye-witness accounts of the effects of the bomb, until recently the largest *conventional* bomb in existence, during *Operation Iraqi Freedom*. The massive pressure wave generated by the explosion and the firestorm "literally mashes and kills any human beings (in) the blast area causing severe internal injuries (and) severe burns..." Reportedly, as the coalition forces moved towards the capitol, the Iraqi Baghdad Division—about 12,000 men—was decimated—killed outright, or severely injured. After the blasts, *Apache helicopters* moved in to strafe the Iraqis, living and dead.

The daisy cutter, originally employed to clear vegetation, had graduated to serve a more useful function—killing people—otherwise known more discreetly as the antipersonnel effect.

dead-enders: those who, driven by motives which may include despair, political or religious fanaticism, and hatred of the aggressor, fight on when there may be little or no hope of their ultimate success.

The term, although of much older origin, became associated with Secretary of Defense Donald Rumsfeld in his dealings with the Middle East. He described the Taliban leader Mullah Omar in November 2001 as "a rather determined dead-ender type...He just doesn't feel to me like the surrendering type." The expression later graduated to a description of the sporadic, deadly resistance which became an almost daily occurrence after May 1, 2001, the official end of major combat in Iraq. Rumsfeld observed "Where pockets of dead-enders are trying to reconstitute...[the Army is] rooting them out" (see *pockets*).

There was some confusion as to the identity and motives of the resistance. In August 2003 Rumsfeld labeled them as "dead-enders," who were streaming into Iraq to help Hussein's followers. He compared them to the isolated gangs of Nazis who fought on after World War II (see *dead-enders*). Condoleezza Rice, the national security adviser agreed, and referred to them as "Baathist and Fedayeen remnants." In an all too optimistic analysis, Rumsfeld predicted that "The coalition forces can deal with [these] terrorists now in Iraq, instead of having to deal with these terrorists elsewhere..."

On December 15, 2003, *Boston Globe* columnist Thomas Oliphant reported that U.S. officials were convinced that "the former elements of [Saddam's] murderous regime have been responsible for the majority of the lethal attacks on other Iraqis, occupying forces, and international aid workers." However, as L. Paul Bremer III, the U.S. civil administrator of Iraq and other officials weighed in with their description of the dead-enders, the "remnants" included "Iran-backed militias," "foreigners" of indeterminate origins, as well as members of "Ansar al Islam," a small resistance group from northern Iraq.

By November 2004 the devastation of the city of Fallujah by U.S. forces resulted in the capture of over 1000 Iraqis—just 15 of whom were confirmed foreign fighters. The term "dead-enders" was no longer in vogue, having been replaced by the more neutral "insurgents".

As the *casualties* mounted in the tragic aftermath of the war, disturbing opinions circulated about the nature of the threat. The *New York Times* (September 17, 2003), while citing Donald Rumsfeld's description of the attackers as "dead-enders, foreign terrorists, and criminal gangs" wrote that "Defense Department officials" were by then saying that "New intelligence estimates are warning that the United State's most formidable foe in Iraq in the months ahead may be the resentment of ordinary Iraqis increasingly hostile to the American military occupation."

The *Times* noted that "The Defense officials spoke on condition of anonymity...They said it was a mistake to discount the role of the ordinary Iraqis who have little in common with the groups Mr. Rumsfeld cited, but whose anger over the American presence seems to be kindling some sympathy for those attacking American forces."

At the time of the report, 70 American military personnel had been killed since May 1, 2003 compared to 109 during the "official war". By January 30, 2005, the day of the Iraq elections (see *democratization*) the number had risen to 1087 killed—as well as 324 who were listed as "non-hostile" deaths—most from accidents.

According to Iraqi intelligence service director Mohamed Abdullah Shahwani, speaking to Agence France Presse on January 3, 2005 "I think that the resistance is bigger than the military in Iraq. I think the resistance is more than 200,000 people."

decapitation strike: a sudden, powerful attack usually aimed at buildings where the leaders of the *enemy* may be present. The assumption is that if they are killed, the enemy will surrender, and submit to the will of the attacker. This seldom occurs.

The term evolved from its much earlier meaning—a nuclear attack aimed at destroying the most important centers of military and civilian control—into one referring to a non-nuclear offensive. In the case of the U.S. conflicts with Iraq, the major focus of decapitation strikes has been Saddam Hussein. Killing Saddam would have been *assassination*, an act whose legal status, under both U.S. and international law is open to debate. Other targets included Iraqi "command and control" centers, any other military personnel who happened to be at the target, and "regrettably" any civilians who happened to be nearby (see *collateral damage*).

During the 1991 *Gulf War*, the U.S. bombed well over 200 sites with Saddam Hussein as the intended target. Over the years between the 1991 conflict and *Operation Iraqi Freedom* in 2003, there were numerous attempts on Saddam's life, some involving the U.S. Central Intelligence Agency (CIA).

The most well publicized decapitation strike was carried out on April 8, 2003. An Air Force B-1 bomber dropped four 2,000-pound *bombs* (see *bunker-busters*) in the al-Mansur residential district in Baghdad, killing at least 18 innocent civilians. Intelligence sources had intercepted a satellite phone message suggesting that Saddam Hussein and perhaps his two sons would be meeting at a particular site in al-Mansur, along with a number of senior aides and bodyguards. Within forty-five minutes the powerful bombs destroyed at least three houses, and damaged a number of others.

Ever the optimist, Vice President Dick Cheney said, a month later, "I think we did get Saddam Hussein. He was seen being dug out of the rubble and wasn't able to breathe." However, forensic evidence ultimately failed to identify any of the intended victims. The dead did include nine members of one family and two children—but not Saddam and his compatriots. Despite the loss of life, a U.S. military official said that strikes did succeed in demonstrating "U.S. resolve and capabilities."

According to the Pentagon, in the early hours of Operation Iraqi Freedom more than 40 satellite-guided Tomahawk cruise missiles were launched at "leadership targets" from vessels in the Red Sea and the Persian Gulf. Bunker buster bombs were also dropped on what was hoped was a bunker that might be housing Saddam Hussein, his sons and other military leaders. The March 23, 2003 *Sunday Mail* quotes a "senior U.S. defense official" as remarking "The bunker was the primary target, but because we couldn't be sure where all the people were, we had to take out some other buildings as well."

deconflicting the airspace: traditionally, keeping track of aircraft so that they do not collide. During *Operation Iraqi Freedom*, the expression also was used to refer to the massive numbers of *artillery* and rockets fired at targets, sometimes from many miles away. Lieutenant General David McKiernan, the land war commander, said that he wanted "to make sure that the fires are fully coordinated and deconflicted." During the "official" hostilities between March 20-May 1, 2003, *coalition* forces flew 41,404 missions (see *aerial sorties)* and fired over 3,000 missiles. There were no Iraqi aircraft to add to the confusion, as the U.S.-led forces had complete *air supremacy*.

defeat: to achieve *victory* by inflicting sufficient suffering on the people judged to be one's *enemy* so that they cease fighting and submit to one's will. What military scholars label "decisive" victory is illustrated by strategist Thomas C. Schelling's observation: " 'Victory' inadequately expresses what a nation wants from its military forces...It wants the bargaining power that comes from its capacity to hurt, not just the direct consequence of direct military action...How to use that opportunity in the national interest...can be just as important as the achievement of victory itself."

In a 2000 essay written for the U.S. National War College, Nancy McEldowney writes about the "deeply ingrained belief that the unconditional surrender and complete victory of total war are inherently preferable...With a tendency to demonize the enemy and to view war more a morality play than as an extension of policy, this characteristically 'American approach' to war is driven by a sense of national exceptionalism and the belief that 'we can remake the world anew.'"

That epitomizes the George W. Bush administration's program of *endless war* against terrorism. The *Project for the New American Century's* 2000 report, *Rebuilding America's Defenses: Strategy, Forces and Resources for a New Century*—the blueprint for President Bush's 2002 *National Security Strategy*—maintains "The United States...requires a globally preeminent military capability both today and in the future." Otherwise, the United States is in danger of losing "a global security order that is uniquely friendly to American principles and prosperity."

In a late-2001 e-mail exchange with a cadet at West Point (see *academies*), Army Gen. Barry McCaffrey (ret.) offered his plan for the military's role in defeating terrorists. McCaffrey told the cadet "We are going to disrupt these people through preemptive attack... we will deceive them... at selected points and times they will be killed suddenly, in significant numbers, and without warning...We will isolate them from their families...If we can find out...where they sleep we will go there and kill them by surprise."

Will that approach—widely acknowledged as the strategy the United States has adopted—somehow guarantee the defeat of our enemies and safeguard our "American principles and prosperity?" Philosopher and poet Wendell Berry warns: "At the end of the war, if we have won it, we declare peace; we congratulate ourselves on our victory; we marvel at the newly-proved efficiency of our latest weapons; we ignore the cost in lives, materials and property, in suffering and disease, in damage to the material world; we ignore the inevitable residue of resentment and hatred; and we go on as before, having, as we think, successfully defended our way of life."

defense contractors: any one of over 100,000 companies whose products are used to retain U.S. military global supremacy. During fiscal year 2003 the top 10 companies alone received $83.7 billion in contracts from the U.S. government. The defense industry has become an integral part of the U.S. economy.

In 1940, just prior to World War II, President Roosevelt said: "Our present emergency and a common sense of decency make it imperative that no group of war millionaires shall come into being in this nation as a result of the struggles abroad. The American people will not relish the idea of any American citizen growing rich and fat in an emergency of blood and slaughter and human suffering."

By 2004 not only had such exemplary flourishes of rhetoric and ideals vanished, the "war millionaires" proscribed by Roosevelt had become commonplace. They now headed industries that operated on a grand scale, even in the absence of major wars. The 2004 "official" defense budget hovered around $400 billion, with promises of billions more needed to support the *occupations* of Iraq and Afghanistan (see *military budget*). According to United for a Fair Economy (www.ufenot.org) "median CEO pay at the 37 largest defense contractors rose 79 percent from 2001 to 2002... the typical defense industry CEO got $5.4 million."

Current or former defense contractor officials became integrated into the U.S. defense structure. William D. Hartung of the World Policy Institute at the New School points out (*Los Angeles Times*, December 10, 2003) "In the first year in office, the Bush administration named 32 appointees to top policymaking positions who were former executives, paid consultants or major shareholders of top defense contractors."

In the Pentagon, Secretary Donald Rumsfeld chose as Secretary of the Air Force James Roche, a former vice president at Northrop Grumman, and for Secretary of the Navy Gordon England, a former executive at General Dynamics. Peter B. Teets, former Lockheed Martin President became the undersecretary of the Air Force. Lockheed Martin, the nation's leading defense contractor, was also well represented in the inner circles by its VP Bruce Jackson, finance chair of the Bush for President campaign. Lynne Cheney, Vice President Dick Cheney's wife, is a former Lockheed board member.

A March 28, 2003 report by The Center for Public Integrity (www.publicintegrity.org) observes "Of the 30 members of the Defense Policy Board...at least nine have ties to companies that have won more than $76 billion in defense contracts in 2001 and 2002. Four members are registered lobbyists, one of whom represents two of the three largest defense contractors." The *Defense Policy Board* advises the secretary of defense on military matters, including the kinds of new weapons that should be developed.

Given the Bush administration's ambitious plans to spread U.S. military might worldwide (see *forward operating bases*), dominate all other nations on land, sea, air, and space (see *Rebuilding America's Defenses*, *National Security Strategy*), and fight a *global war on terrorism* in what may be an *endless war*, defense contractors appear to be well positioned to take advantage of exciting business opportunities. The Perpetual War Portfolio (www.rationalenquirer.org) tracks "five stocks poised to succeed in the age of perpetual war. The stocks were selected on the basis of popular product lines, strong political connections and lobbying efforts, and paid-for access to key Congressional decision-makers."

Defense Planning Guidance (DPG): A government document written in 1992 as a blueprint for the Pentagon for its post-cold-war strategy. The first draft advocated the perpetuation of the U.S. as the world's only superpower by "deterring potential competitors from even aspiring to a larger regional or global role." This was to be accomplished by being "postured to act independently when collective action cannot be orchestrated" (see *Pax Americana*). This blunt plan for world domination was softened in a second draft. The plan eventually re-emerged after 9/11 as George W. Bush's *National Security Strategy.* The philosophy behind its recommendations led to the 2003 attack on Iraq, known as *Operation Iraqi Freedom.*

The periodically updated DPG is intended as an internal planning guide for the Pentagon. In the first Bush administration, Undersecretary of Defense for Policy Paul Wolfowitz, serving with Defense Secretary Dick Cheney, had the opportunity to draft the 1992 DPG, which was to recommend a set of priorities now that the U.S. had emerged as the world's dominant military force.

The first draft of Feb.18, 1992 maintained "Our [the U.S.] first objective is to prevent the re-emergence of a new rival...if necessary the United States must be prepared to take unilateral action." The document, not intended for public consumption, was widely and sharply criticized after it was leaked to the *New York Times*. A new draft was fashioned which was considerably softer in tone and radically different in its philosophy.

The second draft, which was approved as the *Defense Planning Guidance* 1992-1994, places emphasis on "turning old enmities into new cooperative relationships." The first draft had not mentioned the UN while the second says " There will be enhanced opportunities for political, economic, environmental, social and security issues to be resolved through new or revitalized international organizations, including the United Nations..."

In the years following the DPG formulation, the George Bush, Sr. team, ousted by the election of Bill Clinton in November 1992, would perpetuate the philosophy of the first DPG draft (see *Committee for Peace and Security in the Gulf*, *Project for the New American Century*). The radical aim of U.S. global domination marked by unilateral, *preemptive war*, would re-emerge as the "Bush Doctrine,"—the foreign policy principles of the George W. Bush administration after the tragedy of September 11, 2001 (see *National Security Strategy*). Dick Cheney had become Bush's vice president, and Paul Wolfowitz was deputy secretary of defense. Among others involved in preparing the first DPG draft in 1992 was I. Lewis Libby—who now was Cheney's chief of staff.

Khurram Husain wrote in the November/December 2003 *Bulletin of the Atomic Scientists*: "The quest for an impregnable defense and military supremacy over the rest of the world has brought America to a perilous moment of truth." Husain, anticipating the then impending attack on Iraq warned "This time the quagmire will not be an unwinnable war in one country, but endless war across a vast stretch of the Earth—a war from which extrication will be next to impossible" (see *hegemony, endless war*).

Duane Shank, issues and policies adviser for Sojourners, a Christian peace and social justice organization (www.sojo.org) maintains "There is an alternative to empire and endless war... We must advance the vision of a world where international institutions are strengthened rather than destroyed, where global poverty is seriously addressed, where all countries, including the United States, are disarming their weapons of mass destruction, and where human rights are taken seriously."

Defense Policy Board: a group of about thirty experts, from academics to retired military officers, which was established in 1985 to advise the Secretary of Defense on military matters—at that time chiefly related to the Soviet Union. By 2001, after George W. Bush was elected president, the Board turned its attention to championing an attack on Iraq.

Known officially as the Defense Policy Board Advisory Committee (DPBAC), it numbers among its members individuals with connections to neoconservative causes (see *American Enterprise Institute, Committee for the Liberation of Iraq, Committee for Peace and Security in the Gulf, Project for the New American Century*). Prominent among them had been Chairperson Richard Perle, who as assistant secretary of defense under President Ronald Reagan had been dubbed "Prince of Darkness" for his hawkish views.

Perle resigned from the DPBAC on March 27, 2003, as allegations mounted concerning possible conflicts of interest. He was accused of using his influence on the DPBAC to solicit investments for his company, Trireme. Perle, however, remained as a member of the Board. One year later, he resigned altogether, claiming that he did so as to not distract from George Bush's election campaign—and insisted that his leaving was "absolutely not" related to his business affairs. Perle's controversial dealings are analyzed by investigative reporter Seymour M. Hersh in his 2004 book *Chain of Command: The Road from 9/11 to Abu Ghraib*.

The DPBAC, under George Bush, is a sterling example of an agency marked by numerous "appearances" of conflicts of interest. According to a March 26, 2003 report by The Center for Public Integrity (www.publici.org) "At least nine members [of the DPBAC] have won more than $76 billion in defense contracts in 2001 and 2002. Four members are registered lobbyists, one of whom represents two of the three largest defense contractors"(see *defense contractors*).

Other bedfellows on the DPBAC include former CIA director James Woolsey, whose law firm has represented the *Iraqi National Congress*, Henry Kissinger, an architect of the Vietnam War and most improbable recipient of the 1973 Nobel Peace Prize, Kenneth L. Adelman, former Assistant to U.S. Secretary of Defense Donald Rumsfeld from 1975 to 1979 (see *cakewalk*), and Newt Gingrich, who resigned from Congress following the failure of his "Contract With America."

When Richard Perle was associated with the DPBAC, he introduced his good friend Ahmad Chalabi, the head of the *Iraqi National Congress* (INC) to senior members of Congress and administration officials, seeking their support to oust Saddam Hussein. Jim Lobe reported for the Inter Press Service on February 21, 2004 that Chalabi, in an extraordinarily frank interview, had said "he was willing to take full responsibility for the INC's role in providing misleading intelligence and defectors to President George W. Bush, Congress and the U.S. public to persuade them that Hussein posed a serious threat to the United States that had to be dealt with urgently... 'We are heroes in error...the Americans are in Baghdad. What was said before is not important'" (see *democratization*).

degrade: to kill and wound people (the *enemy*), preferably in large numbers, in order to diminish their capacity and their will to fight. Because coalition forces controlled the skies in both the 1991 and 2003 attacks on Iraq, (see *air supremacy*), this degradation was carried out with great efficiency and deadly effect. Typical media reports that describe the tactic are as follows:

"U.S. forces continued their advance on Baghdad on Wednesday, battling Iraqi Republican Guard troops degraded by repeated coalition bombing." (CNN.com, April 2, 2003)

"After an air bombardment that lasted 70 hours over four nights, Iraqi military capabilities have been significantly degraded...according to a preliminary Pentagon assessment." (CNN, December 12, 1998)

"Heavy Air Force bombing day after day appears to have, to use the Army's word, attrited, that is to say badly degraded the units which are supposed to be defending Baghdad. What we're seeing here is essentially pockets of resistance, but nothing overly serious."(CNN.com, April 2, 2003)

"Some of them [the Republican Guard troops] have been degraded to pretty low percentages of combat capability, below 50 percent in...at least two cases, and we continue to work on them." (Gen. Richard Myers, chairperson of the Joint Chiefs of Staff)(Associated Press, April 1, 2003)

Delta Force: a top-secret, clandestine U.S. military unit whose existence is known to everyone. The main purpose of this group— known also as the 1st Special Forces Operational Detachment-Delta (Airborne)-1st SFOD-D (A)—is to "counter-attack terrorism," with orders to "terminate with stealth and impunity." Members of Delta Force allegedly entered Iraq well before the "official" start of the war in March 2003.

According to Gregory L. Vistica, writing in the *Washington Post* (January 5,2004), Defense Secretary Donald Rumsfeld had been "pressuring the Pentagon to take a more active role in tracking down terrorists...Under Rumsfeld's directions, secret commando units known as hunter-killer [Delta force] teams have been ordered to 'kick down the doors', as the generals put it, all over the world."

According to this report, "The Bush administration is moving away from work with insurgents and favoring more direct-action strikes...Rumsfeld's 'manhunter' plan calls for sending Special Mission Units into a number of countries throughout the world... The capture of Hussein may increase support for Rumsfeld's global vision for the hunter-killer teams."

Tom Engelhardt, in his "regular antidote to the mainstream media" at TomDispatch.com. (January 6, 2004) notes that a hunter-killer team is " a military assassination squad let loose on the world...to hunt down terrorists or assumedly other enemies without regard to national boundaries, declarations of war, or, evidently, [legal] 'niceties' of any sort."

Whatever concerns others might have about the ethics of Delta Force tactics, the *Washington Post* disclosed that members of other Special Operations forces, such as the Green Berets and the Navy SEALS were suffering from "Delta envy." This jealousy "now permeates the ranks, especially among younger soldiers who realize early in their careers that the 'kick down the door approach' is what Washington wants...'All they want to do is strike missions.'"

democratization: a process in which the United States, after gaining only limited support in the U.S. for an overwhelming military invasion of Iraq—and in spite of widespread global objection—attacked Iraq, occupied it, imposed a handpicked governing body, and promised national elections sometime in the future. The U.S. predicted that the elections would somehow result in a Western-style democracy.

The U.S. and a few *allies* launched the attack under the

pretences that Iraq was an imminent threat because the country possessed *weapons of mass destruction*. When this proved not to be the case, the Bush administration claimed—among other rationales (see *Operation Iraqi Freedom*)—that the creation of a democracy in Iraq would be sufficient justification for the enforced occupation.

As liberal philanthropist George Soros puts it, "Introducing democracy by military means is a quaint idea...we may claim to be liberators but even victims of Saddam's repression regard us as occupiers" (see *liberation, occupation*). Political activist and author Noam Chomsky scoffs at the notion that the U.S. is in Iraq to bring democracy to not only that country but to the whole Middle East. He points to the "rapturous acclaim" of Davis Ignatius, *Washington Post* commentator, who "described the invasion of Iraq as 'the most idealistic war in modern times'— fought solely to bring democracy to Iraq and the region." Ignatius describes Paul Wolfowitz, the Bush administration deputy secretary of defense, as a genuine intellectual who "bleeds for (the Arab world's) oppression and dreams of liberating it" (see *Defense Planning Guidance*).

Chomsky cites "[Wolfowitz's] strong support for Suharto in Indonesia, one of the last century's worst mass murderers, when Wolfowitz was ambassador to that country under Ronald Reagan... Wolfowitz oversaw support for the murderous dictators Chun of South Korea and Marcos of the Philippines."

Stephen Zunes, author of *Tinderbox: U.S. Middle East Policy and the Roots of Terrorism*, details the devastating history of the U.S. relationships with non-democratic allies in the Middle East. In a November 8, 2003 article for Common Dreams News Center (www.commondreams.org) Zunes maintains that " U.S. policy has propped up...repressive regimes against their own people through large-scale military, financial, and diplomatic support...There are no indications that the Bush administration is planning to stop its support for governments that deny freedom..."

Zunes adds, "The right of self-determination for Kuwaiti Arabs was vigorously defended while under Iraqi occupation, but not the right of Palestinian Arabs under Israeli occupation or Sahwari Arabs under Moroccan occupation...Despite Bush administration efforts to highlight oppression in Iran...the United States was responsible for the overthrow of that country's secular democratic government in 1953 and armed and trained the Shah's brutal secret police for the next quarter century."

British journalist Dilip Hiro points out that the United States, rather than vigorously abetting democracy in the Middle East finds that "It is much simpler to manipulate a few ruling families—to secure fat orders for arms and to ensure that oil price remains low—than a wide variety of personalities and policies bound to be thrown up by a democratic system."

Downplaying the latter point has been of particular concern to the Bush administration. Bush promised a "transition to full Iraqi sovereignty" by June 30, 2004. Two days earlier than that date, for security reasons, a 33-member interim government received the reigns of government (see *Iraqi Governing Council*). The U.S.-led military force of 140,000 remained in place. It was empowered by UN Resolution 1564 to use "all necessary measures" to bring peace and stability.

The U.S., whose principal aims were to position military bases in Iraq and ensure access to Iraq's abundant oil supplies had no intention of leaving the country. The interim government served until general elections were held on January 30, 2005. Naomi Klein observes "That's [many] months for a non-elected government to do what the CPA [Coalition Provisional Authority] could not legally do on its own: invite U.S. troops to stay indefinitely...Only after these key decisions have been made will Iraqis be invited to have their say."

National elections were no guarantee of implanting a

democracy in Iraq, split among Kurds, Sunni Muslims and Shiite Muslims. Iraq's Shiites make up 60 to 70 percent of the country's 26 million population. Shortly after the interim government was selected, the *Boston Globe* (June 13, 2004) reported "Mainstream leaders have spread a message of patience and inevitable victory: Wait for elections, and then we'll take power." Many "cling to the belief that a theocratic government, run by ...clerics, will ultimately prevail."

As it turned out, that scenario became a real possibility. The top vote getter was the United Iraqi Alliance—a coalition of influential Muslim groups backed by Iraq's leading cleric Grand Ayatollah Ali Sistani. Prominent among its members and a prime candidate for the job of prime minister was none other than Ahmad Chalabi, once favored by the Bush White House, but now looking for more independent influence (see *Defense Policy Board*, *Iraqi National Congress*).

Concerns immediately arose as to whether the more conservative elements in the United Iraqi Alliance might insist on a constitution which followed an Iranian style theocracy—the imposition of strict Islamic rule. While reassurances were given that such a constitution—which would be unacceptable to the U.S.—was unlikely, the question of the attitude of the newly elected parliament towards the exit of the occupying forces was equally troubling. For example, Abdel-Azziz al-Hakim—the head of Iraq's largest party—told Time magazine (January 31,2005) "We want this foreign army out of our country immediately. We cannot tolerate this presence on our soil."

Drake Bennet, writing in the *Boston Globe* (January 16, 2005) pointed out "Democracy...does not consist simply of voting...there remains the question of what happens after January 31, when the work of governing begins. When asked whether the elections can bring a semblance of stability and democracy to the country, Iraq experts and democracy scholars here in the United States tend to fall along a continuum of pessimism."

Department of Defense (DoD): the civilian organization in control of the U.S. military whose traditional role has been to defend the country against attack, and has recently assumed the role of the attacker.

In 1781 Congress established a War Office to be headed by a Secretary at War. Seven years later, under President George Washington, Congress re-named this the Department of War, led by a Secretary "of" rather than "at" War. Many years and wars later the various components of the military began an extended period of wrangling over how best to unify the land, sea and air forces. Finally, President Truman signed the National Security Act of 1947 that set up the National Military Establishment under the direction of a Secretary of Defense. In 1949 this became the Department of Defense, created by combining the War Department with the Navy Department.

Back in 1947, Congress, concerned about maintaining a diversity of opinions about defense matters, had appointed a "weak" Secretary of Defense, allowing him only three assistant secretaries and a staff of about fifty. The power of the office grew, especially under President Eisenhower, and by 2004 the Secretary of Defense had a staff of about 2000, and oversaw 2,036,000 employees. Defense had become big business, as reflected in the annual *military budget.*

William D. Hartung, Senior Fellow at the World Policy Institute (www.worldpolicy.org) described the theme of President Bush's 2003 defense budget of $358.2 billion as "Leave no defense contractor behind." That defense budget alone was 53% of the money spent by Congress and the Administration—and dwarfed the $12 billion allotted for non-military foreign aid.

Under the tutelage of George W. Bush's Secretary of Defense Donald Rumsfeld, according to the DoD's (www.defenselink.mil)

backhanded compliment "the missile defense research and testing program has been reorganized and revitalized, free from the restraints of the ABM treaty"(see *nuclear weapons*). Rumsfeld, in his second coming as secretary of defense—having held that office in 1975-1977 under President Gerald Ford—presided over the tortuous, expensive and dangerous redefining of the meaning of "defense." The Department of Defense would now go on the offensive.

The 2002 *National Security Strategy* promises that "America will act against ...emerging threats before they are fully formed... The United States will, if necessary, act preemptively." The DoD had been given *carte blanche* to invade any region where it could claim to have evidence of any intention to harm the U.S.—an unprecedented broad mandate. Rumsfeld would oversee the first dramatic application of such a first-strike mentality in *Operation Iraqi Freedom.* Billed as an attack necessary to prevent the Saddam Hussein regime from using *weapons of mass destruction*, the war had been urged for many years for other reasons (see *Committee for the Liberation of Iraq, Defense Planning Guidance, Defense Policy Board*).

In sharp contrast to the philosophy of using overwhelming military force at the slightest provocation was the legislation introduced by Congressman Dennis Kucinich (D-Ohio) in July 2001 and again in April 2003. The Congressman and his supporters were seeking to establish a Department of Peace— headed by a cabinet-level Secretary of Peace—whose mission would include making peace an "organizing principle," and "work to create peace, prevent violence, divert from armed conflict and develop new structures in nonviolent dispute resolution; and take a proactive, strategic approach in the development of policies that promote national and international conflict prevention, nonviolent intervention, mediation, peaceful resolution of conflict and structured mediation of conflict."

Most of the media, busy with wars and rumors of wars, yawned. Congressman Bob Barr (R-Georgia) reportedly answered the plea of a constituent by writing " I think this is a nonsensical proposal, especially while we are at war. I support our President, military, and our Department of Defense. We do not need a 'Department of Peace.'"

Since 1952, the organization Promoting Enduring Peace (www.pepeace.org), has been conducting "peace education activities to promote sustainable world peace." Their annual Gandhi Peace Award has been given to, among others, Dr. Helen Caldicott, Cesar Chavez, Dorothy Day, and Dr. Daniel Ellsberg. The 2003 recipient was Dennis Kucinich. His radical idea that the U.S. should actually prefer mediation to the military, and discussion to destruction, was not "nonsensical" to everyone.

depleted uranium (DU): Depleted uranium is not simply tired uranium. Depleted uranium can kill. It is a dense, toxic, radioactive byproduct of the technique by which uranium is processed for making *nuclear weapons* and nuclear reactor fuel. Hundreds of thousands of tons of leftover depleted uranium (DU) languishing in U.S. storage facilities were considered hazardous and useless, until the U.S. military discovered the material could be fashioned into wonderfully potent weapons as well as into armor for tanks (see *Abrams tank*).

Shells tipped with DU easily pierce through concrete bunkers (see *advanced unitary penetrator*) and armored vehicles. These burst into flames, incinerating those inside. The DU then oxidizes into tiny airborne particles of uranium oxide, easily inhaled and ingested. They lodge in the lungs indefinitely. Approximately 320 tons of DU were used in *Operation Desert Storm* in 1991, mainly in desert areas. Somewhat less may have been used during *Operation Iraqi Freedom* in 2003, but for the most part it was employed in heavily residential sites. After NATO's use of DU in

Kosovo in 1999, the Council of European Parliamentarians had urged a worldwide ban, citing the "long term effects on health... affecting future generations."

The debate over the hazards of military use of DU (besides the issue of the people killed directly) is an excellent example of the care that needs to be taken when activists and military officials clash over controversial issues involving medical and environmental effects. Exaggerations and unsubstantiated claims regarding DU have been made on both sides. An excellent, detailed report, *Depleted Uranium: Scientific Basis for Assessing Risk* was published in July 2003 by the Nuclear Policy Research Institute (NPRI) (www.nuclearpolicy.org). NPRI's president is Dr. Helen Caldicott, founding president of Physicians for Social Responsibility (www.psr.org).

The study points out that "the health risks of depleted uranium tend to be substantially understated by government bodies...the toxic effects for cancers and possible birth defects have latency periods of a few years to possibly a couple of decades... the most vulnerable population is children. In conflict areas such as Iraq, where residential areas have been ravaged by tanks and munitions, the DU-contaminated debris has become the children's new playground."

They cite the August 2002 report by the UN Sub-Commission on Prevention and Protection of Minorities, which states that the use of DU shells is a breach of numerous laws, including the Universal Declaration of Human Rights and the Genocide Convention. NPRI's extensive recommendations end with the following plea: "Given the potential long-lasting risk to noncombatants, the Pentagon should investigate alternative sources of ammunition...and immediately halt the production, sale and use of depleted uranium weapons."

The Defense Department continues to maintain, "allegations that DU has caused ill health effects have been proved unfounded in numerous independent studies..." Col. James Naughton of the Army Material Command said that DU gives the U.S. an "edge" and "we don't want to give that up."

Meanwhile, an Army training manual requires that anyone who comes within 25 meters of any DU-contaminated equipment or terrain wear respiratory and skin protection, warning: "contamination will make food and water unsafe for consumption."

desertion: an unauthorized absence from one's assigned post for more than thirty days during wartime. The maximum penalty is death. A severe punishment for desertion is necessary, otherwise the military would risk the defection of too many people naturally reluctant to kill or be killed.

In earlier wars, when men were called to war with little preparation, desertion rates tended to be high. During the Civil War, for example, deserters were regularly executed near the White House, to the distress of President Lincoln. He is said to have replied to the Generals who were critical of his frequent pardons, "God help me, how can I have a butcher's day every Friday in the Army of the Potomac?" Given the traumatic and often terrifying experiences of battle, the rarity of desertion in more modern times is a testimony to the effectiveness of *military training.*

A powerful counterweight to the natural fear of injury and death and the repugnance toward killing is the conviction, instilled by training, that a soldier's ultimate obligation is towards his comrades. A March 20, 2004 *Boston Globe* account of the struggles of several seriously wounded veterans of *Operation Iraqi Freedom* included the story of David Pettigrew, 26, whose leg was severed by a rocket-propelled grenade. He admitted "I ultimately lost my leg not for a cause, but for my buddies, for my unit." This useful attitude promotes faithful service in the face of the horrors of war.

Of course, the prospect of condemnation and shame—possibly followed by the death penalty—is another powerful incentive to stay put. During the First World War, the British executed 245 men for desertion. Historian Lawrence James writes that in the British Army at that time "Top level pressure for exemplary death sentences was transmitted downwards in an army where only officers with an aggressive spirit secured promotion." The Americans did not execute any of their own soldiers in that period, and just one unfortunate private in the Second World War (see *cowardice*).

By mid-2004 the trauma of *Operation Iraqi Freedom* had not lead to any convictions for desertion (see *cowardice)*—but conditions were ripe for just such an occurrence. Two young soldiers, Brandon Hughey and Jeremy Hinzman, fled to Canada in early 2004 when their units were about to leave for Iraq. By 2005, six had arrived. They objected to the war for a variety of reasons including its illegality as a war of aggression, and the futility of killing to eliminate injustice. They faced an uphill battle to achieve refugee status. They would have to prove that they were fleeing persecution in the U.S.. According to *The Village Voice,* April 27, 2004, Hughey and Hinzman's attorney planned to put "the war itself on trial by contending that the U.S. wants to send these young men to jail—or worse—for choosing to comply with international law."

He did so in the case of Hinzman, but Canada's Immigration and Refugee Board ruled that the claims of the war's illegality was not relevant to the case. He would have to prove that Hinzman would face "social persecution" if he returned home. The case could be taken all the way to Canada's Supreme Court.

According to *The Toronto Sun* (January 29, 2005) "An estimated 5,500 men and women have deserted since the invasion of Iraq." Jeremy Hinzman's attorney, Jeffry House said that "Two hundred (American soldiers) have contacted him...mostly since

George W. Bush was re-elected in November, looking for a way out."

By February 2004 twenty-one military personnel had taken another way out—*suicide*. By that time a national soldier's support service, GI Rights Hotline, (girights.objector.org) was taking 3,500 calls per month from soldiers, many of whom were on leave and asking about the consequences of not returning to Iraq. Some reported that they had been encouraged to take their leaves in Germany rather than the U.S., to reduce such temptations.

Lt. Col. (U.S. Army, ret) Ralf W. Zimmerman, writing for *DefenseWatch*, January 7, 2004 offered a suggestion to ease the temptation to leave the fighting to others. "The lesson for the Army as a whole is obvious: Combat proves that being all you can be isn't as easy as the slogan sounds. At minimum, the Army should ensure that all soldiers being sent to a war zone have adequate indoctrination and training to prepare them for the 'shock and awe of' such gory sights."

Controversy still swirls around the contention that President George W. Bush fulfills the definition of deserter. Many accusers point to what they considered lack of solid evidence that Bush actually had completed his tour of duty in the Air National Guard (see www.michaelmoore.com) during the time of the Vietnam War. It seemed unlikely that the President would be charged with desertion, although there is no statute of limitations for that offense.

detainees: prisoners. Many were imprisoned for years under the George W. Bush administrations without any recourse to legal assistance.

President Bush issued an executive order in November 2001 that permitted the secretary of defense to allow the indefinite detention of any alien—even those that are U.S. residents—who is suspected of terrorist activities. The *American Lawyer* (February

2004), in its review of James Bovard's book *Trampling Freedom, Justice and Peace to Rid the World of Evil* reports "more than 1,200 'special interest' suspects—temporary and resident aliens—were arrested in the months after 9/11... No evidence surfaced linking any of those people to the terrorist attacks...The government refused to release the names of the detainees...almost all were denied access to counsel either overtly or by subterfuge."

The *American Lawyer* review regarded the "Patriot Act, and the Bush administration's increasingly aggressive assertion of executive authority to curtail or eliminate judicial review of decisions about whom to surveil, detain, and prosecute for what conduct represents a dangerous, unprecedented—and above all— unjustifiable—threat to civil liberties."

By early 2004, over six hundred detainees of another sort were being held at the U.S. military base in Guantanamo Bay, Cuba, and an unknown number in Afghanistan and elsewhere. Many had been captured in 2001-2002 near the battle zones during the Afghanistan war, while others were taken far from the areas of conflict. The Bush administration regarded them all as members of a military force at war with the U.S.—that is, either Al Qaeda or the Taliban—and therefore they were to be treated as *enemy combatants.*

In avoiding the label of prisoners of war (POWs) for the captives the U.S. did not feel obliged to grant them the rights accorded to such prisoners under the *Geneva Conventions.* Moreover, because the Guantanamo military base is not on U.S. territory, the Bush administration claimed that the captives could not claim any due process rights guaranteed under the U.S. Constitution.

New York-based Human Rights First (HRF) (www. humanrightsfirst.org) points out that "Under international humanitarian law, combatants in an armed conflict who are captured by the enemy may be held in detention until the cessation of 'active hostilities'...In this instance, the administration construes this term to mean the end of the 'war against terrorism.'" Those detained are, according to HFC, "In the legal equivalent of outer space."

That began to change on June 28, 2004, when the U.S. Supreme Court ruled, by an 8-to-1 margin that "Due process demands that a citizen held in the United States as an enemy combatant be given a meaningful opportunity to contest the factual basis for that detention before a neutral decision-maker." According to the *New York Times,* June 28, 2004 this decision was "the court's most important statement in decades on the balance between personal liberties and national security."

A series of other legal decisions followed at the federal level, and by early 2005 the Bush administration's claim that they could deny detainees basic legal rights was severely challenged (see *enemy combatants*).

In early 2004 there were still about 8,000 Iraqi detainees being held at various sites around Iraq. Paul Garwood (Associated Press, March 9, 2004) cited the case of 500-900 Iraqis said to be in military detention in Tikrit. "In many cases, innocent Iraqis have been arrested...but getting them out of jail has been difficult. No formal system exists to track them down, verify their stories, and hear representations by family members...tribal leaders complain that tensions are reaching the boiling point in their communities." The Supreme Court decision did not speak to their plight.

The fact that thousands of individuals were languishing in indefinite imprisonment both in Guantanamo, Cuba, and in a war zone under U.S. auspices was not the only issue surrounding their detention. The shocking story of their often-inhumane treatment began to surface in April 2004 with the publication of pictures of cruel, degrading punishment of prisoners in Iraq's Abu Ghraib jail (see *extraordinary rendition*).

The Iraq excesses appeared to have had their roots in

Guantanamo. *Newsweek,* March 24, 2004 explains how General Goeffrey Miller, then commander of the task force running Guantanamo prison, had toughened up the interrogation rules there to the point where the Pentagon felt they were wringing useful information from the detainees. Miller's "72-point matrix for stress and duress" included "naked isolation in cold, dark cells for more than 30 days at a time, prolonged hooding, and threatening by dogs."

As the U.S.-led *occupation* in Iraq faced escalating violence, Miller was sent to Baghdad in September 2003 to "improve" the interrogations. *Newsweek* recounts that "Miller delivered a blunt message to Brig. Gen. Janis Karpinski, who was then in charge...according to Karpinski, Miller told her that the prison would thenceforth be dedicated to gathering intel[ligence]...On November 19, Abu Ghraib was formerly handed over to tactical control of military-intelligence units (see *mercenaries*). In March 2004 Miller was transferred from Guantanamo and named head of prison operations in Iraq.

George W. Bush has called for a *crusade* to "rid the world of evildoer*s*" in a *global war on terrorism.* In an October 17, 2001 interview the President remarked "You mark my words, people are going to get tired of the war on terrorism. And, by the way, it may take more than two years. There are a variety of theatres. So long as anybody's terrorizing established governments, there needs to be a war." Complete with, one must assume, plenty of detainees, who would have to rely on legal protections supported by the courts against the wishes of the Bush administration.

deterrence: the theory held by the George W. Bush administration that increasing the U.S. nuclear arsenal, creating an elaborate missile defense system, deploying military forces worldwide, equipping those forces with high-tech weaponry, and gaining military control over space and cyberspace will usher in a new era of global peace and stability, over which the U.S. will reign as the sole superpower (see *hyperpower*).

Historically, the notion of deterrence was based on the idea that—because the U.S. as well as the Soviet Union had an overabundance of *nuclear weapons* and means to deliver them—those two great military powers would survive because of the fear that any nuclear attack by either would mean certain destruction of both—the situation known as "mutual assured destruction (MAD)". Behind this notion, of course, is the terrible truth that those who possess these weapons, which could destroy the Earth and its people, must make a moral commitment to use them.

Has deterrence in this classical sense worked? Not according to some key participants in its history, practically or ethically. Among them is General Lee Butler, former commander of the U.S. Strategic Command. In the January/February 2000 *Bulletin of the Atomic Scientists* Butler maintains that deterrence has in practice led to "a continuing nightmare of proliferation, crises spun out of control, and the dreaded headline that a city somewhere in the world has been vaporized." Writing about the relations between the Soviets and the U.S. he points out the "the presence of these weapons inspired [them] to take risks—especially in the launch-on-warning force postures— that brought the world to the brink of nuclear holocaust and left it there...the capacity for human and mechanical failure, and for human misunderstandings, was limitless."

Gen. Butler, a strong supporter of conventional (non-nuclear) military forces, is by no means a pacifist. Nevertheless, he stresses that "The United States cannot at once hold sacred the mystery of life while we retain the capacity to utterly destroy it... It is morally wrong to continue to adhere to a national doctrine that accepts the possibility of shearing away entire societies."

The blueprint for achieving a new form of deterrence through global domination, or *Pax Americana*, is clearly outlined in the

2000 document *Rebuilding America's Defenses: Strategy, Forces and Resources for a New Century* (RAD), prepared by the *Project for the New American Century*. The RAD report is assumed to be the basis for the Bush administration's 2002 *National Security Strategy* (NSS).

RAD proclaims the urgent need for a "globally preeminent military capability both today and in the future." This is to include the classic nuclear deterrence based on "a global, net assessment that weighs the full range of current and emerging threats, and not merely the U.S.-Russia balance." Now, instead of the old "wholesale" deterrence of the Soviet Union, the U.S. needs to acquire deterrence at the "retail" level, "by deterring or, when needed, by compelling regional foes to act in ways that protect America's interests and principles." The document goes on to detail the need for "safer and more effective nuclear weapons," "a transformation of war made possible by new technologies," a "worldwide network of operating bases," and "control of space and cyberspace" (see *bunker buster*).

The 2002 *National Security Strategy* spells out this new deterrence in a startling departure from what it calls "deterrence based only on the threat of retaliation." Now, with the threat of *"rogue states"* obtaining nuclear and other *weapons of mass destruction*, the U.S. must be proactive. In their December 2002 Policy Brief #13 (The Brookings Institution, (www.brook.edu), Michael E. O'Hanlon, Susan E. Rice and James B. Steinberg describe the crucial change: "The administration is broadening the meaning [of preemptive force—used in the face of imminent attack] to encompass preventive war as well, in which force may be used even without evidence of an imminent attack to insure that that a serious threat to the United States does not 'gather' or grow over time" (see *preemptive war, preventive war*).

They warn that "Developing doctrines that lower the threshold for preemptive action could...exacerbate regional crises already on the brink of open conflict...Countries already on the brink of war...might use the doctrine to justify an action they already wished to take, and the effect of the U.S. posture may make it harder for the international community...and the U.S....to counsel delay and diplomacy."

Professor Sir Joseph Rotblat, the 1995 Nobel peace laureate, points out that "By utilizing the tremendous advances in technology for military purposes, the United States has built up an overwhelming military superiority, exceeding many-fold the combined military strength of all other nations. It is claimed that this is necessary for world security, but actually what such a policy amounts to is to rest the security of the world on a balance of terror."

The current U.S. policy of maintaining a "balance of terror" can hardly be what Gen. Lee Butler had in mind when he insisted "If we truly subscribe to the principles that give meaning to the worth and dignity of the individual and if we cherish freedom and the capacity for us to realize our potential as human beings, then we are obligated to relentlessly pursue the capacity to live together in harmony with other nations."

died: was (were) killed. In war, people do not simply "die"— they are killed by other people, or sometimes, by themselves (see *suicide*). These news accounts from CNN.com are typical:

"Three Iraqi civilians died when U.S. forces launched attacks in Baghdad and Tikrit aimed at finding former Iraqi leader Saddam Hussein." (CNN.com, July 28, 2003)

"As they once again face the possibility of a military attack, Iraqis have entered a week of official mourning...to remember countrymen who died in the [Gulf] war." (CNN.com, February 13, 1998)

"A service has been held in St. Paul's Cathedral in London to commemorate those who died during the Iraq war." (CNN.com,

October 10, 2003)

dismounts: *soldiers* on foot. As human beings, even if they are wearing some sort of protective gear, they are particularly vulnerable as *soft targets.* Because the U.S. had a disproportionate number of armored vehicles at their disposal in Iraq (see *Abrams tank)* the Iraqi dismounts were typically overwhelmed. For example, an *Operation Iraqi Freedom* battle report written by a U.S. soldier says " I identified a large number of enemy dismounts near the bridge, which was our objective...I was told to move up to the bridge with one of the M1 tanks. While we were moving up the M1 engaged the dismounts with coax and .50 cal. which had no effect. So I opened up with 25mm HE which literally 'laid them out'. Note: the next day our CO counted 65 KIA there" (www. scgonline.net) (see *engage, body count).*

Another account of the same battle reports, "Lead Knight elements and scouts engaged the dismounts ending the silence with machine gun fire. Yelling 'Stop shooting, they're dead!' into his hand mike, 1LT Gleason confirmed the first Task Force battlefield damage assessment, two enemy dismounts...His scouts engaged 10 more dismounts killing six and wounding the remainder. Frantically waving injured arms in the air, the remaining dismounts desperately signaled surrender."

The enemy on foot was at risk even in the dark of night. In a March 27, 2003 interview, CNN senior international correspondent Walter Rodgers—in his characteristically breathless enthusiasm for *high-tech* warfare—asked a U.S. soldier: "You were atop your tank turret with a machine gun. You had night vision goggles on. What could you see? What were you shooting at?" The answer, "Initially we returned fire just at the tracers...But myself and the gunner would drop down and use the night sight, the thermals, to engage the dismounts that we could see."

It is not always necessary to shoot dismounts. One can hope

that they will self-destruct. As a 2001 manual on *antipersonnel devices* (see *area denial munitions*) puts it—concerning landmine safety mechanisms—"They are intended to prevent someone from moving or removing the individual mine, not to prevent reduction of the minefield by enemy dismounts."

dispatch: One can send a dispatch (a message), or one can dispatch (kill) a person. In addition to the directions for killing found in *military training* manuals, there is plenty of advice available elsewhere. For example, (www.self-defense-guide.com) suggests that "In most combat situations, small arms and grenades are the weapons of choice. However, in some scenarios, soldiers must engage the enemy in confined areas...In these instances... the bayonet or the knife may be the ideal weapon to dispatch the enemy."

In support of President Bush's *global war on terrorism,* conservative columnist David Limbaugh (Rush's brother) advised on (www.worldnet.daily.com) "We should use that amount of force that is prudent and necessary to dispatch the enemy as quickly as possible."

Instead of being merely once removed from the actual violence of dispatching, one can order a videogame (see *action figures, military games*) from the Wargamer (www.wargamer. com)— among many other suppliers—in which killing becomes virtual reality. The game "Panzer Elite" assures the user that "If you feel a surge of testosterone and want to dispatch the targets yourself, enjoy, because every crew station is accessible and functional."

dissent: in the realm of good citizenship, expressing one's disagreement with a prevailing policy. Dissent, protected in the Bill of Rights under the First Amendment, has been a hallmark of American democracy. Under the George W. Bush administration, public dissent against its proactive, imperialistic military establishment (see *National Security Strategy*) has come to be widely regarded as unpatriotic.

Soon after the tragedy of 9/11, the President, speaking to a Joint Meeting of Congress on September 21, 2001, warned the world: "Every nation in every region now has a decision to make. Either you are with us or you are with the terrorists." His words were addressed to the nations of the world, but the simple distinction he expressed soon began to apply to all levels of political dissent within the United States. The *flags*, which festooned the autos, homes and workplaces of the country, became a symbol of the dichotomy between those individuals "with" the administration or "against" it.

It was quite obvious that few supported those who had committed the crime of 9/11. However, it became clear that the tenor of the times was not receptive to the suggestion that the U.S. may somehow have fueled the rage expressed in that act.

When comedian and political commentator Bill Maher remarked, shortly after 9/11 "We have been the cowards, lobbing cruise missiles from two thousand miles away...Staying in the airplane when it hits the building—say what you want about it, it's not cowardly." It was poor timing, particularly for a comedian, and an inflammatory distinction, but no more than an exercise in free speech. White House Press Secretary Ari Fleischer responded angrily, warning that "There are reminders to all Americans to watch what they say, watch what they do, and this is not a time for remarks like that. It never is." The tone had been set. In 2003, Fleischer would describe the widespread criticism of the President's public relations gimmick—landing decked out in full flight gear aboard the U.S.S. Abraham Lincoln (see *mission accomplished*)—as "a disservice to the men and women of our military."

The American Council of Trustees and Alumni (www.goacta.

org), a conservative academic group founded by Lynne Cheney, the wife of Vice President Dick Cheney, published a report in November 2001 in which they harshly criticized 40 college professors as well as the President of Wesleyan University for lack of *patriotism* in the aftermath of September 11th. The report names professors who had made statements that were "short on patriotism and long on self-flagellation."

Wesleyan's President, Douglas Bennet, wrote a letter to the Wesleyan community on September 14, 2001 in which he condemned the attacks. However, to the Council's displeasure, he had warned that "disparities and injustices" in America and elsewhere can lead to hatred and violence. He urged that societies should try to see the world "through the sensitivities of others." According to the Council, expressing such radical notions means that "the message of much of academe [is] clear: BLAME AMERICA FIRST."

In December 2001, Attorney General John Ashcroft, the nation's top law enforcement officer, admonished those who were speaking out against curtailment of civil liberties during the *global war on terrorism.* He told the Senate Judiciary Committee "Those who scare peace-loving people with phantoms of lost liberty... your tactics only aid terrorists, for they erode our national unity and diminish our resolve. They give ammunition to our enemies." Press reports described the senators as "astonished."

In mid-2003—when Senate Democratic leader Tom Daschle of South Dakota remarked that Bush had failed at diplomacy before launching *Operation Iraqi Freedom*—House Speaker Dennis Hastert (R-Illinois) said Daschle's remarks "may not give comfort to our enemies, but they come mighty close." By the fall of 2003, the President had apparently come to the conclusion that criticism of his policies was tantamount to a national security threat. Bush described the Democrats who were holding up legislation for a Homeland Security Department as "not interested in the security of the American people."

President Bush managed to remain insulated from worrisome exposure to dissent. The President, who by his own admission does not read newspapers, was kept at a comfortable distance from dissenters during his public appearances. According to the January 4, 2004 *San Francisco Chronicle*, "the Secret Service visits the location ahead of time and orders local police to set up 'free speech' or 'protest zones' where people opposed to Bush policies...are quarantined. These zones routinely succeed in keeping protestors out of presidential sight and outside the view of the media."

The *Chronicle* report cites "the FBI's 'belief that dissident speech and association should be prevented because they were incipient steps toward the possible ultimate commission of act which might be criminal,' according to a Senate report."

In what amounted to almost comic relief, in February 2003— as the U.S. was cobbling together a coalition to attack Iraq— First Lady Laura Bush was about to host a selected group of American poets at the White House. The conference, "Poetry and the American Voice" was to feature the works of Emily Dickinson, Walt Whitman, and Langston Hughes. One of the invited poets, Sam Hamill, had invited friends and colleagues to send him anti-war poems, or statements expressing dissent over the imminent invasion. Hamill intended that the collection—which grew quickly to over 1,500 responses—would be presented to Mrs. Bush at the conference. When her office heard about this shocking display of outspokenness, she canceled the event.

Her spokesperson said "While Mrs. Bush respects and believes in the right of all Americans to express their opinions, she too has opinions, and believes that it would be inappropriate to turn what is intended to be a literary event into a political forum." The fact that Mrs. Bush once remarked, "There is nothing political about American literature" perhaps explains why she may have been unaware of the radical writings of the poets who had been chosen as the subjects of the conference. Had the meeting taken place she might have heard the words of Langston Hughes, "O, let my land be a land where Liberty is crowned with no false patriotic wreath," or perhaps Dickinson's lament for young men killed in war—their lives an "Enormous Pearl" dissolved in "Battle's—horrid Bowl."

Writing at the height of the protests against the Vietnam War, former Supreme Court Justice William O. Douglas observed, "The dissent we witness is a reaffirmation of faith in man; it is protest against living under rules and prejudices and attitudes that produce the extremes of wealth and poverty and that makes us dedicated to the destruction of people through arms, bombs, and gases, and that prepare us to think alike and be submissive objects..."

dropped ordnance: Weapons of death and destruction dropped from aircraft. This may include *bombs* (see *bomblets*), as well as various types of missiles and landmines (see *area denial munitions*). CNN.com reported on April 8, 2003: "A-10 Warthog tank-buster jets circled the sky above the battle, diving every now and then...to drop ordnance, each bomb exploding with a burst of fire and black smoke. As the battle wore on, Iraqi resistance appeared to be diminishing."

dumb bomb: a *bomb* so stupid that it can only obey the law of gravity but so smart that it can explode upon impact, tearing to pieces and/or incinerating anything or anyone within its effective radius.

Dumb bombs are dropped from aircraft and fall to the ground. Their accuracy depends on the skill of the pilot and the vagaries of the weather. The Air Force uses a calculation known as circular error probability (CEP) to determine bomb accuracy. The CEP is the radius of the circle in which a bomb will land at least half the time. For example, if a bomb hits within a 300 foot-wide circle half the time, it has a CEP of 150 feet. A dumb bomb dropped from 2,000 feet generally has a CEP of about 100 feet. In other words, it can miss by, for example, the width of two crowded apartment buildings near the intended target.

During *Operation Desert Storm* in 1991, approximately 256,000 bombs were dropped, of which only 6-7% were *smart bombs*, the type using some kind guidance system (see *precision-guided munitions*). Most were of the dumb variety. In the 2003 *Operation Iraqi Freedom* the U.S. and British dropped about 27,000 bombs, approximately 9,000 of which were dumb bombs. When *smart bombs* go astray, however, their guidance systems may send them even further from their targets than their errant dumb counterparts.

E

"You need courage not to drop bombs. Otherwise, your war will be endless.

Vyacheslav Izmailov

elements: groups of human beings. During *Operation Iraqi Freedom* Fox News, December 17, 2003 reported that the coalition would "target, isolate and eliminate former regime elements" (see *eliminate)*. When elements come under attack they are killed, injured and mutilated (see *camps, barracks, enemy positions, garrisons, units*).

eliminate: kill. The September 1, 2003 *Teacher's Guide* (www.usnewsclassroom.com), suggests a lesson on American Government, entitled "Troops or Consequences." The lesson directs, after reviewing " why President Bush is reluctant to cede authority in Iraq to the international community," that the students role-play as members of either the State Department or the Department of Defense. The latter group will argue that "Increasing U.S. strength in Iraq would eliminate enemy forces..."(see *assassination, collateral damage, degrade, dispatch, mopping up, neutralize, reduce, take out*).

embedded media: an effective Pentagon propaganda technique. Plans were made months before the March 20, 2003 invasion of Iraq to have journalists travel within military units during the war. They would experience fatigue, stress and danger, bonding them to their military protectors. Not planned was the sad fact that within a period of three weeks, twelve would be killed or die.

The Pentagon had vivid memories of what they perceived as pessimistic reporting that had turned the tide of public opinion against the Vietnam war—in the face of the repetitive official government position that *victory* was just around the corner. No reporters were allowed to witness the 1983 invasion of Grenada, and most were kept away from the 1989 attack on Panama. The absurdities of both "wars" were never fully detailed. During the 1991 *Gulf War*, access to information was limited, and reports were often censored or delayed. Whatever information the Pentagon wished to reveal, as in the later Afghanistan war, was relayed in official briefings.

This time around in the war that was about to unfold—a war based on deceit (see *weapons of mass destruction*) and against a military force that was artfully overrated—there was no room for disgruntled media. Nothing makes journalists happier than access, and they would get that in a way that was unique, and to the Pentagon, unthreatening.

According to Sheldon Rampton and John Stauber, in their insightful 2003 *Weapons of Mass Deception: The Uses of Propaganda in Bush's War on Iraq*, the Pentagon's assistant secretary of defense for public affairs Torie Clarke had put together the strategy for placing reporters with the troops. Clarke had moved to the Pentagon "after running the Washington, D.C. office of the Hill & Knowlton public relations firm, which had run the PR campaign for the government-in-exile of Kuwait during the buildup to *Operation Desert Storm.*"

The approximately 600 "embeds" were not alone. For each military division, which took 40-60 journalists, there were 5 or 6 Pentagon public affairs officers along for the ride as well. Officially, these officers duties included, according to Pentagon officials, "keep(ing) tabs on them... (to) assist them if their primary needs failed i.e. help charge their batteries..." Perhaps they also could remind the reporters of the elaborate ground rules which they had signed with the warning that "violation of the ...rules may result in immediate termination of the embed and removal."

Some of the regulations were justifiable safeguards against revealing information that might jeopardize the troops. But Robert Jensen, journalism professor and founder of the Nowar collective (www.nowarcollective.org), writing in the May 2003 *Progressive,* points out that "The rules said that reporters could not travel independently (which meant they could not really report independently), interviews had to be on the record (which meant lower-level service members were less likely to say anything critical), and officers could censor copy...(which) could be defined as whatever field commanders want to censor."

What ultimately emerged from this unique experience of commingling media with military was pretty much what the Pentagon had intended. Vice President Dick Cheney, a few days before the official end of the war, said, "the troops have come to know reporters who are willing to accept the hardships and dangers of war to get the story straight."

The Pentagon had, according to Torie Clarke, "put the same planning and preparation into this [embedding] as military planners put into the war effort." Despite a few outbursts about military tactics, referred to by Secretary of Defense Donald Rumsfeld petulantly as "media mood swings," the media accounts of the fighting centered around the courage and stamina of the U.S. troops, the awesome firepower of their weapons, the technology of modern warfare such as night vision goggles, the expertise of pilots landing on aircraft carriers, and the excitement of *liberation.*

Some could not restrain their awe. CNN's Walter Rodgers, embedded with the Seventh Cavalry, rhapsodized to CNN anchor Aaron Brown "The pictures you are seeing are absolutely phenomenal...if you ride inside that tank, it's like riding inside the bowels of a dragon." Brown replied, "Wow, look at that shot." Rodgers answered, " [this] is truly historic television and journalism." Some went considerably further, according to the

Washington Post, April 28, 2003. "An armed bodyguard with CNN's Brent Sandler returned Iraqi fire near Tikrit. *Boston Herald* reporter Jules Crittenden pointed out three snipers for his soldier's unit to kill."

In the final analysis, according to Robert Jensen, the success of embedding was in the "technical sophistication... the ability of journalists demonstrating considerable skill and fortitude to deliver words and pictures from halfway around the world with incredible speed under difficult conditions." But he adds, "The failure was in journalist's inability...to help people come to the fullest possible understanding...not only of what was happening in the war, but why it was happening and what it meant."

In a more caustic appraisal, the distinguished journalist Russell Baker portrayed the embeds as "serving as megaphones for fraud." Colonel Kenneth Allard, an expert on military strategy, claims that *Operation Iraqi Freedom* "will be remembered as a conflict in which information fully took its place as an instrument of war" (see *information dominance*).

Quite understandably, the "embeds" bonded with their military units. As ABC's John Donovan expressed it "they're my protectors." Bob Franken, experienced national correspondent for CNN, admitted that "One of my proudest moments came when this Marine colonel, a John Wayne type if there ever was one, came up to this riffraff group of reporters...and he said. "You guys are like the Marines."

Not everyone who covered the war was embedded, at least officially. There were foreign correspondents, and a few Americans who were on their own, as unilaterals. Two of the best known of the latter were Bing West and Major General Ray L. Smith, both former Marines. In their 2003 book *The March Up: Taking Baghdad With the 1st Marine Division,* which overflows with praise for the Marines and loathing for the *enemy*, they used a style not employed by the embeds. They write, "The Marines didn't think of their prey as human. They were not men who would joke with one another and write dirt-stained letters assuring their mothers or wives that they were fine. No, as far as the Marines were concerned, they were vermin—rats or weasels— sneaking onto battlefields in civilian buses, hiding behind women, wearing civilian clothes. If it weren't for them, the Marines wouldn't have shot up civilian cars."

end of hostilities: a common reference to the May 1, 2003 announcement by President George W. Bush that "major combat operations have ended" in Iraq. The announcement was not to be interpreted as the "legal end to hostilities" according to White House Press Secretary Ari Fleischer. Such a move would complicate matters, including requiring the U.S.-led coalition to release and repatriate their prisoners of war (see *detainees, enemy combatants*). Besides, Fleischer added, U.S. forces still were at risk from "pockets of resistance.*"* In the months ahead those *pockets* of resistance would account for the killing and wounding of more coalition military than had occurred during the period of "official" hostilities.

In what later would be widely regarded as an embarrassing and inappropriate publicity stunt, Bush had arrived for his speech in a fighter plane which landed aboard the aircraft carrier U.S.S. Abraham Lincoln, waiting just off the coast of San Diego, California. He emerged decked out in an Air Force flight suit (see *mission accomplished, action figures*). Ari Fleischer defended the unique arrival, saying the president wanted "to see an aircraft landing the same way that the pilots saw an aircraft landing. He wanted to see it as realistically as possible."

After his exciting experience, Bush addressed the assembled officers and sailors, telling them that he was there to announce, "major combat operations in Iraq have ended." The President continued, "The battle of Iraq is one victory in a war on terror that began on September 11th, 2001, and still goes on." While not offering any evidence of a link between that tragic event and Iraq, the president maintained, "The liberation of Iraq is a crucial advance in the campaign against terror." Noting that "We will defend the peace"(presumably through war), he told the military audience that they had "taken up the highest calling of history... wherever you go, you carry a message of hope, a message that is ever ancient and ever new" (see *soldier*).

The echoes of the *bombs*, the groans of the wounded, and the screams of the dying had faded far from the shores of sunny California.

endless war: the new *global war on terrorism* promised by the George W. Bush administrations. The barely concealed goal of the protracted march toward global domination is to secure and maintain access to the world's oil supplies. According to the President, the rationale for the endless war is to "rid the world of evil."

During an interview on October 19, 2001 Vice President Dick Cheney promised "It [the new war on terrorism] is different than the Gulf War was, in the sense that it may never end. At least not in our lifetime." Standing in front of a map of Afghanistan, then already under a U.S.-led massive bombardment featuring *cluster bombs*, Cheney explained "The way I think of it is, it's a new normalcy...We're going to have to take steps, and are taking steps, that'll become a permanent part of the way we live."

Jeffrey Record, professor in the Department of Strategy and International Security at the U.S. Air Force's Air War College, warned in December 2003 "The administration has postulated a multiplicity of enemies, including rogue states; weapons of mass destruction (WMD) proliferators; terrorist organizations of global, regional, and national scope; and terrorism itself." He cautions that the objectives, including "destruction of transnational terrorist organizations" "the transformation of Iraq into a prosperous, stable democracy" and "the forcible (if necessary) termination of WMD proliferation" are "unrealistic and condemn the United States to a hopeless quest for national security."

In the words of the administration's own documents and their precursors (see *Defense Planning Guidance, National Security Strategy, Rebuilding America's Defenses,*) the demands of this endless war will permit us unprecedented latitude. We may attack whomever we wish ("if necessary, act preemptively"), with new "bunker-busting" nuclear weapons if needed, on our own authority ("they demand American political leadership rather than that of the United Nations") anywhere in the world ([we] must pursue them across the geographic spectrum").

Those same documents clearly reveal that this unabashed drive for global preeminence was formulated years before the tragedy of 9/11 (see *constabulary duties, critical regions, Defense Planning Guidance*). In the aftermath of 9/11, because there was no credible evidence linking the perpetrators to Iraq, the long-planned attack had to be delayed—but crushing and occupying Afghanistan was easier to defend on the basis of its ties to Al Qaeda. On October 21, 2001 Air Force General Richard Myers described Afghanistan as only a "small piece" of a campaign that might last more than a lifetime. He added "I would say, since World War Two, we haven't thought so broadly about a campaign."

Soon, however, the doctrine spelled out in the 2000 *Rebuilding America's Defenses* would become politically manageable. That document, the blueprint for the 2002 *National Security Strategy*, says "The United States has for decades sought to play a more prominent role in Gulf regional security. While the unresolved conflict with Iraq provides the immediate justification, the need for a substantial American force presence in the gulf transcends the issue of the regime of Saddam Hussein."

The "American force presence" would be established, not by

"transcending" concerns over Saddam's regime, but by trumpeting the imminent threat of Iraq to the U.S. and Iraq's neighbors from Hussein's supposed stockpiles of *weapons of mass destruction.* This pretext served the administration well, and the U.S.-led *coalition of the willing* occupied Iraq by deadly force in mid-2003, under the guise of *liberation.*

Jeffrey Record cautions that any war sold as a global war on terrorism sets itself up for strategic failure. "Terrorism is a recourse of the politically desperate and militarily helpless, and as such, it is hardly going to disappear...the problem is that there are countless millions of people around the world who are, or believe they are, oppressed and have no other recourse than irregular warfare, including terrorism, to oppose oppression."

That eloquent warning that speaks to the structural causes behind our current crises is in marked contrast to President Bush's admonition in his November 11, 2001 press conference: "We cannot let the terrorists achieve the objective of frightening our nation to the point where we don't conduct business or people don't shop."

The Bush administration's global ambitions achieved a new focus in the President's January 20, 2005 inaugural address. He called for "the expansion of freedom in all the world," warning "America's influence is considerable, and we will use it confidently in freedom's cause."

Martin Luther King, Jr. observed "Wars are poor chisels for carving out peaceful tomorrows." In that spirit, Representative Dennis Kucinich (D-Ohio) included in his February 17, 2002 "Prayer for America" "Let us commit ourselves to the slow and painstaking work of statecraft, which sees peace, not war as being inevitable."

enemy: the other. Typically the enemy is identified by one's government as an entity that must be defeated. The intensity and duration of attempts to deal with the enemy peacefully tends to be inversely proportional to the benefits to be gained from their defeat—such as acquisition of their natural resources.

In order to encourage citizens to support a particular war with enough enthusiasm to sacrifice their sons and daughters —generally not those from the more affluent families—the government must generate several traditional, time-honored motivations within civilians as well as *soldiers.*

Chris Hedges, an experienced war correspondent, points out in *War is a Force That Gives us Meaning* "A soldier who is able to see the humanity of the enemy makes a troubled and ineffective killer." Lt. Col. Dave Grossman, former West Point psychology instructor explains in *On Killing: The Psychological Cost of Learning to Kill in War and Society*, "Men have always used a variety of mechanisms to convince themselves that the enemy was different, that he did not have a family, or that he was not even human." Grossman details some of the mechanisms to facilitate this process, some of which apply to civilian motivation as well.

These include emphasizing "Cultural distance, such as racial and ethnic," "Moral distance...an intense belief in [our] moral superiority," and "Social distance...thinking of a particular class as less then human in a socially stratified environment." He alludes to another "distance" as well, one particularly relevant in this era of modern *high-tech* warfare. "Mechanical distance" involves the "sterile...unreality of killing through a TV screen, a thermal sight, a sniper sight, or some other kind of mechanical buffer that permits the killer to deny the humanity of his victim."

The creation of these "distances" is not a modern invention. David Hume, the famed 18th century Scottish philosopher wrote in 1740 "When our own nation is at war with any other, we detest them under the character of cruel, perfidious, unjust and violent: But always esteem ourselves and allies as equitable, moderate and merciful."

The tragedy inherent in this effective approach to whipping up a war frenzy is not just in the dehumanization of the enemy and the exaltation of one's cause, but in what is deliberately omitted. The crucial omission is any serious consideration of a nonviolent means of resolving the crisis. When a government decides that war is in its best interests, violence must be presented as the only alternative.

There will inevitably be at least a small body of citizens who will plead for moderation and a peaceful resolution. They tend to be regarded at best as hopelessly idealistic and at worst as unpatriotic or even as traitors. In the months before the U.S.-led attack on Iraq in March 2003, literally millions of people took to the streets in the U.S., England, and across the world in protest against what was billed as a war of necessity. President Bush dismissed them, not by any reasoned argument, but because he doesn't listen to "focus groups" (see *focus groups*).

enemy combatants: According to the George W. Bush administrations this category includes all those, including U.S. residents, who are suspected of committing hostile acts against the U.S. They can be arrested anywhere in the world and held for as long as the government decides is necessary, without access to legal counsel (see *detainees*).

Because the enemy combatants are to be held "until the war on terrorism is over" according to Defense Secretary Donald Rumsfeld, and that war is considered by the administration to be of indefinite duration (see *endless war*) these prisoners are in what has been described as a "legal limbo."

By early 2004 over 600 such prisoners were being held at the U.S. military base in Guantanamo, Cuba and an unknown number in Afghanistan and elsewhere. Two U.S. citizens labeled as enemy combatants were held at the Navy brig in Charleston, S.C.—Jose Padilla, arrested in Chicago under suspicion of plotting to detonate a radioactive bomb in the U.S., and Yaser Hamdi, picked up on a battlefield in Afghanistan.

On June 28, 2004 the U.S. Supreme Court ruled, by an 8-to-1 margin that "Due process demands that a citizen held in the United States as an enemy combatant be given a meaningful opportunity to contest the factual basis for that detention before a neutral decision-maker." As for the prisoners at Guantanamo the court ruled "Aliens at the base, like American citizens, are entitled to invoke the federal courts' authority...United States have traditionally been open to nonresident aliens."

However, the U.S. Department of Defense maintained, "The United States and its coalition partners remain at war against Al Qaeda and its affiliates...Therefore, the law of armed conflict governs this war...and establishes the rules for detention of enemy combatants. Those rules permit the U.S. to detain enemy combatants without charges or trial for the duration of the hostilities."

Even the chief architect of the U.S. Patriot Act objected to this unprecedented exercise of power. Viet Dinh, who until May, 2003 had headed the Justice Department's Office of Legal Policy, said in November 2003 that the administration's position was "untenable...there must be an actual process or discernible set of procedures to determine how they will be treated."

The June 2004 Supreme Court decision did not specify how the detainees' rights should be exercised. Military tribunals commenced at Guantanamo to try detainees as war criminals. These were brought to a halt by a November 2004 decision by Judge James Robertson of the United States District Court in Washington. He ruled that these tribunals ignored basic provisions of the *Geneva Conventions*, international treaties governing the conduct of war. The Justice Department objected strenuously, maintaining "By conferring protected legal status under the Geneva Conventions on members of Al Qaeda, the judge has put terrorism on the same legal footing as legitimate methods of waging war."

On January 31, 2005 Judge Joyce Hens Green, also of the United States District Court in Washington, ruled against the Bush administration, declaring that the Guantanamo detainees were entitled to have federal courts determine if they were lawfully detained. Judge Green objected to the government's "illogically broad definition of 'enemy combatant'" which condoned holding individuals in many cases "simply for being alleged members of groups that do not like Americans."

The administration had argued that because those detainees had been captured by the military outside the United States and were held on "foreign property leased by the United States" they were not entitled to constitutional rights.

Judge Green's ruling also questioned "Whether some of the information used against the detainees had been obtained by torture and was thus unreliable." In July 2004 the International Red Cross, in a confidential report, had charged the U.S. military at Guantanamo with using psychological and physical methods "tantamount to torture" on their prisoners. According to the *New York Times* (November 30, 2004) President Bush's legal team had "concluded that Mr. Bush was not bound by either the International Convention Against Torture or a federal antitorture statute because he had the authority to protect the nation against terrorism." (see *extraordinary rendition*)

That legal stance had been offered by the President's White House counsel Alberto Gonzales. The Senate confirmed Gonzales as attorney general—the nation's chief law enforcement officer—on February 3, 2005.

The protracted legal wrangling over the status of enemy combatants did not center on the guilt or innocence of the accused, but on their rights. This issue is seen as another glaring example of the insistence of the Bush administration on acting without the constraints of law. This further reinforces the growing sense that the United States is determined to use its unrivaled power to further its own interest at the expense of whoever it decides are adversaries.

According to the Pentagon there has been at least 31 suicide attempts at Guantanamo, none successful.

enemy positions: places where the *enemy* is located. When positions are attacked, the people there are killed and wounded (see *barracks, camps, garrisons, units*). For example:

"Even with the bad weather, the U.S. continued to use satellite-guided bombs to soften up Republican Guard positions." (CNN.com, March 25, 2003)

"At least eight bombs fell Monday on Iraqi front-line positions near the Kurdish-controlled town of Chamchamal in northern Iraq..." (CNN.com, March 24, 2003)

"The A-10s also strafed Iraqi positions with 30mm cannons in the center of the city." (CNN.com, April 9, 2003)

engage: to make contact with and try to kill. Among many examples, media reports during *Operation Iraqi Freedom* included: "The sound of automatic fire could be heard as they engaged the enemy." (Army News Service, December 17, 2003)

"My gunner would drop down and use the night sight, the thermals, to engage the dismounts." (CNN.com, March 27, 2003)

evil: In President George W. Bush's worldview—formed by the advisors supplying his scripted remarks—America, in its prosperity and way of life is good, and anyone who threatens that is evil. Terrorism has replaced communism as the global *enemy.* The only effective response is a military one.

Therefore, America must become even more powerful and establish global military superiority, as well as dominate space and cyberspace (see *Rebuilding America's Defenses*). Any group or nation that harbors terrorists is also evil. The U.S. may feel free to attack and destroy them. Once all the evil ones are killed, life can return to normal. Unfortunately, because the evil ones are difficult to find, appear to be numerous, and have infiltrated many countries, the *global war on terrorism* will be *endless.*

America will use almost any means of violence necessary in that war. It may be necessary to deceive (*weapons of mass destruction*), use horrendous weapons that kill indiscriminately and cruelly (*area denial munitions, cluster bombs, dumb bombs, fuel-air explosives,*), torture (*extraordinary rendition*), and kill hundreds of thousands of innocent civilians (*sanctions*), but we must apply these regrettable means in the fight of good versus evil.

Author James Carroll (*Boston Globe*, July 8, 2003) points out that "Something entirely new, for Americans at least, is animating their government. The greatest power the Earth has ever seen is now expressly mobilized against the world's most ancient mystery. What human beings have proven incapable of doing ever before, George W. Bush has taken on as his personal mission..."

David Frum, former Bush speechwriter responsible for the inflammatory term *axis of evil*, and Richard Perle, a former assistant secretary of defense (see *Defense Policy Board*) spell out a systematic approach to the fight against evil. The Amazon. com editorial review of their 2003 book *An End to Evil: How to Win the War on Terror* says that this "stirring call to arms" urges the United States "to overthrow the government of Iran, abandon support of a Palestinian state, blockade North Korea...disregard much of Europe as allies, and sever ties with Saudi Arabia."

In marked contrast, philosopher Laura J. Rediehs, in her chapter on the uses of the word "evil" in the 2002 *Collateral Language: A User's Guide to America's New War* offers a more nuanced, intelligent, and necessary analysis. She distinguishes two attitudes towards evil. One sees evil as a force rooted in individuals, while the other sees it as "arising when people make significant errors of judgment that result from reaching their intellectual or psychological limits." As a result, "When people are severely stressed or feel very hurt or fearful, they can make serious mistakes."

Accepting the former attitude makes it much easier to "[regard] ourselves as 'good' and the ones whose actions we dislike as 'evil'...we do not have to engage in the difficult process of trying to understand and communicate with people we hate or fear." The enemy "seems monstrous and irrational, incomprehensibly hating what we regard as unquestionably good."

Even thoughtful analyses of "evil" leave many unanswered questions. However, the simplistic notion of evil, as sponsored by the Bush administration in order to support unrestricted militarism, brings only more pain to an already suffering world. James Carroll asks "What is evil, anyway...Is evil the thing, perhaps, that forever inclines human beings to believe that they are themselves untouched by it? Moral maturity...begins in the acknowledgement that evil, whatever its primal source, resides...in the human self. There is no ridding the world of evil for the simple fact that, shy of history's end, there is no ridding the self of it."

exit strategy: a plan for the U.S.-led coalition to appear to withdraw from Iraq and hand over the reigns of that country's government to its inhabitants, while maintaining sufficient political, economic and military influence to remain in charge.

The Pentagon has plans to establish an as yet undetermined number of permanent military bases in Iraq (see *forward-based forces*), part of a plan to span the globe with an even more pervasive U.S. military presence. U.S. forces are now in place on every continent, except Antarctica, in more than 700 overseas bases. The U.S. Embassy in Iraq is one of the world's largest, with a staff of at least 1,700 (see *Green Zone*).

The U.S., in its determination to invade and gain control over Iraq, had written off the UN as irrelevant. As *casualties* mounted well beyond the official *end of hostilities* in an increasingly rebellious Iraq, the Bush administration was forced to turn to the UN for a political exit strategy. UN Secretary-General Kofi Annan agreed in early 2004 to offer the services of that organization to "play a constructive role in helping to find a way...to move forward to the formation of a provisional government" (see *Iraqi Governing Council*).

Political conservatives, including William Kristol and Robert Kagan (see *Project for the New American Century*), architects of much of George W. Bush's foreign policy were dismayed with the possibility that the Pentagon might actually withdraw some forces from Iraq, handing over the dangerous security duties to Iraqis. They asked in *The Weekly Standard*, November 17, 2003, "Is it to be a victory strategy or an exit strategy?... As Senator John McCain put it this week, the only acceptable exit strategy is victory" (see *victory*).

As it turned out, the coalition military forces did not exit when an interim governing body took office on June 28, 2004. The June 8, 2004 UN resolution that set the framework for the transfer of sovereignty to the interim government supported the request from the "Prime Minister of the Interim Government of Iraq...to retain the presence of the multinational force." L. Paul Bremer III and the *Coalitional Provisional Authority* withdrew, ending the "official" *occupation*—and leaving behind the occupation forces.

Following a plan laid out by the Coalition Provisional Authority, national elections were held on January 30, 2005. The objective was to elect a 275-seat legislature, whose first task would be to choose a President and two Vice Presidents. They would choose a Prime Minister. The legislature's main task would be to draw up a constitution in preparation for another election in

December 2005.

The top vote getter turned out to be the United Iraqi Alliance—a coalition of influential Muslim groups backed by Iraq's leading cleric Grand Ayatollah Ali Sistani. Prominent among its members and a prime candidate for the job of prime minister was none other than Ahmad Chalabi, once favored by the Bush White House, but now looking for more independent influence (see *Defense Policy Board, Iraqi National Congress*).

Concerns immediately arose as to whether the more conservative elements in the United Iraqi Alliance might insist on a constitution which followed an Iranian style theocracy—the imposition of strict Islamic rule. While reassurances were given that such a consitution—which would be unacceptable to the U.S.—was unlikely, the question of the attitude of the newly elected parliament towards the exit of the occupying forces was equally troubling. For example, Abdel-Azziz al-Hakim—the head of Iraq's largest party—told Time magazine (January 31,2005) "We want this foreign army out of our country immediately. We cannot tolerate this presence on our soil."

Certainly the U.S., having invaded Iraq in order to establish a powerful military presence there and to achieve control over Iraq's vast oil supply, preferred a government that was much more welcoming to their long term presence. That remained to be seen.

There are other suggestions for a real exit strategy. For example Rep. Dennis Kucinich (D-Ohio) offered this simple strategy throughout his campaign for the Democratic presidential nomination: "Reach out to the world community through the United Nations, to bring UN peacekeepers in and to bring our troops home...[this] represents the best plan to ensure the stabilization of Iraq, the end of the war and the beginning of world security" (see www.denniskucinich.us).

A more "radical" approach—one not involving a military solution—is offered in the January 2005 Washington Newsletter of the Friends Committee on National Legislation. The Quaker lobby says "While the U.S. cannot fulfill its dual responsibilities to withdraw its forces and support Iraqi rebuilding easily or without cost, these steps could help break the cycle of violence, undercut the insurgency, save lives, and give control of Iraq's future back to Iraqis."

extraordinary rendition: a covert procedure used by the U.S. Central Intelligence Agency (CIA) to gather information from captives by torture. Torture is illegal in the United States under U.S. and international human rights law, so the CIA sends terrorism suspects to other nations known to practice such cruel interrogation (see *Geneva Conventions*).

An investigative report published in the December 26, 2002 *Washington Post* details how the CIA hands over these suspects "to foreign intelligence services—notably those of Jordan, Egypt and Morocco—with a list of questions the agency wants answered. These 'extraordinary renditions' are done without resort to legal process."

An "unnamed official" who had been involved in these transfers told the *Post* "We don't kick the [expletive] out of them. We send them to other countries so *they* can kick the [expletive] out of them." However, U.S. officials who defended the transfers maintained, according to the report, "the prisoners are sent to these third countries not because of their coercive questioning techniques, but because of their cultural affinity with the captives... their intelligence services can develop a culture of intimacy that Americans cannot."

Following the CIA model, almost 3,000 suspected Al Qaeda members and supporters were taken into custody after September 11, 2001, and held at various locations around the world. By early 2004 about 600 were confined at the U.S. military base at Guantanamo, Cuba (see *detainees, enemy combatants*), and nearly

100 had been "rendered" to other countries.

One of those sites is the Bagram air base in Afghanistan—another is Diego Garcia, an island in the Indian Ocean that the U.S. leases from Britain. The *Washington Post* describes the interrogations at those sites as a "brass-knuckled quest for information." One official told the reporters "If you don't violate someone's human rights some of the time, you probably aren't doing your job."

In February 2003, as part of his efforts to build public support for an invasion of Iraq President Bush declared that "Bringing stability and unity to a free Iraq will not be easy, yet that is no excuse to leave the Iraqi regime's torture chambers...in operation." Later, in June, he proclaimed "The United States is committed to the worldwide elimination of torture and we are leading this fight by example."

The President's hypocrisy was revealed in shocking detail In April 2004 with the publication of graphic photographs from the Abu Ghraib prison in Iraq showing naked prisoners in humiliating postures, taunted by their grinning captors. The sadistic, cruel and degrading treatment of the prisoners displayed in the images was, according to the International Red Cross "tantamount to torture." The abusers—no longer confined to the CIA—now included military police, military intelligence officers, and civilian interpreters.

The mistreatment of prisoners in Iraq, Afghanistan and Guantanamo had been well known within the Pentagon and the White House for many months prior to the Abu Ghraib scandal. They had been warned repeatedly, including detailed mid-2003 reports by the International Committee of the Red Cross (www.icrc.org), and Amnesty International (www.amnesty.org).

On January 25, 2002, Alberto Gonzales—then the White House Counsel and later confirmed in 2005 as the U.S. Attorney General—wrote a memo to President Bush, saying that "the war on terrorism is a new kind of war." This new situation "renders obsolete Geneva's strict limitations on questioning enemy prisoners and renders quaint some of its provisions"(see *Geneva Conventions*). The memo reassures the President that regarding these prisoners as exempt from humane treatment "substantially reduces the threat of domestic criminal prosecution under the War Crimes Act."

This advice—now known widely as the "torture memo"— aimed at suspected Taliban members captured in Afghanistan— would be applied forcefully at Abu Ghraib prison in Baghdad after the U.S.-led invasion in March 2003(see *Operation Iraqi Freedom*).

In August 2002 Gonzales as well as other White House officials approved a Justice department memo that advised laws prohibiting torture "do not apply to the President's detention and interrogation of enemy combatants"(see *enemy combatants*). Torture, according to the memo, must include "injury such as death, organ failure, or serious impairment of bodily functions."

By the end of 2004, according to Associated Press, "A total of 130 American troops had been punished or charged in cases involving the abuse of prisoners in Iraq, Afghanistan, and Guantanamo Bay." The guilty were at the far end of a long chain of command stretching back to the Pentagon and the White House. On January 1, 2005, after President Bush nominated Alberto Gonzales to be the nation's attorney general, the Justice Department published a revised definition of torture. Now, torture was "abhorrent both to American law and values and international norms", and the department's August 2002 memo was repudiated. Torture henceforth did not necessarily have to provoke excruciating or agonizing pain, and could include "physical suffering" and "lasting mental anguish."

Francis A. Boyle, an international law professor at the University of Illinois told the Inter Press Service on November

12, 2004 " As White House Counsel, Alberto Gonzales originated, authorized, approved and aided and abetted grave breaches of the Third and Fourth Geneva Conventions of 1949, which are serious war crimes...in other words, Gonzales is a prima facie war criminal. He must be prosecuted under the Geneva Conventions and the U.S. War Crimes Act."

Some reactions to the Abu Ghraib scandal were more optimistic than most. On his May 3, 2004 radio broadcast, conservative host Rush Limbaugh offered this analysis: "This is no different than what happens at the Skull and Bones initiation and we're going to ruin people's lives over it and we're going to hamper our military effort...I'm talking about people having a good time, these people, you ever heard of emotional release? You [ever] heard of [the] need to blow some steam off?"

extremist: Those who take positions considered by most to be far from the norm, even highly radical or fanatical. Islamic fundamentalism, which seeks to enforce its strictly literal interpretation of the Koran by persuasion or force, is religious extremism.

When the Soviet Union attacked Afghanistan in 1979, funds from the Middle East and the United States supported the creation of the resistance—mujahadeen fighters who streamed into that country from the Muslim world as "freedom fighters." Mainstream Islam, a peaceful and moderate religion, would become infested with extremist strains of violence, practiced by groups, including veterans of that conflict, seeking to overthrow what they considered to be forces of corruption and spiritual degradation. Among those extremists were Osama bin Laden and his followers.

The 1991 *Gulf War*, followed by 12 years of unrelenting *sanctions*, and *Operation Iraqi Freedom* in 2003 were extremist acts of extraordinary violence, carried out by the United States and its allies. Iraq, long befriended and subsidized by the U.S.

as a barrier to Islamic fundamentalism, would be brutalized by military might which would reduce that country to ruins.

Denis Halliday, former Assistant Secretary General of the United Nations had resigned in protest over the imposition of punishing sanctions on the people of Iraq. He told reporter John Pilger (zmag.org, August 25, 2003), "They [sanctions] became, in my view, genocidal in their impact over the years, and the Security Council maintained them, despite its full knowledge of their impact, particularly on the children of Iraq...we probably killed over a million people...It's a tragedy that will not be forgotten."

F

"You would expect front-line soldiers to be struck and hurt by bullets and shell fragments, but such is the popular insulation from the facts that you would not expect them to be hurt, sometimes killed, by being struck by parts of their friends' bodies violently detached...my buddy's head...his sergeant's heel...or the West Point ring on his captain's severed hand."

Paul Fussell

firebomb: a *bomb* packing volatile, kerosene-based jet fuel laced with benzene. When a firebomb explodes, it creates a massive fireball, incinerating anyone in the area. Those who are not killed suffer burns that are particularly difficult to treat, even if skilled medical care is available.

Firebombs are very similar in their effect to *napalm,* which had been dropped by the millions of pounds, often indiscriminately, during the Vietnam War. The U.S. used napalm in the *Gulf War*, in the infamous *turkey shoot*, attacking and burning defenseless Iraqis fleeing from Kuwait.

When reporters accused the U.S. military of again dropping napalm on Iraqi troops during *Operation Iraqi Freedom*, the Defense Department firmly denied the allegations, pointing out that the U.S. had destroyed its last stocks of napalm in April 2001. Eventually they did admit that Mark-77 firebombs were used on Iraqi troops on several occasions, but not napalm, a distinction lost on the incinerated dead and severely burned (see *atrocity*).

Napalm and other "incendiaries"—weapons that burn—are restricted by the 1980 Convention on Conventional Weapons (CCW) (see *conventional weapons).* They are not banned outright, but are confined to military targets. The U.S. has not signed onto that particular CCW protocol.

flag: A piece of cloth, variously colored, often displayed in order to stimulate feelings of patriotism among citizens. The American flag bears thirteen stripes of white and red, representing the thirteen colonies established on land taken by force from the original inhabitants. The flag represents honor, hope and pride, often justifiably. Those citizens who display the flag—on their vehicles or elsewhere—are regarded by many to be the more loyal to their country. Military personnel are taught to have a particular devotion to the flag. When they are killed in the line of duty, their coffins are draped with the flag. It is removed before interment, because burying a flag is considered to be disrespectful.

focus groups: President George W. Bush's description of the largest anti-war demonstrations since the Vietnam era. In February 2003, in response to millions of people across the U.S. and Europe who turned out in public demonstrations against the impending war against Iraq, Bush told reporters "You know, size of protest, it's like deciding, well, I'm going to decide policy based on a focus group." The president added "Democracy is a beautiful thing...I welcome people's right to say what they believe."

According to the marketing research firm T.L. Grantham and Associates: "A focus group is a form of qualitative research that measures the opinions and concerns of a desired population. This is done by taking 8-12 participants that are selected to each represent 10,000 other people...The information provided by research groups is always helpful because it gives solid feedback on how your target audience will respond to a new product, service, or ad campaign."

The president's cavalier analogy between focus groups—a marketing research technique well suited for the selling of soap or cereal—and the agonized cry of millions of people attempting to halt the death and destruction that was about to begin once again in Iraq—contradicts his own use of that propaganda tool.

In early October 2001, the Pentagon hired a Washington public relations firm to bolster public support for its military strikes in Afghanistan. The Rendon Group (TRG) was given a no-bid $397,000 contract with which, according to the *San Jose Mercury News* (October 19, 2001), they were to "monitor news media in 79 countries, conduct focus groups...and recommend the way the U.S. military can counter disinformation and improve its own public communications."

The Rendon Group was no stranger to the PR efforts of the U.S. Government. Back in the early 1990s TRG had received a $100,000 monthly retainer from the Kuwait government as part of a concerted PR effort to bolster public support for George Bush the elder's invasion of Iraq—*Operation Desert Storm.* After the war, the company cranked up its spin machine to minimize the negative images of what would be years of crippling *sanctions* against Iraq. Soon they were working with the CIA, funneling millions to put together the *Iraqi National Congress*, headed by Ahmad Chalabi (see *Defense Policy Board, exit strategy*).

Whatever focus groups TRG may have put together, they had no discernible influence on the people of Turkey. The Pentagon had every intention of using that country's military bases to launch coalition troops into Iraq. After all, the leaders of Turkey's ruling Justice and Development Party had agreed (for $15 billion) to allow access to their bases. The Turkish Parliament turned down the proposal. As a former ambassador to Turkey explained "The biggest problem is that 94 percent of the Turks are opposed to war."

forces: *soldiers* and their equipment. When forces are attacked, people are killed and wounded (see *barracks, camps, enemy positions, garrisons, units*). The following are examples taken from media reports during *Operation Iraqi Freedom*:

"Warplanes bombed Iraqi forces in the area..." (*Lansing*

State Journal, April 12, 2003)

"U.S. Air Force B-52s bombed Iraqi forces Thursday..." (CNN.com, April 3,2003)

"[a] flanking attack designed to trap and destroy the Republican Guard forces..." (*Diplomatic History,* Winter, 2000)

"...ordered a 'strong, sustained' series of air strikes on military and security forces in Iraq..." (CNN.com, December 16, 1998)

forward-based forces: the *soldiers* and weapons which the George W. Bush administration began to spread throughout the world in order to fulfill the aims of the 2002 *National Security Strategy* (NSS). That document maintains that "The presence of American forces overseas is one of the most profound symbols of the U.S. commitments to allies and friends...to contend with uncertainty...the United States will require bases and stations well beyond Western Europe and Northeast Asia, as well as temporary access arrangements for the long-distance deployment of U.S. forces."

This major expansion of an already vast network of at least 700 foreign military bases, spread across every continent but Antarctica, is spelled out in somewhat more detail in the precursor to the NSS, *Rebuilding America's Defenses: Strategy, Forces and Resources For a New Century* (RAD), published in 2000. Calling the armed forces stationed abroad "the cavalry on the new American frontier" the RAD outlines a variety of moves to place this imagined cavalry "along an expanded American security perimeter around the globe." The Air Force, for example, should expand to the Philippines and Australia, and the Navy needs a "new, permanent forward base in Southeast Asia."

Written well before the 2003 U.S.-led *coalition* attack on Iraq, the RAD points out "The value of such [Middle East] bases would endure even should Saddam pass from the scene...and even should U.S.-Iranian relations improve, retaining forward-based forces in the region would still be an essential element in U.S. security strategy given the long-standing American interests in the region" (see *exit strategy*).

In TomDispatch.com, January 15, 2004, scholar and author Chalmers Johnson wrote a detailed analysis of the then current and planned global reach of the U.S. military. Chalmers writes that Pentagon planners "have identified something they call the 'arc of instability,' which is said to run from the Andean region of South America (read: Colombia) through North Africa and then sweeps across the Middle East to the Philippines and Indonesia. This is, of course, more or less identical with what used to be called the Third World—and perhaps no less crucially it covers the world's key oil reserves."

Johnson concludes "Once upon a time, you could trace the spread of imperialism by counting up the colonies. America's version of the colony is the military base."

friendly fire: the accidental killing or wounding of one's fellow combatants while trying to kill the *enemy*. This tragedy is also called fratricide, amicicide, or more recently, blue on blue. Friendly fire is not unusual. During World War 1, 75,000 *soldiers* were killed by "friendly" *artillery* fire. Fratricide caused 25% of the killings of coalition forces during the *Gulf War*.

The various factors cited as responsible for friendly fire include the stress of combat with its resultant confusion, and the accidental detonation of unexploded munitions (see *area denial munitions, bomblets, cluster bombs*). Another recent major contributor is the "Glass Cockpit Syndrome,"—the proliferation of targeting by computers, leading to technical errors—such as missiles downing the wrong aircraft (see *Patriot missile*). Understandably, the military is undertaking detailed analyses of friendly fire incidents and applying preventive measures, centered around training and technical methods for identifying fellow *soldiers*.

An official military definition of fratricide, offered by the General Officer Steering Committee, reads "...the employment of friendly weapons and munitions with the intent to kill the enemy or destroy his equipment that results in unforeseen death or injury to friendly personnel." Webster's Unabridged Dictionary simply defines it as " the act of killing one's brother."

Who is asking what disqualifies the enemy from brotherhood in the family of humanity?

fuel-air explosives (FAE): enormously powerful weapons that destroy and incinerate structures and people. Delivered as various types of *bombs* and missiles, FAEs burst, dispensing a fine mist of fuel, which is then detonated to create a massive explosion and fireball. They are not now prohibited under the Convention on Conventional Weapons (CCW) (see *conventional weapons*).

According to the U.S. Defense Intelligence Agency, the killing power of FAEs " is unique—and unpleasant...what kills is the pressure wave and, more importantly, the subsequent rarefaction [thinning out], which ruptures the lungs...if the fuel deflagrates [burns] but does not detonate, victims will be severely burned and will probably also inhale the burning fuel. Since the most common FAE fuels, ethylene oxide and propylene oxide, are highly toxic, undetonated FAE should prove as lethal to personnel caught within the cloud as most chemical agents."

The *New York Times* (December 3, 2001) notes, "the above-ground blasts [of FAEs] produce twice the pressure of conventional high explosive charges and searing temperatures above 5,000 degrees—far hotter then the fires that toppled the World Trade Center Towers."

The Federation of American Scientists (FAS)(www.fas.org) has detailed the use of FAEs during the 1991 *Operation Desert*

Storm. They note that the Marine Corps dropped over two hundred 550-pound *cluster bombs* (CBU-72s) modified to carry ethylene oxide. They add that although the fiery bombs were used mostly " against mine fields and personnel in trenches...FAE was primarily useful as a psychological weapon." That distinction was no doubt lost on the nameless and uncounted Iraqis who were shredded and incinerated.

The *Gulf War* FAEs were not used during the 2003 *Operation Iraqi Freedom.* However, the popular *Hellfire missile* was fitted with a new non-liquid fuel-air explosive containing aluminum particles. A Naval Air press release reports that the "number one requirement" for the development of this new weapon for use in Iraq was "to increase the probability of personnel lethality or incapacitation."

The Russian Army is known to have used fuel-air explosives in the suppression of rebels in Chechnya, as well as during their occupation of Afghanistan in the 1980s. In 2001, when the U.S. decided that it was their turn to ravage that country once again, the U.S. military quickly developed a potent modification of the original FAE, in order to get at people hiding in deep caves. These 2,000-pound "thermobaric" bombs first detonate, forcing a fine mist of explosive powder, rather than liquid, far into the cave. A split second later the powder ignites, creating an enormous blast pressure.

A U.S. Central Intelligence Agency report describes the effects: "Those near the ignition point are obliterated. Those near the fringe are likely to suffer many internal injuries, including burst ear drums, crushed inner ear organs, severe concussions, ruptured lungs and internal organs, and possibly blindness." BBC News (March 4, 2002) commented, "These [thermobaric weapons] are, by any standards horrible weapons, but U.S. spokesmen insist that in Afghanistan they are being employed solely against military targets."

full spectrum dominance: the published goal of the U.S. *Department of Defense* to develop an enhanced military—equipped with advanced high-technology weapons and tools—which can operate swiftly and powerfully anywhere in the world, as well as in space and cyberspace, in order to preserve America's interests.

The Defense Department's *Joint Vision 2020*, released on May 30, 2000 spells out this blueprint for world domination. The achievement of full spectrum dominance will require the "ability of U.S. forces, operating unilaterally or in combination with multinational or interagency partners, to defeat any adversary." Those forces must have "access and freedom to operate in all domains—space, sea, land, air and information...achieving full spectrum dominance means the joint force will fulfill its primary purpose—victory in war" (see *information dominance, information operations*).

Rebuilding America's Defenses: Strategy, Forces and Resources for a New Century (RAD), published in 2000 by *The Project for the New American Century* is widely regarded as the model for George W. Bush's 2002 *National Security Strategy.* The RAD elaborates on the aims of *Joint Vision 2020* in vivid terms. Included are such goals as "an ability to deny others the use of space," "... a need to develop a new family of nuclear weapons designed to address new sets of military requirements," "The United States should seek to establish a network of...forward operating bases to increase the reach of current and future forces," and "the Air Force needs to be restructured...to assure 'global reach, global power'" (see *hegemony*).

Joint Vision 2020 promises that "We will win—but we should not expect war in the future to be either easy or bloodless..." The invasion of Afghanistan in 2001, and Iraq in 2003 were elements in this grandiose plan—and as predicted, difficult and bloody— but without the decisive *victory.*

G

"What an absolute savage is the passion of military conquest...the only safeguards against the crimes to which it infallibly drags the nation that gives way to it is to keep it chained forever."

William James

garrison: a site where *soldiers* are stationed. On October 17, 2001, CNN.com reported "U.S. forces focused their bombardment on Taliban troop garrisons and barracks across Afghanistan late Wednesday and early Thursday." Soldiers live, sleep, dream, and eat in garrisons. When a garrison is attacked, many of the people there are killed and wounded (see *camps, barracks, elements, enemy positions, units).*

Geneva Conventions: a set of rules agreed upon by the international community, under which nations at war agree to act with some degree of restraint while they kill each other. The rules are described variously as "attempts to codify the rules of appropriate military conduct," an effort to try "to bring a measure of civility into warfare," or regulations aimed at "limiting the suffering and barbarity of war."

The First Geneva Convention in 1864, inspired by Henri Dunant, founder of the Red Cross, aimed at protecting the sick and wounded in wartime. Four Geneva Conventions in 1949 expanded the earlier rules to some 400 legal provisions, including the treatment of prisoners of war and protection of civilians during wartime. These laws of war continue to evolve, such as, for example, the ongoing discussions in other forums on the regulation of landmines (see *area denial munitions, conventional weapons*).

The Geneva Conventions require a clear distinction between

civilians and combatants. The latter must wear uniforms and carry their weapons openly. Armies dislike "irregular" combatants who may prefer not to be earmarked for death by wearing a distinguishing outfit. Also, a civilian who shoots a *soldier* may be liable for murder, while a soldier who shoots an *enemy* soldier is simply doing his duty.

The rules of war proscribe indiscriminate attacks against areas in which civilians are present, a common practice during *Operation Iraqi Freedom* (see *area denial munitions, cluster bombs*). Also, there is to be no destruction of property unless justified by military necessity—a rationale offered for the destruction of private homes during that war—actions labeled as unnecessary by Human Rights Watch (HRW) (www.hrw.org).

HRW and others have pointed out that the Geneva Conventions do not allow holding prisoners indefinitely without determining their status, as exemplified by the thousands of *detainees* held by the United States. Many of those detainees were considered to be prisoners of war (POWs) by legal experts, and therefore, under the rules of war should have been released after the *end of hostilities.* The Bush administration's answer was that the announcement of *mission accomplished* was not a "legal" end of hostilities—and besides, the United States had never formally declared war on Iraq in the first place.

POWs, according to the Geneva Conventions, "must at all times be humanely treated...Prisoners of war must at all times be protected, particularly against acts of violence or intimidation and against insults and public curiosity." Soon after 9/11 the Bush administration decided that such restrictions would get in the way of their fight against Al Qaeda and other terrorists. The captured suspects sent to the U.S. naval base at Guantanamo, Cuba as well as "high-level" suspects sent to undisclosed locations away from the U.S. would be treated without regard to Geneva constraints.

The U.S.-led *coalition* arrested thousands of Iraqis during

Operation Iraqi Freedom. According to the May 23, 2004 *St. Louis Post-Dispatch,* the International Committee of the Red Cross found that most of those imprisoned were not POWs but civilians. Seventy to ninety percent of those "may have been arrested by mistake, and the arrests were accompanied by shocking brutality." The Geneva Conventions requires that civilians be treated "with dignity and respect." The cruel mistreatment of prisoners in Guantanamo, Iraq, Afghanistan, and elsewhere were blatant violations of what had been accepted for decades as fundamental obligations of the international community (see *detainees, extraordinary rendition*).

On April 24, 2003, when UN Secretary Kofi Annan called on the U.S.-led *coalition,* as "occupying powers," to follow the dictates that the 1949 Geneva Conventions and the 1907 Hague Convention described for that status, the U.S. said it did not regard itself as an occupier. It was, rather, a "liberating force." That category does not appear in either of the Conventions (see *liberation, occupation*).

The Geneva Conventions and other associated international agreements, such as the Hague Conventions, are uncomfortable reminders of the paradox of war. In response to humanitarian impulses, and prompted by the work of concerned individuals and organizations, humans have tried to sanitize their cruelest acts of aggression probably even before the earliest recorded regulations suggested by the sixth century BCE Chinese warrior Sun Tzu.

As a result, many lives have been saved and some excesses, once condoned, are now prohibited. Accompanied by a set of rules of conduct, applied or sometimes disregarded as military exigencies permit, nations continue to wage violent, bloody war, giving in to their instincts of aggression rather than searching first for the high ideals of respect for our common humanity which inspired the Geneva Conventions.

global war on terrorism (GWOT): as stated and implied by the documents and pronouncements of the George W. Bush administrations, a protracted (see *endless war*) worldwide battle against an ill-defined *enemy* towards a goal so nebulous as to be unattainable (see *evil*). The war will employ the overwhelming might of the U.S. military wherever the U.S. sees fit (see *critical regions, Rebuilding America's Defenses*). At home it will necessitate curtailment of civil liberties. Elsewhere the GWOT will allow repressive regimes, in their role as allies, to disregard human rights. The result, already partially realized in Afghanistan (see *Operation Enduring Freedom*) and Iraq (see *Operation Iraqi Freedom*) will be to foster the fear and hatred that breeds acts of terror. The endless war will become a self-fulfilling prophecy.

The term "global war on terrorism" is derived from the President's vow—announced soon after the Al Qaeda attacks on the World Trade Center and the Pentagon on September 11, 2001—that the U.S. would wage a "war against terrorism of global reach." The Bush administration's plans for forcible removal of Saddam Hussein's regime and the establishment of a U.S. military presence in Iraq (see *Defense Planning Guidance, Rebuilding America's Defenses*), not politically viable before 9/11, was now put on a fast track (see *Gulf War*).

The clearly stated aim of attaining U.S. global military dominance (see *Pax Americana*) over all nations, with forcible emphasis on any that appear to interfere with our *national interests* (see *preventive war*) would now be pursued under the guise of national security (see *National Security Strategy*).

Objections to a global war on terrorism do not assume the absence of widespread hatred and violence on the part of many disparate (and desperate) individuals and groups against the United States and other affluent nations. The voices that rise up against the violence planned and already implemented against this threat are a chorus of anguish over the realization that the purported cure for violence breeds even more violence in an endless spiral.

One long-respected voice is that of the world's largest human rights organization, Human Rights Watch (HRW)(hrw.org), founded in 1978. HRW emphasizes "support for terrorism feeds off repression, injustice, inequality and lack of opportunity... global security is thus enhanced by the success of open societies that foster respect for the rule of law, promote tolerance, and guarantee people's rights of free expression and peaceful dissent."

This crucial emphasis on the root causes behind acts of terror is not limited to those who typically espouse nonviolent solutions. Jeffrey Record, a former staff member of the Senate Armed Services Committee, and a Professor at the U.S. Air Force's Air War College is the author of *Bounding the Global War on Terrorism,* written in 2003 for the Strategic Studies Institute (www.carlisle.army.mil/ssi).

Record warns that the objectives of the GWOT are "unrealistic and condemn the United States to a hopeless quest for absolute security." He emphasizes " Absent any prospect of a political solution, what options other than terrorism (often a companion of guerilla warfare) are available to the politically desperate and militarily helpless?...The problem is that there are countless millions of people around the world who are, or believe they are, oppressed and have no other recourse than irregular warfare, including terrorism, to oppose oppression...it is well and good to counsel those with grievances to seek political solutions, but this is hardly useful advice if there is no political process for doing so."

The resolve to consume the world in violence in the name of peace is a potentially fatal contradiction. Martin Luther King, Jr. pointed to the difficult but necessary road to global peace — at least as close to peace as fallible humanity can get—when he said "Only a refusal to hate or kill can put an end to the chain of violence in the world and lead us toward a community where [we] can live together without fear."

glory: an attribute often assumed to be the reward for a hard fought military *victory,* and earned by those who participate in those battles. Wang Chen, a 9th century Chinese military commander, in his widely read *The Tao of War* warns against this notion: "Victories achieved are not glorified for glorifying them is to take pleasure in killing man...After killing masses of the enemy's men, weep for them with grief and sorrow...implement the rites of mourning."

Chen's admonition, in his book which traditionally is studied by most military leaders and scholars, is in marked contrast to Michael Wolff's March 7, 2003 account of the aftermath of the 1991 *Gulf War* (www.MikeHersch.com). Wolff writes, "Time magazine called the war's aftermath 'a stunning military triumph that gives Americans something to cheer about'...Americans filled with joy and young women [threw] kisses at Abrams tanks. Tip Hale, a Chicago insurance salesman, summed up the mood perfectly 'if there was a war you could be proud of, this is it.'"

American history is fond of the notion of the "glorious dead." *A Historic Context for the African-American Military Experience,* published by the U.S. *Department of Defense* says that "The...300 blacks who comprised this unit...achieved their crowning glory on the hills and dales surrounding Providence...The slaughter was terrible." In another account "Despite the glory surrounding the assault at San Juan...more than 1,000 Americans were killed and wounded."

In the face of these literary descriptions are reactions of men who were required to participate in the presumed glories of battle. Donald Murray, longtime *Boston Globe* columnist who fought in World War II writes "Our war was necessary because diplomacy and responsible government failed. There is no such thing as a good war...I marched with the 82nd Airborne in the

Victory Parade in New York in December 1945...the people lining the sidewalks and hanging out windows cheered. It was one of the worst experiences of my life. I saw, walking with me, the ghosts of the American and German dead, and the legs, arms, and heads that never found their bodies to be buried together."

Dennis Kistler, a helicopter pilot during the Vietnam War responded to the hype surrounding *Operation Iraqi Freedom* (see *Countdown Iraq*) in a letter to the *Boston Globe*, March 18, 2003. Writing of the "reality TV" selling of the war, Kistler says "Of course, this fascination ends abruptly in the mind of the young soldier, American or Iraqi, who realizes that his wound is beyond repair. For the dying there is no glory in that moment, only disbelief, and a hopeless desire to be made whole again..."

Glory is a concept more familiar to *war buffs*, military historians or to politicians who, far removed from the awful demands of battle, paint a patina of glamour onto its grim realities. It is the *soldiers* who agree to do the *job* of war, and who suffer while inflicting suffering, who know better.

God bless: an invocation popular in the U.S., especially among its elected leaders, asking the Divinity (generally regarded as Christian) to look favorably on the United States and its troops as they fight the *enemy*, who are not to be considered worthy of God's protection.

From the days when George Washington claimed, in his inaugural address, that every step towards independence had been "distinguished by some token of providential agency"—to the message on Vice President Dick and Lynne Cheney's 2003 Christmas card: "And if a sparrow cannot fall to the ground without His notice, is it probable that an empire can rise without His aid?" —God has widely been considered to be a special friend of the United States (see *crusade*).

A corollary of that belief is the conviction that military

service in obedience to the state is not only a duty, but is pleasing to God. Chris Hedges, in *War is a Force That Gives us Meaning* warns "Once we sign on for war's crusade, once we see ourselves on the side of the angels, once we embrace a theology...that defines itself as the embodiment of goodness and light, it is only a matter of how we will carry out the murder." Writer James Carroll (*Boston Globe*, October 21, 2003) observes "As violence is one of the notes of the human condition, religions often attribute it to God, and then divine violence cycles back to justify the human propensity to act violently. The omnipotent warrior God is...firmly entrenched in the human imagination."

The *global war on terrorism* features excesses of Western religion and Islamic extremism—both infused with and bolstered by a belief in God's special blessings. James Carroll points out a way beyond the polarity that fuels such hatred and violence: "There can be such a thing as an inclucivist religious faith...instead of polarity, this other way of being religious assumes unity—unity between God and God's creation, which serves in turn as a source of unity among God's creatures...A respectful religious pluralism is no longer just a liberal hope but an urgent precondition of justice and peace."

The American Friends Service Committee (www.afsc. org) offers a path to a "peaceable kingdom" in very concrete terms. They identify the true *axis of evil* as "pandemic poverty, environmental degradation, and a world awash in weapons." Peace requires " a world where security and fundamental human rights eclipse violence and oppression; where opportunities to make a living as part of a sustainable community supplant poverty; where appreciation of diverse gifts and cultures replaces exclusion and rejection; where commitment to love and dialogue prevails."

Green Zone: the heavily fortified area in Baghdad where the leaders of the U.S.-led occupying forces, the major U.S. consulting companies, and the *Iraqi Governing Council* were forced to seek relative safety after the official *end of hostilities* was declared in May 2003. It is distinguished from the more dangerous Red Zone—the rest of Iraq. By 2005 at least 5,000 Westerners and 12,000 Iraqi civilians were hunkered down in the four-square-mile refuge.

Flanked by the Tigris River on one side, and hidden behind a 15-foot high concrete wall, the Green Zone was described by the *New York Times* (December 7, 2003) as "the biggest, most secure American base camp in Iraq—but there is little connection between the troops in the field and the bottomless pit of planners and deciders who live inside..." The *Times* related an officer's description of the "two camps, military and civilian, inhabiting the heavily fortified, gold-leafed presidential palace inside the Green Zone" as "a divorced couple who won't leave the house."

As armed resistance to the *occupation* increased, the Green Zone came under almost daily attacks by mortar and suicide bombers, shattering the illusion of a completely safe retreat.

Saddam Hussein's former palace—built by the British occupiers in the 1940s—houses part of the new American embassy, which set up in nearby temporary headquarters shortly after the transfer of "sovereignty" to the Iraqis on June 28, 2004. Remaining behind the walls of the Green Zone, the embassy—with a staff of 1,700—was, until early 2005, headed by John Negroponte, the former U.S. ambassador to the UN. On February 17, 2005, President Bush nominated Negroponte to be the first director of national intelligence.

During his brief confirmation hearings before the Senate Foreign Relations Committee, scant attention was paid to Negroponte's role in building a U.S.-backed contra force against Nicaragua in the early 1980's. During Negroponte's tenure as ambassador in Honduras, according to Jim Lobe (April 30, 2004, Inter Press Service), a death squad "trained by the CIA and the

Argentines...kidnapped and tortured hundreds of real or suspected 'subversive', 'disappeared' at least 180 of them—including U.S. missionaries...Now he goes to Iraq to oversee its democratization." Negroponte had served under President Ronald Reagan, after whose death many members of the American media suffered from collective amnesia about the atrocities caused by Reagan's administration.

The *Washington Post* (March 9, 2004) noted that "the administration had originally considered opening a token embassy in a facility outside the Green Zone, where an ambassador could at least carry out ceremonial functions —and avoid the imagery of remaining in Hussein's Republican Palace...But Washington has abandoned that idea because the facility and the U.S. Embassy personnel would be too vulnerable to attacks."

Gulf War: a slaughter of horrific proportions unleashed against Iraq in early 1991 by a U.S.-led coalition of 34 nations following Iraq's August 1990 invasion of Kuwait. The war—known also as the Persian Gulf War or *Operation Desert Storm*—was portrayed as necessary to liberate Kuwait, restore its rightful government and protect Iraq's neighbors from Iraqi aggression.

Less publicized at the time, but far more important, were the motives contained in President George H.W. Bush's National Security Directive 54, issued on January 15, 1991. The document states "Access to Persian Gulf oil and the security of key friendly states in the area are vital to U.S. national security...the United States remains committed to defending its vital interests in the region, if necessary through the use of military force, against any power with interests inimical to our own."

The long, complicated and bitter history of Iraq—created in 1919 by an artificial division of the ancient lands of Mesopotamia by the occupying British—discloses the greed and cruelty of powerful, affluent nations, most notably the British and later the

United States. The appalling saga is documented clearly, concisely and powerfully in Larry Everest's *Oil, Power & Empire: Iraq and the U.S. Global Agenda.*

Everest, a writer with extensive experience in the Middle East and Central Asia (see www.larryeverest.com), emphasizes that the U.S. was determined "not merely to expel Iraq from Kuwait, but to crush it as a regional power and forcefully assert U.S. global power in the post-Soviet world... [they] wanted to destroy [Iraq's] future economic and military capabilities as well, goals which continued to drive U.S. Iraq policy well into the 1990s."

Iraq, on the other hand, having just fought a bloody eight-year war against Iran with U.S backing, assumed that the Washington-Baghdad alliance strengthened their status in the Gulf region. Desperate for greater access to the Persian Gulf, $80 to $90 billion in debt—and driven by other long-standing resentments against a country they considered part of their rightful territory—Iraq massed troops along the Kuwait border.

However, Saddam Hussein went no further before he consulted with the United States. Summoning U.S. Ambassador April Glaspie on July 25, 1990 Saddam Hussein told her his grievances and intentions. The transcript of this meeting, according to Larry Everest's account "shows the head of a small state trying to defend its regional interests, while trying to maintain a relationship with the world's dominant superpower. And the transcript makes it clear that the U.S. did indeed give Iraq a green light for some sort of a military action against Kuwait."

The U.S. apparently did not anticipate the full extent of that military action. Nor did Iraq understand that its forcible annexation of Kuwait's land and treasured oil supplies would hand the U.S. an opportunity to teach the world a lesson on the ramifications of aggression against America's interests. Despite "at least 11 peace proposals" between August 1990 and February 1991, Iraq's fate was sealed. Even if Iraq were to withdraw peacefully, "with its military intact, it could then exert greater influence over Saudi Arabia and the small Gulf Emirates, eroding U.S. hegemony, and bolstering its own regional strength." As Dick Cheney put it "[the] marriage of Iraq's military of 1 million men with 20 percent of the world's oil presented a significant threat."

Veteran reporter Chris Hedges, in *War is a Force That Gives us Meaning* defines the Gulf War succinctly. He says "We did not fight [the war] to liberate Kuwait, but to ensure that we would continue to have cheap oil...The message that was sent to them was this: We have everything and if you try to take it away from us we will kill you."

U.S. public support for the impending invasion was skillfully stimulated by a professional publicity campaign headed by Hill & Knowlton, then the world's largest PR firm. Sheldon Rampton and John Stauber, in *Weapons of Mass Deception: The Uses of Propaganda in Bush's Latest War on Iraq* describe the $11.9 million PR blitz which included "public rallies," "news releases and information kits," and publication of 200,000 copies of a book titled *The Rape of Kuwait.* Hill & Knowlton's crowning achievement was an impressive recounting of "hundreds" of Kuwaiti babies torn from their incubators by invading Iraqis and left to die. The account was fictional (see *Kuwaiti babies*).

On January 16, 1991 the U.S.-led coalition unleashed 43 days and nights of massive bombardment against Iraq, killing unknown thousands of Iraqi and at least 3,000 civilians. The assault decimated the country's vital infrastructure— including its electrical systems, bridges, and communications network. International Physicians for the Prevention of Nuclear War (www. ippnw.org) reported that the aftermath of that attack, during which U.S. and British aircraft dropped 88,500 tons of bombs—six times the explosive force of the Hiroshima atomic bomb—caused the deaths of over 100,000 civilians in 1991 alone, 70,000 of who were children under 15 years of age.

The bombing was followed by a ground war launched from Saudi Arabia. Coalition troops took back Kuwait, and moved deep into southern Iraq to cut off retreating Iraqi *forces*. The land war lasted a mere 100 hours, during which an estimated 25,000 to 50,000 Iraqi soldiers were killed. Several massacres of Iraqi troops were later reported, among them the infamous *turkey shoot*, in which Iraqi forces retreating from Kuwait city were mercilessly strafed, bombed and incinerated. This was very much in keeping with General Colin Powell's earlier warning regarding the Iraqi military: "First we're going to cut it off, then we're going to kill it."

Larry Everest notes "Bush promised that America's 1991 Gulf War would usher in a 'new world order' in which 'the nations of the world, East and West, North and South, can prosper and live in harmony.' In reality, Operation Desert Storm was a war by the imperialist 'north' against an upstart regime of the Third World 'south' designed to tighten the U.S. hold on the Middle East and preserve an oppressive regional order."

At the conclusion of the Gulf War, the crushing economic *sanctions* against Iraq, first imposed by the UN Security Council on August 6, 1990, were left in place. There is ample documentation that this embargo, which left Iraq unable to generate the oil revenues that had fed and supported the Iraqi people, combined with the deliberate destruction of their infrastructure during the bombardment, would result in the deaths of at least 500,000 Iraqis—many of them children. Robert Gates, the Deputy National Security Advisor under George H.W. Bush warned in 1991 "Iraqis will be made to pay the price while Saddam Hussein is in power. Any easing of sanctions will be considered only when there is a new government."

The then Secretary of State Madeline Albright, during a 1996 CBS *60 Minutes* appearance was asked by host Leslie Stahl concerning the ongoing sanctions "We have heard that half a million Iraqi children have died. I mean, that's more children that died in Hiroshima. And—and you know, is the price worth it?" Albright answered, "I think this is a very hard choice, but the price—we think the price is worth it."

The "worth" of that bloody "price" was unimpeded access to the region's oil. Saddam Hussein, supported in the 1980s during Iraq's prolonged war against Iran, could no longer be tolerated. In 2003, with the sanctions still in place and the country of Iraqi still devastated from the unparalleled destruction of the Gulf War, George H.W. Bush's son—President George W. Bush—would cobble together a *coalition of the willing* and invade Iraq once more. Bush Jr., coached by many of his father's former colleagues, had come to liberate Iraq from Saddam Hussein by launching *Operation Iraqi Freedom* (see *liberation*).

Gulf War Syndrome: a collection of physical and mental symptoms suffered by many thousands of 1991 *Gulf War* veterans for which the U.S. and British governments have been reluctant to admit liability. Because a syndrome technically is a set of symptoms characterizing a specific disorder, many prefer the term "Gulf War Illness" for these often-serious problems. The name change has not been reported to have alleviated any of the veterans' symptoms.

Government authorities acknowledge that Gulf War veterans get sick at two to three times the rate of the *soldiers* who did not deploy there. But despite repeated research studies, until late 2004 there was no widely accepted conclusive scientific evidence that their often debilitating symptoms—which can include fatigue, anxiety, muscle and joint pain, intermittent diarrhea, difficulty concentrating, headaches, memory loss, and neurological problems—could be definitively linked to their military service.

Reports differ widely on the numbers of veterans who have suffered from these chronic and sometimes debilitating illnesses since participating in the Gulf War. Some estimates are as high as one-third of the 697,000 deployed troops—according to *USA Today*, July 15, 2003—or as low as 15,000 to 20,000, according to Gina Kolata in the *New York Times*, March 25, 2003.

In January 1997 President Clinton received the *Final Report of the Presidential Advisory Committee on the Gulf War Veterans' Illnesses*. The Committee could only point to "stress" as "an important contributing factor" and advised further study.

By early 2003 medical researchers claim to have ruled out a number of what had been widely regarded to be prime suspects as causative agents—including nerve gas, chemical exposures, vaccinations, antidotes, pesticides, exposure to burning oil fields, and *depleted uranium.* Here and there, studies continued to provide intriguing questions. In January 2004, Lieutenant Colonel Graham Howe, clinical director of psychiatry in the British forces health service claimed to have made a link between vaccines administered and an immune system triggering of osteoporosis in a veteran. He cited a high incidence of osteoporosis—a thinning of bone density—among Gulf War veterans.

Despite the fact that the British veteran was awarded a 50% disability pension, a six-year-long multimillion-pound legal battle on behalf of thousands of British veterans ground to a halt in early 2004. Their legal experts could not come up with definitive evidence linking service in the war to their health problems.

In October 2004 the Research Advisory Committee on Gulf War Veterans Illnesses—in a report prepared for the federal Department of Veterans Affairs—concluded that the perplexing disorders were "not explained by wartime stress or psychiatric illness." They cited a "probable link" to nerve poisons to which many veterans had been exposed.

The *Department of Defense* and the Department of Veteran's Affairs were concerned about the health risks of troops who would be posted to Iraq during the 2003 *Operation Iraqi Freedom.*

The *soldiers* would certainly be exposed to much of the same potentially toxic environments as their Gulf War predecessors— as well as much higher levels of depleted uranium.

In 1997 Congress mandated that the Pentagon require physicals and blood sampling for all soldiers before and after deployment. According to Steve Rosenfield, TomPaine.com, April 8, 2003 "In a House hearing on March 25 on that requirement, Pentagon officials said the military had not conducted those baseline tests...saying they had asked troops to fill out a questionnaire instead." Rosenfield quotes Dr. Doug Rokke, former director of the Army's depleted uranium project as postulating, "If you don't look, you don't find. If you don't find, there's no correlation. If there's no correlation, there's no liability."

In 1994 the U.S. Congress agreed on a compensation benefit for Gulf War veterans who qualified as suffering from a "disabling, but undiagnosable, illness." As of March, 2003, 3,166 veterans claims had been granted. The maximum monthly payment allowable for a completely disabled individual in this category is $2,193, tax-free.

H

"No other nation possesses even first-generation Stealth Aircraft. Holding this sledgehammer over the world is a grave responsibility. Let's pray that our nation is always governed by leaders who will tell us the truth and swing the hammer only when necessary. But let's also hope that our leaders will not hesitate to swing it, and swing it hard, when our America's best interests call for it."

Joe Oldham, Editor, *Popular Mechanics*

hammer: to inflict severe damage to objects, and deliver death and destruction to people. Note the following media reports:

"Explosions shook the besieged city of Fallujah after dark Tuesday as new fighting erupted, and a U.S. AC-130 gunship hammered targets in the city." (*St. Petersburg Times*, April 28, 2004)

"Air support was called in; A-10s and B-52s hammered the Iraqis, and the Army didn't have to fire a shot." (*St. Louis Post-Dispatch*, March 24, 2003)

"Allies Hammer Iraqis into Submission" (*Herald Sun*, March 22, 2003)

hard target: the object of violence. "Hard" may mean difficult to attack, e.g. "Hawaii...is generally considered a 'hard' or difficult target [because] of a heavy military presence" (*Hawaii Business Magazine,* May, 2003). It may refer to the amount of damage that can be created, e.g. "A Stinger [missile] will do... no damage to a hard target like a city block" (www.razorworks. com).

Armored military equipment may be considered hard, e.g. "The alleged health risks occur when the shells are fired at hard targets like tanks" (*Guardian Unlimited*, February 21, 2001). Concrete bunkers qualify, e.g. "...hard target, deep penetration, and DBHT (deeply buried hard target) weapons that combine uranium with high explosives" (Uranium Medical Research Centre, www.umrc.net)(see *advanced unitary penetrators, bunker busters, depleted uranium*).

People often qualify as targets. Sometimes they are hard, as in "An unpredictable target is a hard target," or " A hard target is a military person and a soft target is a civilian" (*Comeford's Art and its Development*, librarythinkquest.org) (see *soft target*).

harm's way: liable to be killed or injured. Often used by politicians to sound concerned without being graphic. The phrase originated with John Paul Jones—considered by many a *hero* of the unnecessary, bloody Revolutionary War. He wrote in 1778 "I wish to have no connection with any ship that does not sail fast; for I intend to go in harm's way."

CNN.com reported on March 26, 2004, almost one year after the official *end of hostilities* in Iraq; "Soldiers headed for Iraq are still buying their own body armor—and, in many cases, their families are buying it for them—despite assurances from the military that the gear will be in hand before they're in harm's way."

The Associated Press (AP) explained (March 24, 2004) that "Assailants in urban Iraq are often inexperienced, missing on the first shot...They also tend to be armed with AK-47s rather than more accurate rifles, giving soldiers time to return fire or get out of harm's way."

A White House press release (December 2003) told of President George W. Bush's visit to Walter Reed Army Medical Center. Bush told several hundred medical workers "We've put a lot of fine troops into harm's way to make this country more secure...and the world more peaceful...I remember coming here a couple of months ago to pin the Purple Heart on a fellow who lost both legs and one arm. Today, I saw him walking" Bush's remarks brought cheers from his listeners. Neither the amputee nor his family was quoted.

hegemony: the announced aim of the U.S. under the George W. Bush administrations to dominate the world, if necessary, through military force. Any state perceived to be a present or even future threat to the U.S. will be attacked. The global superiority of the U.S. will be maintained on land, sea, air, as well as in space and cyberspace. All nations have two choices, either to be with us or against us. The latter will be subject to the military and economic power of the U.S. without regard to any international regulation (see *constabulary duties*, *critical regions*, *forward-based forces*, *full spectrum dominance, preemptive war, preventive war*).

What seems like hyperbole is simply a synthesis of the far-reaching ambitions of a large cadre of Bush administration officials and advisers—Vice President Dick Cheney, Deputy Secretary of Defense Paul Wolfowitz, Defense Policy Board member Richard Perle among others—whose long-standing, well publicized ambitions for the U.S. finally gained ascendancy upon the questionable election of the younger Bush. They saw the diminution of the Soviet Union as a golden opportunity to establish the U.S. as the pre-eminent global power—provided the U.S. revamp, reposition and impose its military might, free from United Nations and international law restraints (see *Defense Policy Board*, *Defense Planning Guidance*, *Rebuilding America's Defenses, Project for the New American Century*).

The expression of the ambition is found in somewhat muted form in the 2002 *National Security Strategy* (NSS), inspired by the more blatant 2000 *Rebuilding America's Defenses: Strategy, Forces and Resources for a New Century.* The NSS, according to Noam Chomsky, "is a declaration saying that the U.S. must dominate the world by force if necessary, a dimension in which the U.S. reigns supreme, will do it permanently and that it reserves the right to prevent any potential challenge to its domination by the use of military force if necessary."

In Noam Chomsky's compelling *Hegemony or Survival: America's Quest for Global Dominance* he warns why this aggressive philosophy is a recipe for disaster. He underlines that "potential targets of America's imperial ambition are not likely simply to await destruction." Chomsky explains, echoing other leading foreign policy experts that Washington's policies are actually leading to *weapons of mass destruction* proliferation as a means of deterring U.S. aggression.

Iraq was a perfect target to signal the new imperial strategy. According to the *New York Times*, April 10, 2000, "Publication of the [National Security Strategy] was the signal that Iraq would be the first test, not the last...Iraq became the petri dish in which this experiment in pre-emptive policy grew." *Operation Iraqi Freedom*, initiated under blatantly false pretenses, showed the world that it could no longer expect the world's only superpower to operate within the restraints of the United Nations or international law.

The ramifications of the drive for U.S. hegemony are ominous. Jonathan Schell, peace and disarmament correspondent for *The Nation*, lamented in that publication (March 29, 2004), "The American imperial solution has interposed a huge, unnecessary roadblock between the world and the Himalayan mountain range of urgent tasks that it must accomplish no matter who is in charge:... inventing a humane, just, orderly, democratic, accountable global economy; redressing mounting global inequality and poverty; responding to human rights emergencies including genocide; and, of course, stopping proliferation as well as rolling back the existing arsenals of nuclear arms. None of these exigencies can be met as long as the world and its greatest power are engaged in a wrestling match over how to proceed."

Hellfire missile: a 6-foot, 100 pound self-guiding miniature aircraft packed with explosives, usually launched from a helicopter against armored vehicles carrying people, or sometimes targeted directly at people (see *Apache helicopter).*

The AGM 114 Hellfire, traveling at a maximum velocity of 950 miles per hour hones in on its target along a laser beam. This is billed as a *precision-guided munition*, but the missile can stray from its path due to "cloud cover" or other "obstacles" (see *collateral damage*). The U.S. used 562 Hellfire missiles during *Operation Iraqi Freedom*, at a cost of $57,000 apiece, as well as an unspecified number of a new version—the AGM-114N Metal Augmented Charge Hellfire—at $92,000 each. The latter create a lethal blast wave, killing people while leaving structures intact (see *fuel-air explosives*).

On June 22, 2003 CNN.com reported that in an effort to kill Saddam Hussein "The U.S. military's Task Force 20 struck a convoy of Iraqi military vehicles last week, killing and capturing people with ties to the deposed Saddam Hussein regime... it is not known how many people were killed in the strike that included Hellfire missiles"(see *convoy).* Democratic Senator Jay Rockefeller of West Virginia, vice-chairman of the Intelligence Committee reacted by saying "Pat [Senator Pat Roberts] and I hope that we've scored, but we don't know that." The unnamed dead did not include Saddam.

Unmanned combat aerial vehicles also delivered Hellfire missiles during the war. CNN.com (February 8, 2002) stated "On Monday, a CIA-operated unmanned spy plane, armed with Hellfire missiles, scored what appeared to be a direct hit on three white-robed men, one of whom was believed to be a senior Al Qaeda leader...forensic teams will try to positively identify who was killed."

Captain Adam W. Lange, in his article *Getting the Most from a Lethal Missile System*, in *Armor*, January-February 1998, is an enthusiast for the Hellfire. He advises "Synchronizing its lethal effects with other battlefield weapons systems will enable the commander to mass fires and overwhelm would-be enemy forces, defeating their ability and will to fight."

The public appeal of this *high-tech* killing technology was not lost on toy manufacturers (see *action figures*, *military games*). CNN.com 2002 Christmas Headline News told of "Harried parents...trying to find last-minute technology-driven goodies for their kids...Predators (including those armed with Hellfire missiles that vaporized an Al Qaeda convoy in Yemen this fall) are the next step."

hero: in war, a person who performs acts of courage at great personal risk. In that strict sense there are certainly *soldiers* who, while responding to threats to themselves or their comrades, voluntarily expose themselves to danger. Their courage is undeniable.

In modern warfare however, much of what the public—safe at home—perceives as heroism, is understood by the participants as something very different. Experienced war correspondent Chris Hedges, in *War is a Force That Gives us Meaning* points out that "technological and depersonalized levels of organized killing begun in World War I have defined warfare ever since... even in the age of new warfare we cling to the outdated notion of the single hero able to carry out daring feats of courage on the battlefield. Such heroism is as about as relevant as mounting bayonet or cavalry charges. But peddling the myth of heroism is essential...to entice soldiers into war. Men in modern warfare are in service to technology. Many combat veterans never actually see the people they are firing at nor those firing at them" (see *high-tech battlefield*, *military recruitment*).

The hero in war is both a reality and a myth. The politicians who sponsor the war must perpetuate the image of each soldier as a heroic bearer of a noble cause. The military must recruit young men and women with visions of themselves performing heroic deeds in defense of their country. Those who experience the ferocity of the modern battlefield find instead that their training has resulted in their being driven by their instincts for survival and by the urge to support and protect their comrades—as they unleash the terrible destructive power of their weapons at the *enemy*, often unseen.

When the weapons are silent, citizens and politicians drape the mantle of hero over the survivors and the dead. But for many the fit is too uncomfortable to bear. They have dealt in violence, agony, horrible injury, and death, and will bear war's physical and mental scars for the rest of their lives (see *bravery*, *psychiatric casualties*).

high-tech battlefield: the military's vision for making the business of killing an *enemy* even more impersonal and efficient. Due to recent and anticipated ingenious technological developments, the U.S. military has plans for the battlefield of the future in which soldiers, bearing and wearing sophisticated gear, will be "enhanced" physically and psychologically.

Rebuilding America's Defenses: Strategy, Forces and Resources for a New Century, the influential 2000 publication by *The Project for the New American Century* enthuses: "Future soldiers may operate in encapsulated, climate-controlled, powered fighting suits, laced with sensors...Skin-patch pharmaceuticals [will] help regulate fears, focus concentration and enhance endurance and strength. A display mounted on a soldier's helmet permits a comprehensive view of the battlefield —in effect to look around corners and over hills—and allows the soldier to access the entire combat information and intelligence system while filtering incoming data to prevent overload. Individual weapons are more lethal..."

These technical advances are already under development. Frank Oliveri, writing for the *Gannett News Service*, February 26, 2004 describes Pentagon plans for the Objective Force Warrior ensemble, possibly available by 2008. It is "a full-body, lightweight outfit that will digitally connect soldiers and vehicles. Helmets will come with night vision, digital displays and laser eye protection. Uniforms will be largely bulletproof and will regulate body temperature and control hemorrhaging wounds" (see *military games*).

According to DARPA, the Defense Advanced Research Projects Agency of the *Department of Defense*, researchers "are showing off their 'lower extremity exoskeleton', which straps onto a soldier's legs and lets him (or her) carry a load of 85 pounds without feeling it."

Lest the futuristic soldier, often a recent high school graduate, become anxious about being encased in such sophisticated gear, DARPA has funded research on a silicon microchip which may become the "world's first prosthetic brain part" which could lead to "cyborg soldiers and robotic servants." In 2002, DARPA announced that it was experimenting with the effects of magnetic resonance on the brain in order to trick the mind into believing it was well rested. DARPA officials asserted, "Eliminating the need for sleep... will create a fundamental change in war fighting and force employment."

Assisting the technology-enhanced soldier will be fleets of unmanned aerial, terrestrial, and underwater robotic vehicles. A variety of these were used in *Operation Iraqi Freedom*, including the Predator, which was used for surveillance as well as a launching platform for *Hellfire missiles*. By 2010 DARPA hopes to have its X-45 ready to fly—a pilotless plane able to pinpoint the enemy and attack them. Project Director Colonel Michael Leahy sees his research challenge as the ability "to mix man and machines... eventually the two systems will be linked to each other, sharing information and deciding among them who has the best shot."

Time magazine (November 29, 2004) chose the "Talon" robot, a 2-foot-six-inch device armed with automatic weapons, as one of the year's "most amazing inventions". *Time* warned "Insurgents, be afraid. An armed, unmanned ground vehicle that never gets tired, hungry, or scared is headed your way." The U.S. Army plans to deploy the Talon in Iraq sometime in 2005.

Until technology creates a military force that is completely invulnerable, there may still be some difficulties experienced on the battlefield, and DARPA is there to help. The Human Assisted Neural Devices Program is finding "ways to detect and directly decode signals in the brain so that thoughts can be turned into acts performed by a machine." This could be applied to "our injured veterans, who would be able to control prosthetics in a natural way never before imagined."

homeland: the land of one's birth. The word is generally understood to refer to a specific geographical location to which individuals naturally attach a certain loyalty, based on their attachments to family, friends and familiar surroundings. Any external threat to one's homeland evokes fear, resentment, and often violence against the aggressor. For example, *Operation Iraqi Freedom* may have deposed a despotic government, but substituted for it a foreign occupying military force.

Planet Earth is the homeland of all, yet too few of Earth's citizens respond appropriately against threats to global civilization. The human family is threatening itself, not only by abetting the spreading deterioration of our physical environment—the air, water and soil which sustains us—but by allowing our governments to not only wage war in our names, but to maintain the capacity to wreak unimaginably destructive war on all life with *nuclear weapons*.

If war is accepted even as a last resort, then war inevitably will be chosen to further the interests of one homeland over another. Because Earth is our homeland and we are all members of the human family our common enemies are the poisoning of our environment and saying yes to war—both of which, understood in this context, are truly suicidal.

hordes: When opposing soldiers in Iraq (see *enemy)* attack in large numbers, they are said to do so in hordes. When coalition forces (see *coalition of the willing)* attack they do so in *units*, detachments, or in other conventional military groups. Hordes tend to be uncivilized (see *civilization)* and are thought to be composed of uncultured individuals (see *ragheads*). After most of the members of the hordes are destroyed (killed or wounded) anyone still resisting may have to be *eliminated* (see *mopping up*).

humanitarian intervention: offered as a justification for the 2003 U.S.-led invasion of Iraq after all other pretexts had failed. Human Rights Watch (HRW) (hrw.org) defines humanitarian intervention as "the use of military force across borders to stop mass killing." This rationale for *Operation Iraqi Freedom* was only offered as the prime objective after the principal reasons— the threat from *weapons of mass destruction* and links between Saddam Hussein's regime and international terrorism—had lost their presumed legitimacy.

HRW, a highly respected international advocate for human rights, is not a pacifist organization. The HRW World Report 2004 states "Human Rights Watch ordinarily takes no position on whether a state should go to war...a position of neutrality maximizes our ability to press all parties to a conflict to avoid harming noncombatants."

However, the 2004 report took the unusual step of condemning Operation Iraqi Freedom. HRW insists, "The invasion of Iraq failed to meet the test for a humanitarian intervention. Most important, the killing in Iraq at the time was not of the exceptional nature that would justify such intervention. In addition, intervention was not the last reasonable option to stop Iraqi atrocities. Intervention was not motivated primarily by humanitarian concerns. It was not conducted in a way that maximized compliance with international humanitarian law...it was not designed or carried out with the needs of Iraqis foremost in mind."

The Canadian-sponsored UN International Commission on Intervention and State Sovereignty, in its 2001 report *The Responsibility to Protect* concludes, "Military intervention for human protection purposes is an exceptional and extraordinary measure. To be warranted, there must be serious and irreparable harm occurring to human beings, or imminently likely to occur... large scale loss of life, [or] ethnic cleansing."

Ian Wilson, UN correspondent for the *Nation*, in support of those principles, maintains "In the recent Iraq war...one of the worst misdeeds that George W. Bush committed, in collaboration with Tony Blair, was to bring humanitarian intervention into disrepute...most proponents of humanitarian intervention see it as a tool to be used only very sparingly, and then only with the strictest safeguards against abuse by the unscrupulous such as Bush."

Accepting the principle that a nation or coalition may invade another in order to save it from itself is perilous. In the process the interveners may inflict enormous suffering, as in the 1999 NATO assault on Yugoslavia. Noam Chomsky's *The New Military Humanism* relentlessly penetrates the myths surrounding the 1999 US/NATO "humanitarian bombing" of Yugoslavia, a devastating 14,000 *aerial sorties* over 78 days, complete with *cluster munitions* and *depleted uranium*.

There will continue to be humanitarian crises arising from a complex of ethnic hatred, religious intolerance, and other human failings so often brought to the boiling point by poverty. Given that harsh reality, the international community needs to transcend even the carefully crafted constraints of the UN, and create a large-scale, structured, nonviolent means of intervention, which assists all the suffering parties without adding to their distress.

hyperpower: coined by French foreign minister Hubert Vedrine in 1999 to describe the United States. Vedrine concluded that American global influence had gone beyond "superpower"— a Cold War term referring to the military might of the U.S. and the Soviet Union. Since the decline of the latter, Vedrine concluded that American strength had become unique, even extending further than technological, economic and military might to a "domination of attitudes, concepts, language, and modes of life."

Vedrine's answer to American dominance is "through steady and persevering work in favor of real multilateralism against unilateralism...for cultural diversity against uniformity." Vedrine's application of the "hyperpower" label was particularly concerned with the challenge of elevating Europe's and especially France's level of partnership with the U.S.—which would receive a severe blow when the U.S.-led coalition attacked Iraq in *Operation Iraqi Freedom.*

Despite the fact that the prefixes "hyper" and "super" mean essentially the same, i.e. excessive—although the hyperpower label is intended to include the heavy-handed U.S. attempts to dominate world trade—it has come to more commonly refer to the aim of global military dominance admitted quite openly by the power elite in the George W. Bush administration (see *hegemony*).

The 2000 *Rebuilding America's Defenses: Strategy, Forces and Resources for a New Century*, considered to be the blueprint for the White House's 2002 *National Security Strategy* says bluntly " At present the United States faces no global rival. America's grand strategy should aim to preserve and extend this advantageous position as far into the future as possible...today the task is to persevere an international security environment conducive to America's interests and ideals." Further American preeminence will be preserved "through the coming transformation of war made possible by new technologies" (see *constabulary duties, forward-based forces*).

In the April 27, 2003 *New York Times,* Timothy Garten Ash, director of the European Studies Center at St. Antony's College at Oxford, lamented the "hyperpower unilateralism" of the United States. He urged "We must put the West together again." That means, among other steps, according to Ash "handing back Iraq as soon as possible to the Iraqis and supporting their federal or confederal democracy. Then, and urgently, it means trying to make progress toward secure, viable states of both Israel and Palestine. The Palestinian question is now, for the Arab and Muslim world... the litmus test of whether the Bush administration means what it says about liberating and democratizing the Middle East rather than occupying and colonizing it" (see *democratization, exit strategy, occupation*).

I

"As Sgt. Maj. Henry Bergeron of battalion 1/7 said of the fedayeen much earlier, 'this is the perfect war. They want to die, and we want to kill them.'"

Bing West and Ray Smith, *The March Up: Taking Baghdad with the 1st Marine Division*

incontinent ordnance: typically refers to *bombs* that miss their intended target (see *dropped ordnance*) despite the fact that ordnance is a more general term which may encompass all the weapons used in war. When a pilot drops bombs that go astray, they may kill his fellow soldiers (*friendly fire*) or civilians who happen to be in the way (*collateral damage*).

Dumb bombs may often miss their mark, while *precision-guided munitions* are more accurate, but not always predictable. During the Vietnam War, the term "incontinent ordnance" was used frequently. During the 1991 *Gulf War* it was somewhat less popular. By the next US-led savage attack on Iraq in 2003 the term, perhaps having reached its nadir of absurdity, faded from view. Possibly the Pentagon's dogged insistence on the accuracy of its ordnance prompted its demise.

incursion: an invasion. Commonly used in media reports, e.g.: "Meanwhile 5,000 Turkish troops continued their incursion inside Iraq where they are pounding Kurdish rebel positions with heavy artillery and gunships." (*The Examiner,* February 19, 1999) "The operation, the second incursion by U.S. forces into the heart of the city in three days, came as British troops in the south sought to build on their seizure of Basra yesterday...the 2nd Brigade of the 3rd Infantry Division rolled into central Baghdad at 3 a.m." (www.intellnet.org, April 7, 2003)

information dominance: an aim of current U.S. military strategy, which sees the acquisition, dissemination and control of information as a vital weapon of war. The basic concept is ancient. Chinese military strategist Sun Tzu wrote in 3000 B.C. "The way (propaganda) is what brings the thinking of people in line with their superiors. Hence, you can send them to their deaths or let them live, and they will have no misgivings one way or the other."

However, the current military understanding of information dominance goes well beyond the traditional notion of propaganda. The new notion was reinforced in the 1998 U.S. Air Force document *Information Operations*. That document says that in the "growing [global] information infrastructure" military "psychological operations" are "designed to convey selected information and indicators to foreign leaders and audiences to influence their emotions, motives, objective reasoning, and ultimately their behavior" (see *information operations*).

More traditional information "warfare" tends to concentrate on the military's and the *enemy's* physical information networks. The newer vision is outlined in the Pentagon's *Joint Vision 2020*. That document, released in June 2000, is a blueprint for *full spectrum dominance*, which "implies that US forces are able to conduct prompt, sustained and synchronized operations with combinations of forces tailored to specific situations and with access to and freedom to operate in all domains—space, sea, land, air, and information."

The information domain includes—quite understandably from the military's viewpoint—information networks that allow secure, reliable communications within its own *forces*, and the ability to disrupt those of the enemy. The Internet, now available to all, originated as a closed governmental communications network during the Cold War. However, the information domain, according to David Miller, editor of *Tell Me Lies: Propaganda and Media Distortion in the Attack on Iraq*, now "sees little difference between command and control systems, propaganda and journalism. They are all types of 'weaponized information' to be deployed."

In the January 8, 2004 *Guardian*/UK Miller maintains that "embedding journalists in Iraq was a clear means of building up 'friendly' information...analysis of the print output produced by embeds shows that 90% of their reporting was either 'positive' or 'neutral'" (see *embedded media*).

The move toward information dominance ran into a temporary roadblock after the February 19, 2002 *New York Times* reported that the Pentagon's newly formed Office of Strategic Influence (OSI) was "developing plans to provide news items, possibly even false ones, to foreign media organizations." The OSI "has begun circulating classified proposals calling for aggressive campaigns that use not only the foreign media and the Internet, but also covert operations." The *Times* articles aroused widespread public criticism, and the Pentagon promptly closed down the OSI—but retained its philosophy.

The buildup to *Operation Iraqi Freedom*, as well as its execution, gave ample opportunity to give information dominance techniques a good workout. Aside from the predictable superiority of the U.S. military's sophisticated information technology, there were determined efforts to control the content of information flow, ranging from relatively subtle to heavy-handed.

In 2002 the White House created the Office of Global Communications (OGC)(www.whitehouse.gov/ogc). Its stated purpose is to 'truthfully depict America and Administration policies...these messages are intended to prevent misunderstanding and conflict, build support for and among United States coalition partners, and better inform international offices." The September 17, 2002 *Times*/London reported a planned $200 million "PR blitz" by the OGC "against Saddam Hussein... [using] advertising techniques to persuade crucial target groups that the Iraqi leader must be ousted."

The OGC releases a daily "one-page fact sheet"—the *Global Messenger*—to "disseminate key points." On April 15, 2004, as fierce battles raged across Iraq, particularly in the Fallujah region, resulting in the killing of hundreds of civilians and dozens of U.S. Marines, the daily message was a statement by the President describing his pledge of support for Israel's intention to keep some settlements in the West Bank under any future peace agreement.

Before the "official" 2003 war, a U.S. missile destroyed the Kabul, Iraq offices of the Arab satellite network Al-Jazeera. A spokesperson for the Pentagon maintained, "The U.S. military does not and will not target media. We would not, as a policy, target news media organizations." After the 2003 invasion, the Pentagon quickly set up a new TV and radio service for Iraq—the Iraqi Media Network (IMN)—under the direction of a *defense contractor*, Scientific Applications International Corporation (SAIC). The company—a major recipient of contracts from the National Security Agency and the CIA—specializes in "information dominance" according to its website.

By June 2003 the *coalition's* occupying authority chief L. Paul Bremer III, alarmed at what he considered a growing liberalization of news reporting, had closed down some Iraqi-run newspapers as well as a number of radio and TV stations. Bremer then issued a nine-point list of "prohibited activity." The UK Index on Censorship (www.indexonline.org) notes: "The man in absolute authority over the country's largest, richest and best-equipped network is also his own regulator and regulator of his rivals, with recourse to the U.S. Army to enforce his rulings."

Anthony H. Cordesman of the Center for Strategic and International Strategy (CSIS), a Washington D.C.-based think tank, offered an interesting suggestion in his November 9, 2001 article *The US Bombing and Ramadan: The Real Problems We*

Face Because of our Failure to Understand Asymmetric Warfare and Mistakes that Turn 'Information Dominance' into a Self-Inflicted Wound. Cordesman suggests that the U.S. has "lagged badly in trying to win 'information dominance' with the Taliban and Al Qaeda...in the Islamic world, Middle East and Pakistan."

He explains "We do not seem to understand that it is the perception of bombing civilians over time that creates hostility and not the body count per se. The idea that we pay the same political price for limited levels of bombing in populated areas over time that we do for large-scale bombing does not seem to sink in. Neither does the fact that massive initial bombing at the point when a war begins and getting the job over with in populated areas is critical."

information operations: all of the many ways that the modern military has devised to control the flow of information within its own operations and disrupt the information systems of the *enemy*, so that killing them becomes more efficient. In the process, psychological operations (PSYOP)—a subset of information operations—are playing an increasingly important role both in deceiving the enemy and gaining popular support for whatever expression of violence the government decides is in the *national interest*.

The *Department of Defense* defines information operations as "The integrated employment of the core capabilities of electronic warfare, computer network operations, psychological operations (PSYOP), military deception, and operations security...to influence, disrupt, corrupt, or usurp adversarial human and automated decision making while protecting our own" (see *information dominance, full spectrum dominance*). The Pentagon's 2000 *Joint Vision 2020* says "Information operations are essential to full spectrum dominance...operations within the information domain will become as important as those conducted in the domains of land, sea, air, and space."

There is far more involved here than protecting and interfering with computer networks (see *high-tech battlefield*). Col. Brad M. Ward, in his April 7, 2003 *Strategic Influence Operation— the Information Connection*, written for the Army War College emphasizes "There is a battle in progress that is far subtler than strategic bombing missions...This battle is the 'war of the words,' which is designed to capture the minds of the world's citizenry, influence their attitudes and behaviors and produce responses favorable to U.S. policy."

While he did not suggest that fewer "strategic bombing missions" might assist in that battle, he did maintain that the psychological operations facet of information operations, under the aegis of the DoD, aims to "influence the emotions, attitudes and ultimately behavior of a target audience...DoD PSYOP programs are always based on truth..."

The U.S. public as well the international audience has long been targeted with a stream of misinformation flowing from the White House and the Pentagon in a deceitful mix of military PSYOP and old-fashioned public relations. In his October 2003 paper *Truth from These Podia: Summary of a Study of Strategic Influence, Perception Management, Strategic Information Warfare and Strategic Psychological Operations in Gulf II*, Col. Sam Gardiner (USAF, Ret.) details "50 stories manufactured or at least engineered that distorted the picture of Gulf II [Operation Iraqi Freedom] for the American and British people."

Gardiner's list includes the fictitious links made between terrorism, Iraq, and 9/11, the "discovery" of Iraq's purchase of African uranium—based on a forged document (see *yellowcake*)— the stories about Saddam Hussein's possession of *weapons of mass destruction* and the rescue of Pvt. Jessica Lynch—a carefully choreographed event.

According to the November 7, 2003 *New York Times* "...

news organization were repeating reports, attributed to anonymous American officials, that Ms. Lynch had heroically resisted her capture, emptying her weapon at her attackers. But subsequent investigations determined that Ms. Lynch was injured by the crash of her vehicle, her weapon jammed before she could fire, the Iraqi doctors treated her kindly, and the hospital was already in friendly hands when her rescuers arrived."

He concludes, "The war was handled like a political campaign. Everyone in the message business was from the political communications community. In London, there was a parallel organization and a parallel coordination process. They kept the coordination with secure video conferences."

The U.S. and Britain, before the onset of *Operation Iraqi Freedom*—despite a prolonged world-wide public outcry of agonized opposition to the war—agreed to refer to it officially as an "armed conflict" and to be sure to refer to the Iraq government as "the regime."

intervention: an attack. The use of the term does not diminish the pain of the wounded or the number of those killed. A few of many possible examples include the following 2003 newspaper reports:

"The White House is seeking to protect the coming American intervention in compassionate terms, aimed at constructing images of liberation, reconstruction, and reconciliation in the region." (*New York Times,* February 30, 2000)

"With the Bush administration openly threatening to overthrow Saddam Hussein, a public airing of the pros and cons of intervention is long overdue." (*New York Times,* July 30, 2002)

"James Cardinal Hickey of Washington ...cited the conclusion of 'many well-informed persons' that 'armed intervention has become a necessity to resist aggression.'" (*New York Times,* January 26, 1991)

Iraqi Governing Council (IGC): a group of 25 Iraqis appointed by the U.S. in July 2003 in order to appear to be ceding some authority to the people of Iraq, who had not welcomed the U.S.-led forceful occupation with sufficient enthusiasm. Ahmad Chalabi, the most prominent figure in the Pentagon-backed *Iraqi National Congress*, was one of the appointees. L. Paul Bremer III, the coalition's chief civilian administrator, retained final veto power over the Council's decisions. Bremer had quickly replaced the first administrator, retired General Jay Garner, who was judged unable to control the developing chaos in occupied Iraq (see *viceroy*).

The *Washington Post*, July 11, 2003 reported "occupation forces are trying to create a body that will cooperate with them and support policies that are generally in line with U.S. interests... a more prominent role in postwar governance is intended to place Iraqis at the receiving end of some of the popular discontent that has been directed at the occupation administration."

In November 2003 the U.S. and the IGC agreed to transfer governing authority to a new "legitimate" Iraqi government on June 30, 2004. The plan called for caucuses of handpicked individuals in each of Iraq's 18 provinces. The caucuses would decide on an interim government to whom authority would be transferred. That transitional national assembly would serve until general elections were held no later than December 31, 2004.

In January 2004 Iraqi unrest over the ploy by the U.S to retain power while appearing to transfer it finally led to the U.S agreeing to scrap the caucus plan and ask the UN for assistance in determining an acceptable way to decide on an interim government. Meanwhile, the IGC managed to draft and sign an interim constitution, creating the promise of an unprecedented set of rights for the Iraqi people. However, the reaction of Grand Ayatollah Ali Sistani, the leading Shiite cleric in Iraq was not reassuring.

He wrote "This places obstacles to arriving at a permanent constitution for the country that preserves its unity and the rights of its people in all their ethnicities and sects." The Grand Ayatollah had consistently called for general elections to decide on a legitimate Iraqi government, a prospect discouraged by the U.S., lest the election choose a government inconsistent with their objectives, i.e. to stay in control of Iraq and its resources (see *nation building*).

According to the June 2, 2004 *New York Times,* UN special envoy Lakhdar Brahimi played a secondary role in choosing an interim Iraq government, which was to exercise whatever control might be ceded to them (see *occupation*) until general elections, scheduled for January 2005. The members of the interim government were "essentially negotiated between the United States and the Iraqi Governing Council." However, the *Times* reports, the newly appointed President of the interim body, Sheik Ghazi Ajil al-Yawar—a former IGC member—was unwilling to appear to be the "puppet of the occupation forces." He said, "We blame the United States 100 percent for the security in Iraq. They occupied the country, disbanded the security agencies, and for 10 months left Iraqi's borders open for anyone to come in..."

A suicide bomber killed IGC president Izzadine Saleem and six others on May 17, 2004, while Saleem was waiting at a checkpoint outside the *Green Zone* in Baghdad. Earlier, in September, 2003 Aqila al-Hashemi was assassinated shortly after she joined the Governing Council. The beleaguered IGC dissolved itself on June 1, 2004. It had "lost virtually all legitimacy after its inability to solve the military and political crises that erupted across Iraq in April."

Iraqi National Congress (INC): an organization created by the CIA soon after the *Gulf War* to help organize opposition to the Saddam Hussein regime. The INC, assisted by the PR firm, the Rendon Group (see *focus groups*) began by disseminating propaganda, graduated to sponsoring clandestine military strikes within Iraq, and eventually tried to position itself to become the new Iraqi administration after *Operation Iraqi Freedom.* That grandiose ambition had little popular support in Iraq.

In October, 1992 Ahmad Chalabi became the head of the INC. Chalabi, an Iraq native who had left there in 1956, had become a favorite of U.S. neoconservatives including Richard Perle and Paul Wolfowitz (see *Defense Policy Board, Project for the New American Century*). He worked with them to help persuade Congress to pass the Iraqi Liberation Act in 1998, which made regime change in Iraq official government policy through support of opposition groups (see *regime change*)—and funneled $97 million to the INC and other opposition groups.

After the election of George W. Bush, Chalabi and his INC assumed the role of a government-in-waiting. David Rieff, in the *New York Times Magazine*, November 2, 2003 related how "at the insistence of the civilian administrators in the Pentagon, Chalabi and 500 members of the Free Iraq Forces—[a trumped-up right wing INC military unit]—were flown to Nasiriya in southern Iraq in April, in the first weeks of the war." Rieff adds "But to the surprise and disappointment of American military leaders on the ground, Chalabi failed to make much of an impression on the people he tried to mobilize...in the end, Chalabi sat out the war in the Iraqi desert and was taken to Baghdad only after the city had fallen and the Americans had moved in."

Eventually it appeared that Chalabi still had friends in high places—in the U.S. In July 2003 Chalabi was appointed as a member of the *Iraqi Governing Council.* In January 2004 he sat directly behind Laura Bush during her husband's State of the Union address.

In late February 2004 Chalabi freely admitted that the

INC, under his leadership, had provided misleading intelligence to the U.S. government in order to help make the case that Saddam Hussein posed a serious threat and had to be dealt with immediately. The admission did not deter the Pentagon at first. According to Defense Department officials they continued to pay the INC $340,000 per month for "intelligence collection."

However, as Chalabi began to speak critically of the *Coalition Provisional Authority*, including the plan to allow the United Nations to choose an interim government for Iraq (see *democratization*) the Pentagon abruptly shut off their monthly payment to the INC.

Three days later, a raiding party of Iraqi police officers stormed into Chalabi's home and offices and took computers and documents, as U.S. soldiers looked on. According to the *New York Times*, May 20, 2004 "A spokesman for the United States occupation authority acknowledged that there was American involvement in the operations but asserted that it had been planned and led by the Iraqi police." Chalabi was charged with counterfeiting.

The *Boston Globe,* May 21, 2004 recorded the dismay of an old friend of Chalabi. Richard Perle, a senior Pentagon advisor and key supporter of the war complained, "They did everything they could do to put him out of business...He has devoted his life to freeing his country...and I believe the effort to marginalize him will fail. They will end up looking ridiculous." (see *Defense Policy Board*)

In September 2004 the charges were dropped. Chalabi emerged as a vocal champion of the Iraqi Muslims. After the January 30, 2005 elections he presented himself as a candidate for prime minister of Iraq as part of the victorious United Iraqi Alliance (*exit strategy*).

J

"Next the statesman will invent cheap lies, putting the blame on the nation that is attacked, and every man will be glad of those conscience-soothing falsities, and will diligently study them, and refuse to examine any refutations of them; and thus he will by and by convince himself that the war is just, and will thank God for the better sleep he enjoys after this process of grotesque self-deception."

Mark Twain

job: a term commonly used to describe the *soldier*'s task—to kill and destroy—and the invader's mission—to see to it that their soldiers kill and destroy to the point where the country under attack admits *defeat* (see *victory*). Once the job is assigned, the soldier must carry out the demands of the job despite any moral misgivings. To leave the job is to be considered a *coward* and the offender may be imprisoned (see *deserter*). Those who assign the job to the soldier are usually older men or women, who often may not have been asked in their youth to do a similar job—but they are nonetheless resolute in insisting that the soldier risk his/her life pursuing their leaders' political and economic goals. For example:

"It [the banner] just says 'I support our troops'. Whether you're for or against what's going on, you can at least hope that our soldiers come home safe...They're merely doing their jobs, following orders, and trying to serve their country." (March 22, 2003, binarytoybox.com)

"Well, I believe that the majority of the Australian people want our job in Iraq finished. They want us to see it through." (Australian Prime Minister John Howard, April 16, 2004, foxnews. com)

"I can tell you that where we operate, we're doing the job,

we're performing our mission, we're killing the bad guys and we're making life better for the average Iraqi people in the western part of Iraq." (Maj. Gen. Keith Stalder, April 9, 2003, military.com)

"Condoleezza Rice, Bush's national security adviser [said]: 'The images that are coming from Iraq are hard images to see... The large picture, though, is that we have a job to do in Iraq, we have a job to finish in Iraq...and we're going to finish it.'" (The *Miami Herald*, September 22, 2003)

"We've got a job to do, and we're not going to abandon the Iraqi people. We're going to help build up their forces and their capability and we're going to win." (Donald Rumsfeld, November 2, 2003)

just war: A set of principles for judging the moral legitimacy of a war, which, when applied based on what a nation considers its best interests, leads almost invariably to war.

Augustine (354-430) established a series of criteria by which one could judge the permissibility of a particular war. According to Augustine, " No one must ever question the rightness of a war which is waged on God's command..." In the thirteenth century Thomas Aquinas refined the just war principles. The influence of both of these Catholic philosophers contributed to centuries of bloody conflict.

The basic elements of the just war criteria state that a war can be justified only if (1) there is a just cause (2) if a legitimate authority makes the declaration (3) if the war is the last resort, and (4) if the good achieved is proportional to the violence of the methods.

The *Encyclopedia Britannica* refers to the just war doctrine as "an extremely flexible one, enabling a state to describe its war as just at its own discretion. As a corollary, the enemy would therefore be fighting an unjust war." President Bush, a practicing Episcopalian, is said to have followed just war principles as he pondered initiating *Operation Desert Storm.*

In November 2002, as another bloody conflict with Iraq seemed likely, the U.S. Catholic Bishops stated, "With the Holy See and bishops from the Middle East and around the world, we fear that resort to war...would not meet the strict conditions in Catholic teaching for overriding the strong presumption against the use of military force." They cited, among other considerations, a lack of compliance with the UN Security Council, unpredictable consequences, and "incalculable costs" for the civilian population. Many other religious bodies denounced the impending conflict based on their reading of just war criteria. *Operation Iraqi Freedom* followed.

Francis A. Beer, in his still very relevant 1980 book *Peace Against War,* points out that "on a global scale, secular ideology has partly replaced religion as the definer of legal justice...leaders assert the justice of wars that preserve free institutions, 'make the world safe for democracy' or 'preserve their people from foreign atheistic systems.'" He adds, "contemporary... interpretations of international law uphold the necessity of targeting urban populations in the event of nuclear war." Should one be nostalgic for the days of the sword?

K

"If in some smothering dreams you too could pace
Behind the wagon that we flung him in,
And watch the white eyes writhing in his face,
His hanging face, like a devil's sick of sin;
If you could hear, at every jolt, the blood
Come gargling from the froth-corrupted lungs,
Obscene as cancer, bitter as the cud
Of vile, incurable sores on innocent tongues,—
My friend, you would not tell with such high zest
To children ardent for some desperate glory,
The Old Lie: Dulce et decorum est
Pro Patria Mori."

Wilfred Owen—World War I

kill: to take away a person's life, depriving them of their very existence, and removing them forever from the loving company of their family and friends (see *assassination, degrade, dispatch, eliminate, mopping up, neutralize, reduce, take out).*

Civil society regards killing, i.e. murder, as its most serious crime. That same society, when it condones war, encourages killing on as massive a scale as is necessary to achieve *victory.* States at war train their young people, approaching the prime of their lives, to kill in the name of the State's interests. Those who do not agree to kill are punished.

The word "kill" is not avoided by the military, but is generally used to indicate destruction of inanimate objects which, however, typically contain human beings. *Lessons of Modern Warfare* Vol. IV from the Center for Strategic and International Studies (www. csis.org) refers to "kill rates" of "combat equipment," "tank kill claims," "actual killing effects," and "types of kill capability" while referring only occasionally to killing "personnel."

William Lutz, euphemism expert, notes "in 1984, the U.S.

State Department decided that it would no longer use the word 'killing' in its reports on human rights in various countries. Instead it would talk about 'unlawful or arbitrary deprivation of life.'"

John Taylor, in *Body Horror: Photojournalism, Catastrophe and War* explains "Removing horror from the popular, historical understanding of killing (or dying) for one's country is one effect of recent war management, made easier by the 'virtual' nature of warfare practised by highly developed nations organised and led by the United States."

Colin Powell, Secretary of State in the George W. Bush administration, was the Army Chief of Staff during the *Gulf War*. Powell belied his urbane image when he said—speaking of a "twofold strategy" toward the Iraqi army, "First we're going to cut it off, then we're going to kill it." Kenneth Vaux, remarking on this oft-quoted statement in *Ethics and the Gulf War: Religion, Rhetoric and Righteousness* says "After this initial effort, the bombing continued in order to liquidate Iraq's military capability by eliminating divisions—a euphemism for killing tens of thousands of Iraqi soldiers..."

kill box: an area where pilots are free to kill or destroy anyone or anything. In *Operation Iraqi Freedom* military planners divided up Iraq into a series of grids typically 35 miles square. The technical name for these free-fire zones is Killbox Interdiction/ Close Air Support (KI/CAS) areas, commonly referred to as "Kick-ass."

When pilots bomb or fire missiles at tanks or other armored vehicles in the kill box, the people in those vehicles are wounded and killed. Civilians, while theoretically protected, may find themselves within these lethal grids. Maria Tomchick (Alternet, April 7, 2003) reported "Soon after the war started, U.S. military planners set up 'kill boxes' in the region south of Baghdad, a largely rural area...there is no way that civilians on the ground can know when they've entered a kill box until a bomb falls on them. [12 year-old] Ibrahim and his 17 year-old cousin Jalal left home to have lunch with Abdullah, a friend who owned the neighboring farm. They were torn apart by a U.S. bomb because they were outside, walking, and a kill box had been superimposed over their home."

Soldiers are fair game. John M. Broder (*New York Times*, April 10, 2003) notes "The bombing campaign that accompanied ground actions to squeeze military units into ever-smaller 'kill boxes' almost certainly left thousands of soldiers dead, perhaps tens of thousands. But the world will never know how many, and no Iraqi authority is left to count them and notify their families." He added " Powerful munitions used by American and British air forces" left victims "pulverized, burned or buried in rubble."

Mercury News (April 19, 2003) quotes Air Force Major Greg DeFore concerning his participation in the kill box system in Iraq. "Instead of focusing on an entire country," he said "we can focus on a small subset at a time." "An underlying goal...was to complement the allied strategy of eliminating the Iraqi leadership, or 'cutting off the head' from the field troops." Explained DeFore: "We dealt with beating the body to death."

kinetic targeting: destroying equipment and killing people on the ground with *bombs*, *artillery* shells, and missiles. Brigadier Andrew R. Gregory, a British Armoured Division Commander during *Operation Iraqi Freedom* wrote in the January-February 2004 *Field Artillery:* "It was hoped many Iraqi formations would indicate a desire to surrender, avoiding combat and potentially allowing them to form a nucleus of a new Iraqi army. However, a lack of feedback forced us to revert to kinetic targeting of assessed positions...This issue, in part, resulted in the significant expenditure of artillery ammunition...many soldiers commented during the fighting that it was 'just like being on an exercise.'"

Kuma\War: a revolutionary computer game, released in February 2004, which insults the memory of all those killed in Iraq and Afghanistan, turns organized violence into entertainment, and trivializes death and destruction—all with the blessings of the Pentagon. It deserves a unique place among the wide assortment of *military games* and *action figures.*

An online review of Kuma\War (www.kumawar.com)—the PC game created by New-York based Kuma Reality Games—boasts "Created using real-world missions from breaking news events, the subscription-based online service is a tactical, squad-based game that brings top stories from the war on terror directly to the customer's PC. Just weeks after a military event occurs... Kuma\War will create a re-enactment of the conflict...[it] will give players a 'boots on the ground' experience of recent missions such as Uday and Qusay Hussein's last stand [and] Operation Anaconda in Afghanistan."

The game begins with a TV broadcast in the style of Fox or CNN, designed by former ABC producer William Davis—using real war footage obtained from the U.S. military under an arrangement with the *Department of Defense.* Declassified intelligence reports, advanced satellite imagery, and graphic modeling of the combat scene are presented, along with one's choice of appropriate weapons. The "Operation Anaconda" mission directions, for example, include "Helicoptered into the thick of combat, you must gradually pick off the enemy." If you choose "Samarra Bank Heist" that game "offers insights into the power and tactical advantage of the M1A1 tank, which you'll be commanding as a member of the "Iron Horse" Division in this playable mission."

The authenticity of the re-creations are assured by the staff of "decorated" military veteran advisors, including Major General Thomas Wilkerson, a former US marine commander. In November

2004 Kuma\War players were offered an opportunity to simulate the attack on the city of Fallujah, Iraq, during which that city of 200,000 people west of Baghdad was destroyed in order to root out insurgents (see *dead-enders*). The game describes the "marine's job" as a chance to "investigate each and every structure for signs of the enemy in a deadly game of 'whack a mole.'"

Perhaps anticipating objections that might be raised against this video game—which allows the user to recreate and virtually participate in events in which *coalition* and Iraq soldiers and civilians were killed—Kuma Reality offers the following: "We will proudly donate $1 from all paid subscriptions [to Kuma\War] to the Intrepid Fallen Heroes Fund which was created to assist the families of our nation's fallen heroes killed in the performance of their duty."

Kuwait babies: In September 1990, press reports appeared that claimed Iraqi soldiers had run amok in a Kuwaiti hospital. They reportedly had snatched premature babies from their incubators and had thrown the infants to the floor to die. President Bush and General Norman Schwarzkopf joined a chorus of angry voices denouncing this shocking crime. In October 1990 a fifteen-year-old Kuwaiti girl testified before the Human Rights Caucus of the U.S. Congress. Choking back tears, "Nayirah," as she was named to protect her identity, told the members that she had witnessed the atrocity. Later, during the Senate debate on the necessity of military action, seven senators referred to this horrible act.

Two years later, a different story emerged. John MacArthur, publisher of *Harper's* magazine, explained in the January 1992 *New York Times* that "Nayirah" was the daughter of the Kuwaiti ambassador to the United States. The American public relations firm Hill & Knowlton, which had created Citizens for a Free Kuwait (financed by the Kuwaiti government in exile) to demonize the Iraqis, had coached her for the testimony. The Kuwaiti babies incident had been an invention (see *Gulf War*).

L

"With the might of God on our side we will triumph over Iraq. God will watch over our troops and grant us a victory over the threat of Saddam's army."

President George W. Bush

launch success rate: another fine example of Pentagon propaganda. In April 1992, more than a year after the end of the *Gulf War,* the *Defense Department* released its final report to Congress on that bloody war.

In the report, the Pentagon boasted that the Tomahawk cruise missile had a "98 percent launch success rate." Two hundred ninety-seven Tomahawk missiles were used in the Gulf War. The meaning of "launch success rate," not given in the report, is merely the percentage of missiles that leave their launcher and achieve level flight.

The April 1992 the *Bulletin of the Atomic Scientists* explained that the missiles—each costing 1 million dollars and carrying 1000 pounds of explosives—actually hit their intended target slightly more than half the time. The powerful Tomahawk missiles, streaking to their often-accidental destination at 550 miles per hour, contributed to the war's appalling *collateral damage* (see *dumb bombs, precision-guided munitions*).

liberation: after failing to find *weapons of mass destruction* following the brutal 2003 U.S.-led *coalition* attack on Iraq, this emerged as one of the principal announced motives for having invaded and occupied that country (see *democratization, occupation*). Because the coalition—principally in the form of the U.S. military and administrative officials—remained in Iraq as an occupying force, the repressive government of Saddam Hussein from which the Iraqis had been freed was replaced by new self-proclaimed owners, i.e. the U.S. and a few allies.

On May 22, 2003 the UN passed Security Council resolution 1483, which gave the *Coalition Provisional Authority* permission to govern Iraq, and control its oil revenues. On June 19, 2003, the *Washington Post* reported L. Paul Bremer III, the U.S. chief civilian administrator in Iraq, as admitting "As long as we're here, we are the occupying power. It's a very ugly word, but it's true."

The U.S. formed the *Iraqi Governing Council* in July 2003 to foster the appearance of Iraqi control over their affairs. Paul Wolfowitz, Deputy Secretary of Defense, in a 60 Minutes interview (April 6, 2003) maintained, "We come as an army of liberation, and we want to see the Iraqis running their own affairs as quickly as possible."

On June 8, 2004, UN Resolution 1546 supported the transfer of "sovereignty" to a 33-member Iraq interim government selected through collaboration between the Iraqi Governing Council and the U.S. On June 28, 2004 Bremer handed that "sovereignty" to the handpicked interim government and departed for the U.S., leaving behind a massive U.S. Embassy—and 140,000 troops (see *Green Zone*).

By the time of the Iraqi national elections in January 2005 there were 150,000 U.S. troops present, many under daily siege by Iraqis rebelling against the occupation. President Bush's budget proposal in February 2005 included $1-2 billion for construction of a new U.S. embassy in the Green Zone in Baghdad. No timetable was set for withdrawal of the occupying forces (see *exit strategy*).

In 1917 the British army entered Baghdad. The British commander General F.S. Maude reassured the Iraqis " Our armies do not come into your cities and lands as conquerors or enemies but as liberators (see *carpet bombing*). The British took over control of Iraq in 1920 under the Treaty of San Remo, mandated by the League of Nations. They would remain in power under various guises until 1958.

Norman Solomon, introducing the winners of the 2003 P.U.-Litzer Prizes, presented by AlterNet (www.alternet.org.) for the "stinkiest media performances of the year" named Tom Brokaw as the recipient of the "Liberating Iraq" prize: "Interviewing a military analyst as the U.S. jet bombers headed to Baghdad on the first day of the Iraqi war, NBC anchor Tom Brokaw declared: 'Admiral McGinn, one of the things we don't want to do is destroy the infrastructure of Iraq, because in a few days we're going to own that country.'"

M

"A nation that continues year after year to spend more money on military defense than on programs of social uplift is approaching spiritual death...Our only hope today lies in our ability to recapture the revolutionary spirit and go out into a sometimes hostile world declaring eternal hostility to poverty, racism, and militarism."

Martin Luther King, Jr.

mercenaries: guns-for-hire. By late 2004 there were an estimated 20,000 of these non-governmental employees in Iraq. They prefer to be called "private security forces" or "private contractors". As security threats increased against the *occupation*, many more eventually would be hired from the dozens of firms specializing in these services.

Mercenaries have been used throughout the history of warfare. According to David Isenberg, in *Soldiers of Fortune Ltd.: A Profile of Today's Private Sector Corporate Mercenary Firms,* a Center for Defense Information (www.cdi.org) monograph, "Throughout most of human history it was considered the order of things that the destruction of war should be left to needy foreigners so citizens of rich states could go on making their fortunes."

Fortunes can certainly be made in the mercenary business, and scores of companies have taken advantage of the availability of the spoils of war in Iraq. The *New York Times*, April 19, 2004 cited government estimates that "security forces could claim up to 25% of the $18 billion budgeted for reconstruction, a huge and mostly unanticipated expense that could delay or force the cancellation of billions of dollars of projects to rebuild schools, water treatment plants, electric lines and oil refineries." The private employees were being paid from $500-$1500 per day.

Individuals who take up arms for profit are an eclectic

assortment. They include in Iraq, for example, former British and U.S. *soldiers*, Chileans trained during General Pinochet's cruel dictatorship, and ex-apartheid South Africa security forces. Blackwater Security Counseling (blackwatersecurity.com), a Maryland-based company boasts that its "mobile security teams are comprised of former operators primarily from the ranks of the U.S. special operations and intelligence communities...[they] stand ready to deploy around the world ...in support of U.S. national security objectives, private or foreign interests."

In Iraq, Blackwater employees were hired to guard L. Paul Bremer III, the head of the *Coalition Provisional Authority* (CPA). The Washington Post also disclosed that in March 2004, the CPA had "earmarked $100 million to replace U.S. troops guarding Baghdad's [*Green Zone*] with private security for the first 15 months after the hand over [on June 28,2004]."

The *Washington Post* (April 6, 2004) reported "An attack by hundreds of Iraqi militia on the U.S. government's headquarters in Najaf on Sunday was repulsed, not by the U.S. military, but by eight commandos from a private security firm...Before U.S. reinforcements could arrive, the firm, Blackwater Security Consulting, sent in its own helicopters amid an intense firefight to re-supply its commandos and to ferry out a wounded Marine... Thousands of armed private security contractors are operating in Iraq in a wide variety of missions and exchanging fire with Iraqis every day..."

Despite the fact that the military does not offer contracts for security forces to engage in direct combat, the nature of their employment makes it inevitable. Military officials and security contractors insist that they only respond to attacks, but do not initiate them, but some admit the distinction is "blurring."

There are no figures available on how many mercenaries or Iraqis have been killed or wounded in these encounters featuring "outsourced" fighters. Meanwhile, Senator John W. Warner,

Virginia Republican and Armed Services Committee member said in an interview "I regard them as our silent partner in this struggle."

A new category of private contractors was revealed in May 2004 when the Abu Ghraib prisoner abuse scandal erupted (see *detainees*). According to the May 16, 2004 *Toronto Star,* "Of the 37 interrogators at Abu Ghraib prison, 27 did not belong to the U.S. military but to a Virginia private contractor called CACI International. Twenty-two linguists who assisted them were employed by California-based Titan International. Two of these workers were cited in Maj.-Gen. Anthony Taguba's damning report on the "sadistic, blatant and wanton" treatment of detainees..."

The two accused did not come under military law, and it was unclear if Iraqi or U.S. laws would apply to the their alleged misconduct. By late May 2004 CACI was under investigation by the US General Services Administration, a probe which threatened the loss of future contracts for CACI, which had already been paid $66 million for its work in Iraq.

The *Progress Report,* May 28, 2004 revealed " In a stunning move this week, with investigations currently underway, CACI international was rewarded with a new $88 million contract to provide computer systems engineering support for the Navy."

military budget: Obscenely large and growing bigger. The $2.6 trillion federal budget proposed by President Bush for fiscal year 2005 (October 1, 2005 to September 30, 2006) featured a request for $419.3 billion for the *Department of Defense*, an increase of 5 percent from the previous year, and 41 percent higher than the fiscal 2001 budget.

The budget plan, which did not include the ongoing military expenses in Iraq and Afghanistan, did include plans to reduce funding for Medicaid, the No Child Left Behind education law, food stamps, as well as other social programs such as child-care assistance for low-income families and home heating aid. According to Joshua Bolten, Bush's budget director (*Boston Globe,* February 8, 2005) "We must exercise even greater spending restraint than we have in the past."

The President planned on asking Congress at a later date for about $80 billion in new funding for the military in Iraq and Afghanistan. This would bring the total for both wars to almost $300 billion. According to Reuters (January 25, 2005) "the administration is also considering including $1 billion to $2 billion to construct a new embassy complex in Baghdad." (see *Green Zone*)

In order to hide the true cost of war and the preparations for war the U.S. government prefers to include Trust Funds (e.g. Social Security) and expenses accrued from past military spending with the nonmilitary portion of the Federal budget.

The War Resisters League (WRL) (www.warresisters.org) is a good source for honest reporting. Each year the WRL publishes accurate budget figures after the President releases a proposed budget. In addition to the monies allocated for the *Department of Defense* for fiscal year 2004 (October 1, 2004 to September 30, 2005), WRL includes military spending from other parts of the budget. This includes items such as veteran's benefits, interest on that portion of the national debt due to military expenses, and spending on nuclear weapons.

In addition, they tally the cost of the Iraq and Afghanistan wars which are not included in the President's budget. By May 2004 the cost of the U.S. military presence in Iraq was costing $4.7 billion a month. When the White House submitted its 2005 budget in February 2004 the administration maintained it had sufficient funds for both the Iraq and Afghanistan operations until 2005. On May 5, 2004 the President asked for an additional $25 billion.

The true military budget for fiscal 2004, according to WRL, is actually over $935 billion—a staggering 49 percent of the total

Federal budget. The entire Human Resources portion—Education, Health/Human Services, etc. is $631 billion.

This disproportionate emphasis on death and destruction raises serious moral issues. For example, columnist Chet Raymo points out in the *Boston Globe* (April 22, 2003) "A billion people do not have access to safe water. Three billion people have inadequate sanitation. Up to 7 million people die each year from water-related diseases...Imagine what a few billion dollars could do to address the global water crisis."

Jaques Diouf, director-general of the United Nations Food and Agricultural Organization warns of practical consequences of the inequity between the amount of money allocated for weapons and for people. Diouf, in the *Boston Globe*, November 27, 2003 says "Allowing 842 million people to suffer the ravages of hunger is not only an unacceptable tragedy, it is a threat to economic growth, political stability, and peace: All too often, a hungry man is an angry man."

Not everyone sees unalloyed tragedy in war. Jeff Fischer, in the January 12, 2003 The Motley Fool (www.fool.com) advised, "War in Iraq seems likely. Rather than worry or flee the stock market, 20th century history in war represents a stock-buying opportunity...If you had bought stock at the outset of any major war in the past 90 years, you could have achieved above-average returns, and often in short order...so, you might dislike war, but don't let it cloud your investment thinking."

military games: an insidious form of popular entertainment aimed at young children and teenagers, in which graphic violence passes for fun. It is highly profitable for the manufacturers, and encouraged by the Pentagon. The genre includes board games, *action figures*, and more recently, video games—the most flagrant example of the interactive interface of youthful curiosity and the military mindset (see *KUMA\War*). The first video game console was created with Pentagon funding in 1966 as a "top secret" project with the aim of using it to teach strategy and sharpen a soldier's reflex skills. The commercial applications would burgeon only a few years later, but the military's connection with the industry would continue.

According to Nick Turse (TomDispatch.com, October 17, 2003) The Institute for Creative Technologies (ICT) in Marine del Ray, California, part of the University of Southern California system, "is a $45 million joint Army/USC venture begun in 1999, designed to link up the military with academia and the entertainment and video game industries." ICT has created a highly realistic video specifically for military training—"Full Spectrum Command"—"to teach the fundamentals of commanding a light infantry company in urban areas."

"Full Spectrum Command" morphed into the commercially available "Full Spectrum Warrior" (FSW) designed for the popular Microsoft Xbox system. FSW is "a realistic combat simulator that allows the gamer to act as an Army light infantry squad leader conducting operations in ...a fictional nation nestled between Afghanistan, Pakistan and China." The fanatical leaders "hatred of the western world is well known." FSW, according to its manufacturer, is replete with opportunities to kill the evil enemy. It "puts you in the dirt with your men, where danger lurks around every corner."

Nick Turse points out that the Institute for Creative Technologies "also draws on the talents of a host of Hollywood's top creative minds to dream up futuristic weapons, vehicles, equipment, and uniforms for the Army." Production designer Rob Cobb (Star Wars, Aliens, Total Recall) helped design "the Army's super soldier of the future" who will be " an integrated system of weapons, armor, camouflage and electronics" (see *high-tech battlefield*).

In January 2005 Lucas Arts Entertainment Company released

"Mercenaries: Playground of Destruction"(see *mercenaries*). They describe it as a "revolutionary action-shooter game" which targets a North Korean General and his advisors. The game offers a player "the firepower to lay waste anything in sight."

In 2002 the Army began using a videogame for recruiting purposes (see *military recruitment*). "America's Army" was created with the assistance of entertainment and gaming industry notables—including Lucasfilm Skywalker Sound, Dolby Laboratories, and Epic Games. It is available for download—or at Army recruiting stations. Now one of the most popular online video games, "America's Army" lets the user "experience" boot camp and kill enemy forces with exciting, powerful weapons.

Not to be outdone, the US Navy's Special Warfare Command advised Sony on the production of Sony's online SOCOM 11: US Navy Seals. The players can act as "an elite SEAL commander" and "strike targets of importance within 12 intense international missions quietly and successfully—and protect freedom across the globe...utilizing the best weaponry."

This melding of the deliberate glamorization of war, immensely profitable graphic entertainment, *military training*, and military recruitment—co-sponsored by the Pentagon, industry, and Hollywood—can only support society's acquiescence to war as an acceptable means of conflict resolution—and help supply our youth to the military to kill and be killed.

military recruitment: the means by which the military convinces young citizens that enrollment in the armed services is a glamorous, exciting, profitable and career-enhancing opportunity. Recruiters tend not to stress that once someone enlists in the military, he or she will be assigned according to the needs of their chosen branch, and will be required to support or participate in killing whoever the Pentagon decides is the *enemy*. Recruits who prefer not to follow those orders face imprisonment and disgrace.

In order to maintain the U.S. military force of 1.4 million, based in 138 countries (see *forward-based forces*, *hegemony*), the 7,000 recruiting offices across the country are issued specific quotas to bring in their share of the over 200,000 young recruits needed each year.

The recruiters target young men and women between the ages of 17 and 21 by an incessant marketing campaign, centered on high schools and colleges. That became much easier in early 2002 with the passage of the federal Elementary and Secondary Education Act (ESEA), better known as the No Child Left Behind (NCLB) Act. In addition to its other deficiencies, the NCLB mandates that schools receiving funds under this Act must provide armed forces recruiters with lists of students' names, addresses and telephone numbers. Students can notify the local authorities if they do not want this information released— although not all school districts publicize that option.

Until late 2004 colleges and universities ran the risk of losing federal aid if they banned recruiters from campus, under the 1995 "Solomon amendment". In November of that year the U.S. Court of Appeals in Philadelphia ruled that those educational institutions could not be forced to allow military recruiters on campus, saying that such a practice was "incompatible with their educational objectives." In early February 2005 the Justice Department said it planned to ask the Supreme Court to hear an appeal to overturn that decision.

There is an increasing emphasis on attracting college age teenagers. Douglas Smith, spokesperson for the Army Recruiting Command at Fort Knox, Kentucky told *USA Today* (January 21, 2004) "What we know is lots of those people start college but don't complete it because they're not ready maturity-wise, or don't have the finances."

The websites for each of the branches of the military offer a mix of generally similar inducements. For example, the Army (goarmy.com) advertises cash incentives for joining, money for education, a chance to learn valuable skills—and a free download of "America's Army," a video game featuring wound-free excitement (see *military games*). Another download allows one to "put a piece of the world's most powerful land force on your desktop."

In the Army website's list of 12 questions for parents of prospective recruits, the first to hint at the true rationale for military recruitment is question number nine—"What is deployment?" The answer given is, in part—"Deployment is the term used to describe when an Active Duty or Army Reserve unit is sent to a specific area of operations, usually on foreign soil...Often times, units are deployed to non-combat regions, including Hawaii, Italy or Germany for humanitarian efforts, such as building hospitals..."

Recruiting is by no means confined to soft-pedaling the realities of military obligations to people old enough to enlist. Programs that try to foster a positive image of military life are aimed at sometimes much younger audiences. For example, The US Navy "Starbase-Atlantis" "exposes fifth graders and their teachers to real-world applications of math and science through... experiments in aviation and space-related fields, sea-going vessels, and tours of Navy activities."

Located in nearly every state, "Young Marines" is the U.S. Marine Corps official youth program, open to children as young as 8 years old. The Marines insist that this "is not a recruiting force...We strive to instill the core values of Honor, Courage, and Commitment."

Membership in the United States Army Junior Reserve Officer's Training Corps (JROTC) is available in 1,555 schools throughout the U.S. and in American schools overseas. Two hundred and seventy three thousand high school age cadets, complete with uniforms, are taught "the value of citizenship, service to the United States, personal responsibility, and a sense of accomplishment."

In terms of citizenship, President George W. Bush offered an added incentive towards that goal when he issued an executive order in July 2002, expediting naturalization for aliens and non-citizen nationals who are willing to serve in the military during the war on terrorism. Non-citizens who enlisted after September 11, 2001 may apply for citizenship as soon as they arrive at their first military base, rather having to wait three to four years.

That executive order raised the concern in the country's Latino community, according to Miriam Kagan (Inter Press Service, September 22, 2003), that " Hispanic men and women are being disproportionately exposed to risk and sent to the front lines." She notes "According to the Pew Hispanic Center, while Latinos make up 9.5 percent of the actively enlisted forces, they are over-represented in the categories that get the most dangerous assignments—infantry, gun crews and seamanship—and make up over 17.5 percent of the front lines."

On the contentious issue of minority representation in the military, the *Washington Post* (February 4, 2003) notes that "38 percent of the military's...enlistees are ethnic minorities, while they make up only 29 percent of the general population." Ronald Walters, a University of Maryland political science professor says, "The playing field outside the military is not level. Life structures you to certain choices, and you wind up in the military." This is often referred to as the "poverty draft."

Miriam Kagan cites the conclusion of Teresa Gutierrez, of Act Now to Stop War and End Racism (ANSWER)(www. internationalanswer.org): "The people who are fighting the war are youths who cannot find jobs or afford university fees because there is an economic draft in the army that is particularly relevant to Latinos."

Jorge Mariscal, professor at the University of California asks in the April 18, 2003 *Counterpunch*, "What can we say of the young Latino men who sacrificed their lives in Iraq? That they fought without knowing their enemy, played their role as pawns in a geopolitical chess game devised by arrogant bureaucrats, and died simply to get an education; trying to have a fair shot at the American Dream that has eluded the vast majority of Latinos for over a century and a half."

Despite the theoretical appeal of some benefits of military life, the life of the recruiter remains a challenging one. Their burden was eased somewhat in 2004 when the Army decided to permit 25 percent more high school dropouts to enlist, and accepted more recruits with borderline scores on a service aptitude test.

According to *USA Today* (January 21, 2004) "officials estimate it takes 120 to 150 contacts to get one person to enlist." Staff Sgt. Katrese Clayton told reporter Charisse Jones "When you make an appointment, you have to interview them in 48 hours." Otherwise, Clayton said, "it's too much time for them to think."

military training: a strict regimen imposed on military recruits which consists of sustained, rigorous physical and mental challenges which diminish their sense of self-identity and stress their membership in an interdependent group.

Young men are taught to kill on command only incidentally for motives of patriotism. Lt. Col. Dave Grossman emphasizes in *On Killing: The Psychological Cost of Learning to Kill in War and Society* "A tremendous volume of research indicates that the primary factor that motivates a soldier to do the things that no sane man *wants* to do in combat (that is, killing and dying) is not the force of self-preservation but a powerful sense of accountability to his comrades in the battlefield."

Indeed, the *US Officer's Guide* points out "What, then, keeps the soldier from giving away to fear? The answer is simple—his desire to retain the good opinion of his friends and associates... his pride smothers his fear." This same theme occurs throughout the writings of those who have experienced war first-hand. In *War is a Force That Gives us Meaning* Chris Hedges quotes a Marine Corps lieutenant colonel about to enter Kuwait during the *Gulf War*; "Just remember that none of these boys is fighting for home, for the flag, for all the crap that the politicians feed the public. They are fighting for each other, just for each other."

Hedges admits, "We are humiliated in combat. The lofty words that inspire people to war—duty, honor, glory—swiftly become repugnant and hollow. They are replaced by the hard, specific images of war by the prosaic names of villages and roads...combatants live only for the herd, those hapless soldiers who are bound into their unit to ward off death. There is no world outside the unit. It alone endows worth and meaning. Soldiers will die rather than betray this bond. And there is—as many combat veterans will tell you—a kind of love in this."

The products of the well-honed techniques of military training—young men who will kill and expose themselves to deadly danger when so ordered—are not automatons. Many leave their homes and loved ones filled with patriotic fervor and a desire to serve their country. The fault lies not in them but in those to whom war is a justifiable solution to conflicts—political, economic, religious—because they lack the will to seek positive, nonviolent means of settling disputes. The insatiable appetite of war is satisfied only by the blood of a nation's youth.

mission accomplished: On May I, 2003, President Bush landed in a fighter jet on the aircraft carrier U.S.S. Abraham Lincoln near San Diego. He emerged decked out in a flight suit (see *action figure*). The President posed before an enormous banner draped across the bridge of the ship (delayed off the coast of San Diego, California for the occasion for hours on its homecoming voyage) as he declared an end to major combat operations in Iraq (see *end of hostilities*). The banner stated, "Mission Accomplished."

By late October 2003 there had been more *soldiers* killed in Iraq than during the so-called combat phase of *Operation Iraqi Freedom.* On October 28, in a rare press conference, the President seemed to disavow the banner, which critics maintained had proclaimed a premature conclusion. "The 'Mission Accomplished' sign, of course, was put up by the members of the U.S.S. Abraham Lincoln, saying that their mission was accomplished," Bush said. "I know it was attributed somehow to some ingenious advance man from my staff. There weren't that ingenious, by the way."

On November 3, 2003, the *New York Times* reported that Scott Sforza, a former ABC producer and a member of the White House communications staff, had overseen the production of the sign. Sforza had been on board the Abraham Lincoln preparing for the media event. It was unclear who had suggested the wording. None of the officers on the U.S.S. Abraham Lincoln could recall who had said at a planning meeting, "You know, it sure would look good if we could have a banner that said 'Mission Accomplished'."

Referring to "those on the ship" at the time, White House Press Secretary Scott McClellan explained, "They're the ones who put it up."

In a September 27, 2004 news conference with Fox News, President Bush told host Bill O'Reilly that he had no regrets about his controversial appearance on the aircraft carrier. Bush added "And by the way, those sailors and airmen loved seeing the commander in chief...you bet I'd do it again." By that date 1049 U.S. military had been killed in Iraq.

mission creep: changing the goals of a military plan beyond their original intent. This may occur in a variety of contexts including the evolving nature of a combat situation, the restless ambition of a military commander, or the political ambitions of a President. The term originated during the Vietnam War—a tragic example of all of the above contexts.

The *New York Times*, February 19, 2002 reported "In a shift, U.S. Uses Airstrikes to Help Kabul." Reporter John Burns wrote "American forces appeared to have opened up a new phase in the war of Afghanistan with two bombing raids...that were aimed at clashing militia forces rather then the Taliban or Al Qaeda...the bombing raids seemed to have placed the United States for the first time in a position of using American air power in defense of the [Karzai] government."

The U.S. Congress had given the President authorization to go to war in response to September 11, but only against those who "authorized, committed, or aided the terrorist attacks." This escalation was a prelude to an even more flagrant "mission creep" proclaimed by President George W. Bush in a February 2003 speech in which he emphasized his resolve to "disarm Iraq by force" if Saddam Hussein did not disarm according to the dictates of the UN Security Council. Further, he promised that a U.S.-led invasion would not simply depose Saddam, but would "ensure that one brutal dictator is not replaced by another."

In November 2003, six months after the "official" end of *Operation Iraqi Freedom*, mired in the middle of an increasingly violent occupation, the President addressed The National Endowment for Democracy, a quasi-governmental agency that funds political activities abroad. He announced a new United States policy he called " a forward strategy of freedom in the Middle East." Bush's perceived mission had now crept to positioning the armed *occupation* of Iraq as "another great turning point" marking the "next stage of the world democratic movement" after the Cold War. He offered no novel suggestions as to how that movement might proceed.

Ironically, twelve years earlier, President Bush the elder had disavowed mission creep after driving the Iraqis from Kuwait in *Operation Desert Storm.* Speaking of that decision, the then Secretary of Defense Dick Cheney told the British Broadcasting

Corporation in 1992 in an eerily prescient interview "If we'd gone to Baghdad and got rid of Saddam Hussein—assuming we could have found him—we'd have had to put a lot of forces in and run him to ground someplace. Then you've got to put a new government in place, and then you're faced with the question of what kind of government are you going to put in place in Iraq? How many forces are you going to have to leave there to keep it propped up, how many casualties are you going to take through the course of this operation?"

Simon Jenkins, writing in the *Times* (London), April 7, 2004 saw this scenario developing: " [Eventually] foreign troops will withdraw to... huge military bases now being constructed...From these bases the West will offer residual firepower to a new regime and protect its oil and reconstruction interests, which are to remain in American hands. This plan is increasingly implausible, as is the European thesis that the UN might be a popular alternative... Already the June handover is seen as cosmetic. The Americans are staying on in Saddam's palace. The longer they stay, the more mistakes will be made and the less likely is a stable and moderate Iraq government to succeed them."

He concluded, "Get out [of Iraq] by July and mean it. All else is wishful thinking and certain mission creep."

mopping up: killing or capturing the *enemy* who may still be alive after a battle. The expression is favored by the media and the military, reducing people to the status of trash to be swept away (see *kill*). For example:

"Forces allied to the United States on Saturday were mopping up in the southern city where the repressive regime of the Taliban began." (CNN.com, December 8, 2001)

"Defense Secretary Donald Rumsfeld, however, said coalition troops were succeeding in mopping up the resistance. 'They're making progress against the dead-enders who are harassing coalition forces,' Rumsfeld said today." (Associated Press, June 25, 2003)

"Mopping up Fallujah but rebs lash out in other restive cities" (headline—*Daily News*, November 12, 2004)

"We are now into the mop-up phase. Roman Nancy Garrett's son, Army Pfc. John Lane Garrett, was supposed to leave for Iraq two weeks ago, but now it looks like, instead of fighting, his energies could go into the mopping up.' I'm hoping if he gets sent, he'll get sent for the cleanup.'" (*Rome News-Tribune*, April 10, 2003)

N

"[Saddam Hussein] can be absolutely confident that in the right conditions we would be willing to use our nuclear weapons."

British Defence Minister Geoff Hoon

napalm: highly flammable, sticky, jellied gasoline used in war to burn vegetation and the *enemy*. Napalm was invented in 1943 by a team of Harvard chemists, led by Dr. Louis Feiser, also well known for his research on the chemical causes of cancer. When a *bomb* packed with napalm explodes, the flaming jelly scatters and sticks to whatever or whomever it hits.

The United States used over 300,000 tons of napalm in the Vietnam War between 1963 and 1971 to burn through dense jungle growth as well as to kill and demoralize *soldiers* and civilians. Many of the antiwar demonstrations during those years were directed against Dow Chemical, the makers of the cruel weapon. Dow President Herbert D. Doan maintained, "It [napalm] is a strategic weapon essential to the pursuit of the tactic we are engaged in without exorbitant loss of American lives."

Harvard's Doctor Feiser, also under attack for his invention, insisted that he could not be responsible for how other people used his ideas, saying "I have no right to judge the morality of napalm just because I invented it...I'd do it again, if called upon, for the defense of the country." As for Dow's role, Feiser felt "If the Government asked them to take a contract, and they're the best ones to do it, then they're obliged to do it."

Napalm and other "incendiaries"—weapons that burn—are restricted by the 1980 Convention on Conventional Weapons (CCW)(see *conventional weapons*). They are not banned outright, but are confined to military targets. The U.S. has not signed onto that particular CCW protocol. The U.S. used napalm during the

Gulf War (see *atrocity*, *turkey shoot*) but destroyed its last stocks of napalm in April 2001. They do, however, have a remarkably similar substitute, which was used to incinerate *soldiers* during *Operation Iraqi Freedom* (see *firebomb*).

Retired Marine Lt. Gen. Bernard Trainor, familiar as a frequent cable TV news commentator (see *Countdown Iraq*), is a 1951 graduate of the College of the Holy Cross, home of the "Crusaders." Trainor had this to say about napalm: "I used it routinely in Vietnam. I have no moral compunction about using it. It's just another weapon." In March 2003 he delivered a lecture at his alma mater entitled "War and the Christian Conscience."

nation building: in the case of the U.S. in Iraq—invade a sovereign country with overwhelming force, killing both *soldiers* and many civilians, further damage an already devastated infrastructure, install administrators of your choice, and try to create a new government that will reflect the will of the populace—provided you remain in control of the military power, and the people's will does not conflict seriously with U.S. *national interests.*

Gary T. Dempsey and Roger W. Fontaine note in their 2001 book *Fool's Errands: America's Recent Encounters with Nation Building,* "Washington said it would bring order to Somalia, but left chaos...it intervened in Bosnia to reverse the effects of civil war, but now oversees a province that is not self-sustaining; and it occupied Kosovo to build a multiethnic democracy, but has instead observed widespread ethnic cleansing."

George W. Bush—campaigning against President Clinton in 2000—asserted in the second presidential debate, " I don't think our troops ought to be used for what's called nation building...I think what we need to do is convince the people who live in the lands they live in to build the nations...I'm not so sure the role of the United States is to go around the world and say this is the way it's got to be."

However, by early 2002 President George Bush would be supporting a radical new doctrine of *preemptive war*, maintaining that the United States was free to strike any foreign state unilaterally if there was a suspicion that U.S. interests and security might be threatened. These were the circumstances under which the U.S. justified its attack on Iraq in 2003 (see *Operation Iraqi Freedom*).

Having failed to produce any evidence of *weapons of mass destruction* in Iraq, the administration needed a new rationale for the invasion. Nation building came back into favor. In a speech at The National Endowment for Democracy on November 6, 2003 Bush said, "The United States has adopted a new policy, a forward strategy of freedom in the Middle East...the advance of freedom is the calling of our time, it is the calling of our country" (see *democratization).*

The *Department of Defense* (DoD) had precedence over the State Department for post-war planning. The DoD expected that the Iraqi citizens, once freed from the tyranny of Saddam Hussein, would gladly embrace a coalition-imposed government, and nation building could begin with national elections. Instead, not only did many Iraqis reject the putative leaders imported by the coalition (see *Iraqi Governing Council, Iraqi National Congress*), an armed rebellion developed, killing hundreds of *coalition* soldiers (see *casualties*).

On June 8, 2004, UN Resolution 1546 ratified "sovereignty" for a 33-member Iraq interim government selected through collaboration between the Iraqi Governing Council and the U.S. (see *occupation*). On June 28, 2004, the new interim government—well stocked with U.S. supporters—officially received the mandate to govern Iraq, and welcomed the continued presence of the coalition military force. Together, they intended to build a new Iraq from the old one that two U.S.-led coalitions had destroyed by two wars and years of *sanctions* (see *exit strategy, regime change*).

national interests: the preservation of America's privileged access to a disproportionate share of the world's resources through the maintenance of absolute global military superiority, domination of the world's economy, and willingness to unilaterally and preemptively attack any state which the U.S. deems is hostile to those goals—according to George W. Bush and those who supply him with ideas.

These "national interests"—sometimes expressed as "America's interests"—are frequently invoked. Often they are implied while not being clearly defined. In the White House 2002 *National Security Strategy* (NSS), for example, the terms are used seven times with no elaboration—although the document does say, "The United States government relies on the armed forces to defend America's interests."

The Pentagon's *Joint Vision 20/20*—the plan for the military of the future—emphasizes "Given the global nature of our interests and obligations, the United States must maintain its overseas presence forces and the ability to rapidly project power worldwide in order to achieve full spectrum dominance" (see *forward-based forces, full spectrum dominance, hegemony*).

Rebuilding America's Defenses: Strategy, Forces, and Resources for a New American Century, the 2000 document widely believed to be a blueprint for the NSS insists that the U.S. must control "space and cyberspace" as well. It maintains "An America incapable of protecting its interests...in space or the 'infosphere' will find it difficult to exert global political leadership." This is part of "preserv[ing] an international security environment conducive to American interests and ideals." "Ideals" was not defined in the document.

Condoleezza Rice, then foreign policy advisor to presidential candidate George W. Bush, wrote a position paper "Campaign 2000—Promoting the National Interest" for the January/February 2000 *Foreign Affairs* magazine. She warned against " a reflexive appeal to notions of international law and norms, and the belief that the support of many states—or even better—of institutions like the United Nations—is essential to the legitimate exercise of power. The 'national interest' is replaced with 'humanitarian interests' or the interests of 'the international community.'...To be sure, there is nothing wrong with doing something that benefits all humanity, but that is, in a sense, a second-order effect."

She went on to state her opinion that national interests are not served by such international agreements as the Kyoto treaty on global warming and the Comprehensive Test Ban Treaty banning nuclear weapons testing—both of which would be later repudiated by President Bush with Rice as his national security advisor. She does invoke the familiar military superiority theme, suggesting that "U.S. technological advantages should be leveraged to build forces that are lighter and more lethal, more mobile and agile, and capable of firing more accurately from long distances." Rice became U.S. Secretary of State in January 2005.

In December 2000, the report *Global Trends 2015* was released by none other than the U.S. Central Intelligence Agency (CIA). It emphasized why America's national interests in terms of its security are, in fact, intimately identified with global "humanitarian interests." The document highlights the escalating regional shortages of water and food, the spread of disease, and "economic stagnation, political instability, and cultural alienation." These will "foster political, ethnic, ideological, and religious extremism, along with the violence that often accompanies it."

The United States government, consumed with preparations for global military superiority, and willing—as amply demonstrated by the *Gulf War* and *Operation Iraqi Freedom*—to kill hundreds of thousands of people to further its concept of "national interests" and to preserve the American "way of life," ignores the cries of humanity for justice at its own peril.

National Security Strategy (NSS): a document released by the White House on September 20, 2002 that is idealistic, threatening, and hypocritical. The NSS is the expression of years of planning towards American global dominance formulated by a number of key George W. Bush administration officials, including Secretary of Defense Donald Rumsfeld, Deputy Secretary of Defense Paul Wolfowitz, and Vice President Dick Cheney (see *Defense Planning Guidance, hegemony, Project for the New American Century, Rebuilding America's Defenses: Strategy, Forces and Resources for A New Century*).

The NSS claims "the aim of this [national security] strategy is to make the world not just safer but better." In order for governments to better themselves by being granted U.S. economic aid, they must "fight corruption, respect basic human rights, embrace the rule of law, invest in health care and education [and] follow responsible economic policies." The document does not point out that many of the allies cooperating with the U.S. in its military adventures, e.g. Saudi Arabia, Pakistan, or Uzbekistan fall far short of these goals.

These seemingly humanitarian aims conflict sharply with the means by which this transformation of society is to come about. Boasting of the current unrivaled power of the U.S., the NSS declares, "we will work to translate this moment of influence into decades of peace, prosperity and liberty. The U.S. national security strategy will be based on a distinctly American internationalism that reflects the union of our values and our national interests."

That translates to an unapologetic policy which sees the U.S. bringing about "democracy, development, free markets, and free trade" to all—provided America's *national interests* are served. Specifically, the NSS announces a radical change in the role of

U.S. military might. First, the U.S. will "require bases and stations within and beyond Western Europe and Northeast Asia as well as temporary access arrangements for the long distance deployment of U.S. forces" (see *critical regions, forward-based forces*).

More importantly, "America will act against...emerging threats before they are fully formed...we will not hesitate to act alone, if necessary, to exercise our right of self defense by acting preemptively." Marcus Corbin, Senior Analyst at the Center for Defense Information (CDI)(www.cdi.org), a Washington, D.C. think tank dedicated to studying national security issues, says "this strategy proposes expanding the relatively uncontroversial topic of true preemption—striking first against an imminent, specific near certain attack—to the far broader concept of striking first to prevent the possibility of a longer term threat even developing, which might be labeled preventive war" (see *preemptive war, preventive war*).

Corbin warns, "What will the boomerang effect be if other nations adopt this policy too? Would Iraq [have had] a justification... to strike the U.S. "preemptively?" Could India be justified in striking Pakistan? What will Russia justify doing? China?"

Noam Chomsky, noted author and social critic, put it more bluntly in a January 28, 2004 interview on the Canadian Broadcasting Corporation. Describing the NSS as a "crucial event" Chomsky portrayed the document as "a declaration saying that the U.S. must dominate the world by force if necessary [and] will do it permanently" (see *endless war, hegemony*).

He warned "If you can announce to people ' I'm going to come and attack you whenever I feel like it,' they don't say: 'gee, thank you, here I am, please bomb me.' So they turn to the weapons that are available to the weak...it led to a sharp spike in recruitment for Al Qaeda style organizations. Experts on North Korea and Iran pointed out right away its probably a factor in stimulating their search for weapons of mass destruction."

The 2003 U.S.-led attack on Iraq could be cited as a test case for the new doctrine of preemptive war. The rationale for war was the putative evidence for *weapons of mass destruction* in Iraq that posed, presumably, an "imminent threat" to Iraq's neighbors and to the United States. It was unilateral in the sense that the U.S., while coercing a number of allies to form a *coalition of the willing,* ignored the United Nations and worldwide protests against the invasion.

However, because the U.S. invoked that rationale—later changing it conveniently to *democratization*—merely as a pretext for a long-planned invasion of Iraq, it was instead simply naked aggression (see *Committee for the Liberation of Iraq*, *Defense Planning Guidance, Operation Iraqi Freedom*).

The NSS warns in several places of the dangers presented by *nuclear weapons.* The document says "Other rogue regimes seek nuclear, biological, and chemical weapons as well. These states' pursuit of, and global trade in, such weapons has become a looming threat to all nations."

Meanwhile, the George W. Bush administration, with the largest nuclear arsenal in the world, has withdrawn from the Comprehensive Test Ban Treaty. It is seeking new funding for research on new, smaller "tactical" nuclear weapons, with the intention of having them available for use in future battles—preemptive, preventive or otherwise (see *bunker buster, nuclear weapons*).

neutralize: to kill people (see *kill, assassination, degrade, dispatch, eliminate, mopping up, reduce, take out*). For example:

"Basra had been largely quiet Wednesday, after British forces 'neutralized' militia fighters." (Associated Press, March 26, 2003)

"The operation is aimed 'against non-compliant groups and individuals, focused on neutralizing paramilitary, former regime loyalists, foreign fighters...within the task force area of responsibility.'" (CNN.com, November 17, 2003)

no-fly zones: two areas in northern and southern Iraq within which the U.S., Britain, and France—under a false interpretation of a UN resolution—forbade the use of Iraqi aircraft, and carried out sustained and escalating air attacks.

In March 1991, after the *Gulf War* cease-fire, the northern Kurds and the southern Muslims rebelled against the Saddam Hussein regime. Stephen Zunes, in *Foreign Policy in Focus*, December 6, 2002, explains "The United States banned the use of Iraqi fixed-wing aircraft, which could be of danger to American personnel, but allowed Iraq to use helicopter gunships, which were crucial in reversing the tide of the rebellion and resulted in brutal repression by the Iraq armed forces against the rebellious populations."

The United Nations passed Security Council Resolution 688, adopted on April 5, 1991. The resolution demanded that Iraq end the repression, but did not provide for enforcement. Nevertheless, the U.S., Britain, and France set up a northern "no-fly" zone in Iraq in April 1991, and a second southern zone in August 1992. The two zones covered most of the country with the exception of Baghdad and central Iraq. The purpose of the zones—forbidding the use of any Iraqi aircraft and meanwhile systematically attacking Iraqi military communications, command and control centers—ostensibly was humanitarian protection of the population (see *containment*).

However, as Stephen Zunes observed " According to two State Department reports in 1994 and 1996, the creation and military enforcement of 'no-fly zones' in fact do not protect the Iraqi Kurdish and populations...the demarcations of the no-fly zones do not correspond with the areas of predominant Kurdish populations. That the United States has allowed the Turkish Air

Force to conduct bombing raids within the northern Iraq 'no-fly' zone against Kurdish targets is but one indication of the lack of concern..."

The history of the no-fly zones is one of periodic escalation (see *mission creep*). In December 1998 President Bill Clinton diverted attention from the investigation of his scandalous personal behavior by ordering a massive bombing attack on Iraq—termed Operation Desert Fox—supposedly to punish the regime for failing to cooperate with UN inspections (see *Operations*). After 1998, according to the Global Policy Forum (www.globalpolicy. org) "'more robust rules of engagement' led to regular bombing of ground targets which resulted in substantial civilian casualties."

By October 1999, according to Tariq Ali (*New Left Review,* September-October 2000) "American officials were telling the *Wall Street Journal* they would soon be running out of targets— 'we're down to the last outhouse.'" President George W. Bush helped out in early 2001 by extending the possible targets to cover anything that might hinder the invasion already in the planning stages (see *Operation Iraqi Freedom*). Those targets extended to areas around Baghdad, far beyond the "official" no-fly zones. U.S. Air Force Captain Kevin C. Albright told the Associated Press (November 11, 2002) "To fly over the same territory you're going to attack is a real luxury."

Operation Iraqi Freedom—the 2003 U.S.-led assault on Iraq—would inflict even more destruction and suffering on a country already ravaged by the incessant bombing and missile attacks throughout the years of the no-fly zones. Combined with the even more brutal program of *sanctions*, the no-fly zones had driven a once relatively prosperous country into misery and despair.

nuclear weapons: the most dangerous and destructive explosive devices ever made. Fashioned by extraordinary human creativity and scientific expertise, these weapons are capable of destroying human civilization. Customarily they are referred to generically as "atomic *bombs*," which, along with *biological* and *chemical* weapons, are known as *weapons of mass destruction.* The United States, the only nation ever to kill people with atomic bombs—at Hiroshima and Nagasaki—has more than 10,000 nuclear warheads, according to the January/February 2005 *Bulletin of the Atomic Scientists*. The first George W. Bush administration, in a startling reversal of a long-standing policy, let it be known that it was willing to use nuclear weapons again, and planned to develop new ones.

In the late 1940s, when the United States alone had nuclear bombs, it threatened to use them as "massive" retaliation in the event of an attack by the Soviet Union. Later, when the Soviet Union had developed these weapons, the 1950s became the era of the fallout shelter as part of a "damage limitation" concept. By the 1960s it became evident that there could be no real "winners" in a nuclear exchange. This understanding became known as the doctrine of "mutual assured destruction" (MAD)—the notion that it made no sense for either side to use their nuclear weapons first because that act would assure their own destruction (see *deterrence*).

This standoff, always prone to accidental mutual destruction by technical or human errors, helped keep nuclear doom at bay. Essential to the admittedly tenuous equilibrium was the knowledge that both sides had the capacity to strike back at the other, even if each suffered enormous damage. This assurance was codified in the 1972 Antiballistic (ABM) Treaty. The United States and the Soviet Union pledged not to build defensive missile systems—interceptors that could destroy incoming missiles, thus upsetting the MAD balance.

In 1983, President Ronald Reagan announced the Strategic Defense Initiative (SDI), or "Star Wars," a multibillion-dollar research program aimed at creating a space-based system to defend the nation against long-range nuclear missiles. Critics blasted the idea as unworkable at best, and at worst, as a serious destabilization of the imperfect MAD standoff, and a direct violation of the ABM Treaty. "Star Wars" in various forms, continued to squander money with few results. President George H.W. Bush introduced the concept of a more limited version in the early 1990s, turning research towards rocket-launched interceptors.

George W. Bush accelerated that research program, known as the National Missile Defense (NMD). In 2001—the first year of his presidency—he withdrew the U.S. from the ABM Treaty because it "prohibits us from pursuing promising technology." Bush then committed $23 billion over the next three years to working on a space-based system that—according to the American Friends Service Committee (AFSC) June, 2003 *Disarmament Report*—"is unlikely to work for the foreseeable future, increases the danger of a regional arms race and of nuclear war, and which fuels nuclear weapons proliferation."

There was more to come. President Bush released the *Nuclear Posture Review* (NPR) in January 2002. This framework for the U.S. nuclear policy affirmed, "nuclear weapons, for the foreseeable future, will remain a key element of national security strategy."

The AFSC report summarizes the NPR as follows: (1) an "explicit threat to use nuclear weapons against potential regional rivals such as Iraq, Iran, and China" (2) "a renewed commitment to so-called 'missile defense' and ...massive nuclear weapons stockpiles" (3) [supports] funding for development, testing and deployment of new nuclear weapons" (see *bunker busters*).

Meanwhile, other treaty obligations were shredded. President Bush boycotted the 2001 UN conference to encourage support for the Comprehensive Test Ban Treaty (CTBT). The CTBT, signed by President Clinton in 1996, forbids all nuclear explosions for any purpose, thus banning testing. U.S. nuclear testing, widely expected to take place, also will further violate the already tattered 1970 Non-Proliferation of Nuclear Weapons Treaty (NPT), in which the U.S. agreed to forego nuclear-weapons development and work towards nuclear disarmament.

These are dangerous times. The George W. Bush administration became intent on unilaterally developing and testing new nuclear weapons, antimissile systems, and space-based weapons. On February 13, 2003 Reuters reported "Defense Secretary Donald Rumsfeld on Thursday refused to rule out the U.S. use of nuclear weapons in a possible war with Iraq, while a leading senator told him such a move would trigger a near-total breakdown in American relations with the rest of the world" (see *bunker buster*).

On February 21, 2003 ten U.S. Senators, including Diane Feinstein (D-CA) and Edward Kennedy (D-MA) warned President Bush "A shift in U.S. [nuclear] policy would deepen the danger of nuclear proliferation by effectively telling non-nuclear states that nuclear weapons are necessary to deter a potential U.S. attack, and by sending a green light to the world's nuclear states that it is permissible to use them. Is this the lesson we want to send to North Korea, India, Pakistan or any other nuclear power?"

The Bush administration, in its request to Congress for fiscal year 2005, asked for $27.6 million to work on a nuclear *bunker buster,* and $9 million to develop small nuclear weapons for battlefield use—so-called "mini-nukes." Senators Kennedy and Feinstein proposed an amendment that would cut those funds. The Senate rejected the amendment in June 2004. However, on November 20, 2004 Congress passed an appropriations bill with no funding for new nuclear weapons. The *Chicago Tribune* (November 23, 2004) said the decision "was hailed...by arms control advocates as the biggest success in more than a decade. Undeterred, Defense Secretary Donald Rumsfeld pressed for the restoration of the funds.

Jonathan Schell's *The Unconquerable World: Power, Nonviolence, and the Will of the People* makes a cogent, compelling case for this proposition: "In our time, we must secure not only peace but survival...we must suppress the menace of annihilation. A decision for non-violence, in our time, is a decision to exist. An agreement to abolish nuclear arms and all other weapons of mass destruction is the sine qua non of any sane or workable international system in the twenty-first century."

O

"One great use of words is to hide our thoughts."

Voltaire

occupation: the forcible seizure of a country by one or more other countries, followed by the establishment of a governmental system that furthers the invader's strategic, economic and political interests. The United States and Britain, along with a smattering of smaller states, invaded Iraq in May 2003 with a massive military force. This *coalition of the willing* established what they promised would be a temporary occupation.

In April 2003, as the invasion was still underway, Deputy Defense Secretary Paul Wolfowitz said, "We don't want it to be an occupation—we also don't want it to be something that the coalition imposes on the Iraqis." On May 22, 2003 the UN Security Council passed Resolution 1483, which recognized the United States and the United Kingdom as the "Occupying Power" in Iraq, thus legalizing what most members of the UN had considered an illegal invasion.

Both the British and the U.S. were no strangers to the role of carrying out occupation by brute, merciless force. Another chapter in the long, cruel history of British colonialism arrived in 1920 when the British—having earlier invaded and seized the area—were given a Mandate by the League of Nations to occupy and govern what had been pieced together as Iraq. According to the Global Policy Forum (www.globalpolicy.org), "In response to Iraqi resistance...British forces battled for over a decade to pacify the country, using airplanes, armored cars, firebombs and mustard gas. Air attacks were used to shock and awe, to teach obedience, and to force the collection of taxes. Winston Churchill, as responsible cabinet member in the early years, saw Iraq as an experiment in high-technology colony control" (see *carpet bombing*).

The Iraqis, having achieved independence of sorts in 1932, were attacked and occupied by the British once again in 1941. In the course of three decades of struggle, 98,000 Iraqis had been killed. The British would return in 2003 to add to that total.

The U.S. forces that led the invasion of Iraq were following a long American tradition of bloody occupation. Some countries, such as Cuba and the Philippines had been subjugated by American force, while others, e.g. Vietnam, resisted the invasion at the cost of over 1 million Vietnamese lives. The U.S. arrived in Iraq as the occupying force in Afghanistan and as avid supporters of the Israeli occupation of Palestinian territories.

When the British arrived in Iraq almost 100 years earlier, they promised that they had come to liberate the Iraqis from oppressive Ottoman rule. They proceeded to impose their own. In 2003, the British stormed into Iraq once again, this time with the U.S.-led coalition, again promising liberation from a despotic regime and a chance for a new democratic government for the Iraqi people.

The invaders appointed a handpicked set of compliant followers, the *Iraqi Governing Council* (IGC), who they assumed would be hailed as the leaders of the new Iraq. The Iraqis soon dismissed the IGC as irrelevant. Widespread unrest among the occupied Iraqis, along with an influx of some insurgents from surrounding Arab countries had sparked a campaign of armed insurrection against coalition forces.

In late May 2004 a 33-member interim government made its appearance. According to the June 2, 2004 *New York Times,* the new temporary rulers were selected by decisions "essentially negotiated between the United States and the Iraqi Governing Council." (see *Iraqi Governing Council, Iraqi National Congress*). Only about one-third of the new Iraqi government had spent any time under Saddam Hussein's regime. Five of the six leading posts were given to Iraqis who had been abroad for years. The June 10, 2004 *Boston Globe* reports, "At least two [cabinet members] are U.S. citizens. In addition to Prime Minister Iyad Allawi, who was involved in a CIA-backed attempt against Hussein, at least seven others were members of exile groups funded by the United States."

On June 8, 2004 the UN Security Council voted unanimously in favor of Resolution 1546 which ended the formal occupation of Iraq and supported "full sovereignty" for the interim government. On June 28, 2004 the *Coalition Provisional Authority,* in a small ceremony in the heavily guarded *Green Zone* in Baghdad, handed over that sovereignty. The "official" occupation was at an end— but the occupiers were still in place.

L. Paul Bremer III left behind some major restrictions on the interim government. Bremer had issued more than 100 orders and regulations, including creating and filling commissions to oversee communications, public broadcasting and securities markets. He also issued an edict that gave U.S. and other foreign contractors immunity from Iraqi law. The rules also included some good examples of micromanagement. According to the *Washington Post,* June 27, 2007 Bremer's orders "[impose] a new traffic code that stipulates the use of a car horn in 'emergency conditions only' and requires a driver to 'hold the steering wheel with both hands'."

The U.S.-led military force, then numbering 140,000, could use "all necessary measures" to bring peace and stability. It would be required to work in "partnership" with Iraq forces, practicing "close coordination and consultation" with Iraqi commanders.

The coalition forces, in the words of the UN resolution, had a mandate that would "expire after completion of the political process..." That referred to the plan to hold national elections by January 31, 2005, after which time an elected "Transnational Assembly" would draft a "permanent constitution" leading to a "constitutionally elected government by December 31, 2006" (see *democratization*).

The elections were held as planned. According to Felicity Arbuthnot (Commondreams.org) "international law expert Sabah Al Mukhtar, the London-based President of the League of Arab Lawyers maintains that the election (was) not only fatally flawed, it (was) illegal." He points out "Under the Vienna Convention an occupying force has no right to change composition of occupied territories socially, culturally, educationally or politically. This election was based on the laws laid down by the former 'Viceroy' Paul Bremer and is entirely unconstitutional."

Earlier (*Knight-Ridder,* May 9, 2004) U.S. Secretary of State Colin Powell had remarked "Obviously, because a large foreign military presence will still be required, under U.S. command, some would say, well, then you are not giving full sovereignty... But we are giving sovereignty, so that sovereignty can be used to say: 'We invite you to remain. It is a sovereign decision.'"

In early 2005 that military presence—by then 150,000 troops—appeared to be staying on indefinitely. Though details were hard to come by, it appeared that 12-14 military bases were being put in place across Iraq. Widely varying predictions of how long the U.S. military would occupy Iraq abounded (see *exit strategy*). Whatever the timetable for the withdrawal of at least some of those troops, the long term goal of the U.S.-led invasion of Iraq had always been the establishment of a permanent, powerful military presence there, and control over Iraq's vast oil reserves. The election results mattered only in determining how that would be accomplished.

Writer Tariq Ali, in *Bush in Babylon: The Recolonisation of Iraq*—his searing indictment of the latest occupation of Iraq—predicted in 2003: "The occupation is still in its infancy. Its aims are simplistic: to impose privatisation and a pro-western regime in Iraq. But its ability to do so permanently is circumscribed by the history and consciousness of the Iraqi people. This is not to imply that that whole country is desperate for a protracted war. If anything, the opposite is the case. If the occupation succeeds in stabilising the country, and if basic amenities are restored together with some semblance of normality, then a Vichy style operation staffed by local jackals could succeed, if only for a limited period."

Tariq Ali, a man with intimate knowledge of the Middle Eastern cultures and history, asks, "What if the Iraqis elect a government that insists on keeping oil under Iraqi control and demands the withdrawal of the occupation armies and U.S. bases? It might not happen immediately, but the medium-term possibility is always present. That would necessitate another regime change."

Oil-for-Food (OFF): a program designed and implemented by the United Nations to alleviate some of the enormous suffering of the Iraqi people caused by another UN program—economic *sanctions*—as well as by the devastation of the UN-supported 1991 U.S.-led attack on Iraq.

On August 6, 1990, four days after Iraq's invasion of Kuwait (see *Desert Storm*), the UN Security Council imposed strict sanctions on Iraq, which effectively cut off that country's access to the outside world. On January 15, 1991 the Council endorsed *Operation Desert Storm*, which destroyed much of the country's infrastructure.

After the March 3, 1991 ceasefire, the sanctions were to be maintained until Iraq was declared verifiably free of *weapons of mass destruction.* By August 1991, the UN, acknowledging the scale of the developing human disaster, stated "The Iraqi people may soon face a further imminent catastrophe, which could include epidemic and famine, if massive life-supporting needs are not rapidly met."

They proposed that Iraq be allowed to sell some of its oil to raise money for food and medicine—as well as for reparations for having invaded Kuwait—and to pay the UN's expenses, including weapons inspections.

The Iraqis rejected the offer, not willing to relinquish sovereignty over their oil resources, but by 1995 agreed to the plan in the face of massive starvation. According to the UN, between 1996 and May 28, 2003—shortly after yet another devastating invasion of Iraq in March, 2003 (see *Operation Iraqi Freedom*)—that country had received $28 billion worth of humanitarian supplies and equipment through the OFF.

What might seem to have been a generous accommodation to a country that had invaded a neighboring state, and was reluctant to allow UN weapons inspectors free access, was quite the opposite. Denis Halliday, who had served as a UN Assistant Secretary-General and Humanitarian Coordinator in Iraq since September 1997 submitted his resignation in September 1998. In an interview in the July 19, 2000 *Al-Ahram Weekly (*Cairo, Egypt) Halliday maintained, "The Oil-for-Food program was not designed to solve the crisis in Iraq...it was designed to stop further deterioration. But the fact is that Oil-for-Food has sustained the humanitarian crisis." He went on to cite "mortality rates of children under five years of age still remain at 5,000 per month, plus an additional 2,000-3,000 [other deaths]." The people were dying "because of bad water, inadequate diets, broken down hospital care and collapsed systems."

Halliday, a native of Ireland and a Quaker, resigned in disgust over the combined effects of the economic sanctions and the inadequate OFF program, which he said had led to "famine conditions." Hans von Sponek, a native of Germany, filled his position on October 26, 1998. In February 2000 Sponek resigned for the same reasons as Halliday. A few days later yet another senior UN humanitarian official—Jutta Burghardt, head of the World Food Program in Iraq—followed their lead and resigned as well. In April 2000 The American Friends Service Committee (www.afsc.org) nominated Denis Halliday for the 2000 Nobel

Peace Prize, along with Kathy Kelly. Cofounder of Voices in the Wilderness (www.vitw.org), Kathy Kelly had brought activists into Iraq to witness and report on the ravages of the Iraqi sanctions.

OFF remained, as did the sanctions, until after *Operation Iraqi Freedom.* The OFF was handed over to the *Coalition Provisional Authority* in November 2003, giving control over Iraqi oil to the U.S.-led *occupation* forces.

A scandal erupted in early 2004 as reports circulated regarding alleged corruption in the OFF program. According to the Inter Press Service, (April 12, 2004), there were allegations that "nearly three-quarters of the suppliers of food and medicine to Iraq jacked up their prices to pay 10 percent kickbacks to Iraqi oil exporters—while UN officials turned a blind eye." The June 2, 2004 *New York Times* reported that UN diplomats "said it was what one called 'common knowledge' that member states were ignoring the widespread complaints about kickbacks and payoffs by Saddam Hussein's government so that their companies could continue being part of the lucrative program." On October 7, 2004 the *Times* summarized a detailed report from Charles A. Duelfer, then the top American arms inspector, revealing that Saddam Hussein had "created a web of front companies and used shadowy deals with foreign governments, corporations and officials to amass $11 billion in illicit revenue." Duelfer disclosed that Iraq directed "lucrative oil vouchers to Russia, France and Belarus and other countries."

UN Secretary Kofi Annan appointed a panel in April 2004 to investigate the charges. The panel estimated that it would need at least a year and $30 million to "determine whether the charges are justified."

Operation: a war, or a phase of a war, under an assumed name. Labeling military offensives for much more than convenience has its origins in World War I, when the Germans tried to inspire their battle-weary *soldiers* with fanciful names for offensives such as "Mars," "Achilles," and "Archangel."

The U.S. applied code names to hundreds of various phases of World War II, mainly for security reasons. The British, under Winston Churchill, were more imaginative in their choices. Churchill, early to understand the public relations value of labels, warned against names "that disparage...in any way, [or] enable some widow or mother to say that her son was killed in am operation called 'Bunnyhug' or 'Ballyhoo'."

Near the war's end, the War Department (see *Department of Defense*) tried out the nickname "Operation Crossroads" for the 1946 atomic bomb tests on Bikini atoll. The name met with general approval, and by the time of the Korean War Lieutenant General Matthew Ridgeway was busy assigning aggressive names— including "Thunderbolt," "Roundup," "Ripper," and "Courageous".

Lieutenant Colonel Gregory Sieminski wrote a detailed history, *The Art of Naming Operations,* in the August 1995 issue of *Parameters*, the U.S. Army War College quarterly. He relates how General Ridgeway was proud of his choice of the nickname "Operation Killer" for a major counteroffensive. The Army Chief of Staff, however, had objected that "the word 'killer'...struck an unpleasant note as far as public relations was concerned." Ridgeway defended his choice, saying " I am by nature opposed to any effort to 'sell' war to people as an only mildly unpleasant business that requires very little in the way of blood."

Ridgeway's philosophy was shared by at least one Vietnam War officer, who came up with "Operation Masher" for a 1st Cavalry Division assault. President Johnson "angrily protested that it did not reflect 'pacification emphasis.'" General William Westmoreland speculated that Johnson "objected...because the connotation of violence provided a focus for carping war critics."

The modern military now has a set of clear guidelines for

nicknaming operations. The Department of Defense, warning that improperly selected names "can be counterproductive," specifies that names must not "express a degree of bellicosity inconsistent with traditional American ideals or current foreign policy." In the last 20 years the military has had ample opportunity to inspire the American public and the U.S. soldiers by operations such as "Urgent Fury"—the 1983 U.S. invasion of the tiny island of Grenada—and "Just Cause," the U.S. invasion of Panama.

The U.S.-led attacks on Iraq in 1991 and 2003 afforded a splendid opportunity to masquerade bloody conquests. From *Operation Desert Shield* and *Operation Desert Storm* to *Operation Iraqi Freedom*, selling war by brand name gained a secure place in the pantheon of propaganda.

Operation Desert Shield: the name given to the massive buildup of coalition forces prior to the *Gulf War*. The title was chosen —true to the spirit of naming a military *operation*— because it reflected the purported attempt to protect Saudi Arabia from an Iraqi invasion.

As *soldiers* and equipment began pouring into the Gulf region in August 1990, resulting eventually in a coalition force of nearly 700,000, a meticulous search began for a title that would convey a favorable image for this largest deployment since the Vietnam era.

Lieutenant Colonel Gregory Sieminski, writing in the August 1995 issue of *Parameters*, the U.S. Army War College quarterly explains, "Central Command (CENTCOM) staff officers managed to compile a list of candidate nicknames three pages long, from which General Norman Schwarzkopf initially selected Peninsula Shield." After due consideration this was rejected, along with "Crescent Shield," in favor of "Desert Shield"—a title which suggested that this was a 'defensive mission" using a shield against the bloody sword of Iraq's aggression. This "played well with domestic and international observers...garnering support for the operation."

As the war began on January 16, 1991 with the coalition bombing assault dubbed "Instant Thunder," "Desert Shield" morphed into *Operation Desert Storm.*

Operation Desert Storm: the fanciful name given to the *Gulf War,* a title more grandiose than "war" that diminished none of the suffering. Having recognized the popularity of the nickname *Desert Shield*—applied to the deployment of coalition military *forces* in the Persian Gulf prior to the 1991 war—the theme continued in labeling as "Desert Storm" the overall massive assault on Iraq. This meshed neatly with the initial aerial bombardment ("Instant Thunder"*)* the ground attack ("Desert Saber"), the later redeployment ("Desert Farewell") and the donation of leftover military food supplies to poor U.S. citizens ("Desert Share").

Operation Enduring Freedom: The first major step in the *endless war* against global terrorism. This massive U.S. and British bombardment of Afghanistan began in October 2001.

In 1979, after the Soviet Union had invaded Afghanistan, the U.S. Central Intelligence Agency (CIA), in collaboration with Pakistan's Inter Services Intelligence (ISI) funded and recruited thousands of Muslim fighters from dozens of countries to bolster the Afghan resistance. The CIA hoped that their support would fuel a holy war against the Soviets. Afghanistan suffered through 10 years of warfare before the Soviets finally withdrew, leaving behind continuous civil war.

Arundhati Roy, in the *Guardian*/London, September 29, 2001 recounts "The CIA continued to pour in money and military equipment but...more money was needed. The ISI set up hundreds of heroin laboratories across Afghanistan. The Pakistan-Afghanistan border had become the biggest producer of heroin in the world, and the single biggest source of heroin on American streets. The annual profits...were ploughed back into training and arming militants...In 1995, the Taliban...fought its way to power in Afghanistan. It was funded by the ISI, that old cohort of the CIA. The Taliban unleashed a reign of terror."

Afghanistan, ravaged by decades of vicious fighting—its economy ruined and its people weakened by crushing poverty—was to be America's first target in the GWOT. The Taliban were sheltering Osama bin Laden, the man held to be responsible for the 9/11 atrocities, and Al Qaeda, his terrorist network. Terrified by the prospect of an American attack, upwards of one million people fled to the Pakistan border. The UN estimated at least eight million other innocent civilians also needed emergency assistance.

On October 7, 2001 American and British forces unleashed an aerial assault on Afghanistan. Initially, Bombers and Tomahawk cruise missiles were used, followed by *cluster bombs* and *daisy cutters.* By early November the Americans were *carpet bombing* their targets. On November 25, U.S Marines arrived to begin the ground offensive.

Independent estimates of Afghan civilian deaths from the bombing range from 1,000 to 4,000 (see *collateral damage*). Within three weeks after the bombing had begun, U.S. planes, flying at 30,000 feet dropped 1,000,000 packets of food and medicine marked with an American flag for whoever might find them. Thomas Gonnet, representing Action Against Hunger (www.actionagainsthunger.org) in Afghanistan called the airdrops an "act of marketing." The food packets were bright yellow—the same color as the dangerous unexploded *bomblets* scattered across the landscape, left over from the U.S. cluster bombs.

President George W. Bush has said that "failure is not an option" in U.S. policy towards Afghanistan. Certainly the U.S. did not fail in killing many Taliban fighters and destroying their bases. But according to the January 2004 Human Rights Watch

World Report, "Unless the United States, the de facto leader of the international community in Afghanistan, develops and implements policies that take into account and protect the rights and well-being of Afghans, failure is a real possibility."

Human Rights Watch (HRW) (www.hrw.org) says that "Afghans know that it wasn't humanitarian concern" that prompted Operation Enduring Freedom. They "fear that the world outside will fail them and banish them again to insecurity, conflict and chaos." HRW maintains, " the signs are troubling. Despite the initial enthusiasm for rebuilding the country, the world seems to have forgotten them...While Iraq received...$26 billion in reconstruction aid in 2003, Afghanistan received less than $1 billion." This, despite the fact that most estimates suggest that "at least...$15-20 billion dollars will be needed over the next five years.

Furthermore, "Warlords, militias and brigands dominate the entire country, including the city of Kabul...Poppy cultivation has soared to new heights, providing billions of dollars to the Taliban, warlords, and petty criminals who resist the central government." By the summer of 2004 the U.S. had 17,000 troops in Afghanistan, along with 6,500 NATO troops. HRW says "the mandate of these troops is to combat the Taliban, not to provide security for Afghans. In fact, as of this writing, these troops freely engage and support local warlords and military commanders who will ostensibly fight the Taliban, with little or no regard for how the warlords treat the local citizenry."

HRW, a highly respected international human rights advocate concludes that in order not to "lose the peace" in Afghanistan, "The U.S. military must cease cooperation with regional warlords outside the purview of the central government. Further, "U.S. military forces must abide by international human rights and humanitarian law while conducting operations in Afghanistan. The use of excessive force...in residential areas has generated

tremendous resentment against the international community...
Continuing in this manner is to court failure."

The October 9, 2004 election in Afghanistan gave the U.S.-
backed Hamid Karzai a landslide victory. The *Los Angeles Times*
reported on November 23, 2004 "The Taliban...still exist in the
countryside, and the bulk of that country is still run, de facto, by
competing warlords dependent on the opium trade, which now
accounts for 60% of the Afghanistan economy...the country
produces 87% of the world's opium."

Christian Parent, in *The Nation* (November 15, 2004)
writes, "Given current dynamics, Afghanistan will remain a weak
and fragmented state...its economy broken, its common people
mercilessly exploited."

Operation Infinite Justice: the name given to the U.S.
military build-up in the Persian Gulf in response to the September
11, 2001 attacks on the World Trade Center and the Pentagon. The
title brought immediate objections from Muslims who hold that
only God, or Allah, can mete out infinite justice.

"Infinite justice" is a term familiar to conservative evangelical
Christians. The U.S. Christian Apologetics and Research Ministry,
whose aim is to "equip Christians with good information on
doctrine" says that the term refers to God's exacting a "terrible
price" to purify from sin "all His created humanity" (see
crusade).

On September 25, 2001 Defense Secretary Donald Rumsfeld
announced that the administration, sensitive to these issues, would
change the name to *Operation Enduring Freedom.* He stressed
that this name referred only to the military build-up, and not the
entire U.S. war on international terrorism. Rumsfeld added that
the new name implied that "this is not a quick fix...it'll take years,
I suspect" (see *endless war*).

Columnist Norman Solomon, in *Media Beat* (October 29,

2002) commented, "The replacement, Enduring Freedom, was well received in the U.S. mass media, an irony-free zone where only the untowardly impertinent might suggest that some people had no choice other than enduring the Pentagon's freedom to bomb."

Operation Iraqi Freedom: a devastating military assault on Iraq carried out in early 2003 by a U.S.-led *coalition of the willing.* The attack was "illegal" according to United Nations Secretary General Kofi Annan (the *Guardian/UK,* September 16, 2004). The announced aim of the war was principally to find and destroy Saddam Hussein's *weapons of mass destruction* and prevent his regime from further aiding terrorist activities. The actual motives, in the planning stages for years, were to establish a U.S. military presence in Iraq as an early stage of a move towards America's absolute global dominance (see *Rebuilding America's Defenses, hegemony*) and to gain control over Iraq's rich oil reserves.

Three hundred thousand troops—mostly U.S., some British, and a few Australian and Polish—launched a massive air and ground attack on Iraq beginning on March 20, 2003. Iraq, already weakened by years of *sanctions*, and still suffering from the massive destruction of the 1991 *Gulf War,* had few defenses against the military might of the invaders. The "official" *end of hostilities* was May 1, 2003, but violent opposition to the subsequent *occupation* continued (see *liberation, mission accomplished*).

During the war, 109 U.S. *soldiers* were killed, and 545 were injured (see *casualties).* Twenty-nine others died from "non-hostile causes" (see *friendly fire, suicide*). From May 1, 2003 to February 2, 2005—the date of President Bush's State of the Union address—1436 U.S. soldiers were killed, and 10,770 had been wounded. There were 336 non-hostile deaths—mostly from accidents.

Accurate data on collateral deaths and injuries as a result of

Operation Iraqi Freedom are difficult to ascertain. However, on October 29, 2004 the noted British medical journal *The Lancet* published a study by a research team at the renowned Johns Hopkins University in Baltimore. They concluded, after extensive interviews across Iraq, that at least 100,000 Iraqi civilians died as a consequence of the 2003 U.S.-led attack on Iraq—mostly from bombing or rocket attacks. The number of Iraqi soldiers killed is not known, but numbered in the many thousands (see *body count*).

All of these deaths, each a personal tragedy, were regarded by the Bush administration as a regrettable but necessary price to pay for a grandiose scheme which had long been an unfulfilled dream among an influential cluster of George W. Bush advisors and administration officials.

Those included Paul Wolfowitz, Bush's deputy secretary of defense, who had written the 1992 *Defense Planning Guidance*—a blueprint for unilateral military action to establish the U.S. as the world's only superpower (see *hyperpower, Pax Americana*). Dick Cheney, who became George W. Bush's Vice President, had served as secretary of defense during the 1991 Gulf War. According to CBSNEWS.com, (April 18, 2004) Cheney "was the driving force in the White House to get Saddam Hussein...to him, Saddam was unfinished business." In 2000—before Bush took office—Cheney, along with Wolfowitz, Donald Rumsfeld, Jeb Bush (George Bush's brother), I. Lewis Libby, Stephen Cambone and others had a hand in putting together the document: *Rebuilding America's Defenses: Strategy, Forces and Resources for a New American Century* (RAD).

Among other radical proposals, RAD calls for "American military dominance" through unilateral aggression against anyone standing in the way of America's *national interests* (see *Project for the New American Century*). This document is considered to be the inspiration for the 2002 *National Security Strategy.* Rumsfeld would become Secretary of Defense, Libby the chief of staff for Cheney, and Cambone would serve as undersecretary of defense for intelligence.

In 1998 Wolfowitz, joined by, among others, Donald Rumsfeld, had written to President Clinton urging him to "turn your administration's attention to implementing a strategy for removing Saddam's regime from power"(see *Committee for Peace and Security in the Gulf*). Clinton was willing only to kill Iraqis through continued, cruel sanctions and regular bombings (see *no-fly zones*). Once they came into power in Washington in 2001, Wolfowitz, Rumsfeld, Cheney and their like-minded colleagues (see rightweb.irc-online.org) were well positioned to try to achieve a takeover of Iraq—and the tragedy of September 11, 2001 gave them the perfect opportunity to do so.

President George W. Bush, who was described by Senator Richard Gephardt (D-MO) on CBS' "Face the Nation" as "a nice man. But he doesn't have experience. He doesn't have knowledge. He doesn't have curiosity," was quick to display the courage of other people's convictions. Bush's Former Treasury Secretary Paul O'Neil, in *The Price of Loyalty*—written by Ron Suskind—revealed that no one in the 2001 National Security meetings had questioned why Iraq should be invaded. O'Neil told CBS News' "60 Minutes" (January 11, 2004), "It was all about finding a way to do it. That was the tone of it. The President saying 'Go find me a way to do this.'"

Intensive planning apparently began very soon after 9/11. Noted journalist Bob Woodward's April 2004 book *Plan of Attack* is a detailed, behind-the-scenes portrayal of the machinations to prepare for and sell an invasion of Iraq. Woodward's account is highly credible because it is based on extensive interviews with 75 of the key participants, including two extensive interviews with the President.

In late November 2001, according to Woodward, the President

instructed Defense Secretary Rumsfeld to draw up a secret war plan. Rumsfeld passed the order along to General Tommy Franks, and gave him a "blank check." By July 2002 the clandestine planning needed money—$700 million—which quickly was siphoned from a supplemental appropriation Congress had passed for the war in Afghanistan (see *Operation Enduring Freedom*).

Public support was needed before open preparation for an invasion on Iraq could get underway. This support was expertly elicited by an elaborate synthesis of the prevailing fears of terrorist attacks with the always powerful threat of *weapons of mass destruction.* Iraq was identified as an "imminent threat" to the safety and security not only of its Middle East neighbors, but to the United States as well. Although the resulting enthusiasm stirred up among many Americans for war was counterbalanced by massive worldwide opposition to an assault on Iraq, the Bush administration disregarded the latter as mere *focus groups.*

President Bush, in an October 2002 speech in Cincinnati, Ohio stated that Iraq is a "grave threat to peace...it possesses chemical and biological weapons" (see *biological weapons, chemical weapons*). Bush added "Iraq possesses ballistic missiles with a likely range of hundreds of miles...[and] a growing fleet of manned and unmanned aerial vehicles that could be used to disperse chemical and biological weapons across broad areas." Further, "[Iraq] is seeking nuclear weapons...does it make any sense for the world to wait to confront him?" He warned, "We cannot wait for the clear proof—the smoking gun—that could come in the form of a mushroom cloud" (see *weapons of mass destruction*).

While that warning might have seemed somewhat contradictory coming from the President of a country with the world's largest nuclear arsenal, and from someone actively engaged in supporting research and development of newer, battlefield-ready *nuclear weapons,* the message was clear. There would be war.

In addition to stoking fears of an impending nuclear attack, Bush also told of "urgent concern about Saddam Hussein's links to international terrorist groups" (see *global war on terrorism*). He said "Iraq and Al Qaeda share a common enemy—the United States of America...[their] contacts go back a decade...Confronting the threat posed by Iraq is crucial to winning the war on terror."

The alleged Iraq-Al Qaeda connection, reinforced by Vice-President Dick Cheney and other administration officials, convinced a majority of the American public that the 9/11 attacks were somehow linked to Al Qaeda and Saddam Hussein. In its July 2004 report the 9/11 commission appointed by Congress found no evidence "indicating Iraq cooperated with Al Qaeda in developing or carrying out any attacks against the United States."

A study published in the September 2004 issue of *Foreign Policy* reveals that "between September 2001 and October 2002 ten key players in the debate over Iraq presented at least 21 rationales for going to war." The then National Security Advisor Condoleezza Rice joined with others in at least ten of these, including "to further the war on terror", "Iraq's violations of UN resolutions", and "to disarm Iraq."

In an op-ed in the January 23, 2003 *New York Times,* Rice warned that Iraq had "failed to account for or explain (their) efforts to get uranium from abroad", a widely discredited claim (see *yellowcake*). During the January 2005 Senate confirmation hearings for Rice's nomination to become Secretary of State, Senator Carl Levin (D-MI) spoke against approving her because of her "participation in the distortions and exaggerations of intelligence that the Administration used to initiate the war in Iraq." Condoleezza Rice's nomination was approved by the Senate on January 26, 2005 by an 85-13 vote.

These growing numbers of rationales for invading Iraq continued in many other public forums, including the 2003

State of the Union speech. What was left unsaid was that the information on which much of the announced threat was based was vague, uncertain, and in some instances, simply false. "Crucial" information had been gladly supplied by Ahmad Chalabi, longtime protégé of Paul Wolfowitz. Chalabi was slated to become the leader of the new Iraqi government after the war, but this ambition was frustrated when he was rejected by the Iraqis after the invasion, and ultimately by the U.S. (see *Iraqi Governing Council, Iraqi National Congress*). The fact that Chalabi freely admitted to supplying the U.S. with false information about Iraq didn't help his cause.

However, by late 2004 Chalabi emerged as a vocal champion of the Iraqi Shiite Muslims. After the January 30, 2005 elections he presented himself as a candidate for prime minister of Iraq as part of the victorious United Iraqi Alliance (see *democratization*).

Secretary of State Colin Powell addressed the United Nations Security Council on February 5, 2003. He was there to make the case that Iraq had failed to fulfill UN Resolution 1441, passed on November 8, 2003. This resolution demanded that Iraq give up its alleged weapons of mass destruction or face "serious consequences." The Bush administration already had decided that the U.S. would administer those "consequences" on its own authority. Powell's presentation included many of the same accusations concerning Iraqi weapons of mass destruction and terrorist links. The coalition forces were already massing in the Gulf region. George W. Bush, who had said in his Cincinnati speech "America is a friend to the people of Iraq" would begin to bomb them mercilessly on March 20, 2003 (see *Shock and Awe*).

During the year after the invasion, as the bloody occupation wore on, not only were no weapons of mass destruction found— and it became even more obvious that the bombing of the World Trade Center and other Al Qaeda atrocities had not originated from Iraq—the Bush administration disengaged itself from its original rationale for Operation Iraqi Freedom.

As early as April 25,2003, during the late stages of the war, John Cochran reported on ABCNEWS.com: "Officials inside government and advisors outside [said] the administration emphasized the danger of Saddam's weapons to gain the legal justification for war from the United Nations and to stress the danger at home to Americans. 'We were not lying' said one official. 'But it was a matter of emphasis.'"

Faced with a systematic dismantling of their "evidence" for the war, the U.S—according to the administration—had been in the business of *liberation* and *democratization* all along. The President announced in a speech at The National Endowment for Democracy on November 6, 2003: "The United States has adopted a new policy, a forward strategy of freedom in the Middle East... The advance of freedom is the calling of our time; it is the calling of our country."

Operation Iraqi Freedom evolved into, according to Bush's 2004 State of the Union address, a means of "delivering justice to the violent." Then, as he entered his second term in office, the President delivered an inaugural address in which the war in Iraq was not mentioned by name. He did mention that "Our country has accepted obligations that are difficult to fulfill and would be dishonorable to abandon" (see *quagmire*).

Death, destruction, and occupation were to be the hallmarks of America's role in the world, whatever the reasons.

P

"I have never known a peace made, even the most advantageous, that was not censured as inadequate, and the makers condemned as injudicious or corrupt. 'Blessed are the peacemakers' is, I suppose, to be understood in the other world; for in this they are frequently cursed."

Benjamin Franklin

Patriot missile: a U.S. missile used in the *Gulf War* and hailed by its manufacturer and by the Pentagon for its stellar performance. It didn't work as advertised.

During the 1991 Gulf War, TV viewers watched in awe as Patriot missiles streaked across the sky and appeared to intercept Iraqi Scud missiles, destroying them in spectacular explosions. U.S. officials, including then Secretary of Defense Dick Cheney and Generals Colin Powell and Norman Schwarzkopf were ecstatic about this awesome defensive weapon. President George H.W. Bush told a cheering crowd at the Andover, MA Raytheon plant—makers of the Patriot—"Forty-one Scuds engaged, 42 intercepted. Thank God for the Patriot Missile." General Schwarzkopf said during the war "the Patriot's success, of course, is known to everyone. It's 100 percent..."

Soon after the war, the story began to change. Independent investigations found little proof that the Patriot missiles had even limited effectiveness. A U.S. General Accounting Office study claimed that the Patriot success rate did not exceed 9 percent, while a 1993 U.S. Armed Services Committee Report concluded, "A post war review of photographs cannot produce even a single confirmed kill of a Scud missile."

The debate has continued ever since. Raytheon spokesperson David Shea told the *Boston Globe* (January 13, 2001), "After extensive analysis, the Army has steadfastly maintained that the Patriot's performance during the Gulf War was excellent." However, the same *Globe* report cites the blunt comment by former Secretary of Defense William Cohen had made a few days earlier, "The Patriot didn't work."

Despite the controversy, the Patriot continued as a key antimissile weapon in the Army's arsenal. Raytheon has sold millions of dollars worth of Patriots to such countries as Israel, Saudi Arabia, and Japan. During *Operation Iraqi Freedom* the U.S. used a newer, "far superior" version of the Patriot, the PAC-3, made by Lockheed Martin.

Despite the $3 billion spent by the Pentagon to upgrade the Patriot, the newer version, according to *USA Today* (April 15, 2003) "apparently downed at least two allied fighter jets and almost brought down a third since fighting began..." Three aviators were killed in these incidents. The *USA Today* report continued "At a Senate hearing Wednesday, Lt. Gen. Ronald Kadish, head of the Pentagon's Missile Defense Agency, said...overall, the performance of the [new] Patriot has been 'very, very good.'"

patriotism: generally understood as a devoted loyalty to and support for one's country. This notion is particularly dangerous when one identifies one's country as the prevailing government. In that case the ideal patriot abets in and obeys the orders of the state, including its injunctions to wage war. Those who rebel against the decisions of the state are considered unpatriotic (see *dissent*).

Professor, writer and social activist Noam Chomsky, in a November 2002 ZNet interview (www.zmag.org) pointed out that "what 'patriotism' means depends on how we view the society." He cites the "totalitarian" view that "identifies the state with the society, its people, and its culture." This contrasts with the "democratic" philosophy that identifies patriotism as "commitment to the welfare and improvement of the society, the people, and its culture."

The former attitude, prevalent in the U.S. today, was echoed in President George W. Bush's warning, shortly after 9/11, "Either you are with us or you are with the terrorists." His words were directed at the nations of the world, but the simple distinction he expressed soon became a litmus test for American patriotism. This totalitarian interpretation, according to Chomsky, "is one of the worst maladies of human history."

Noted historian Howard Zinn, writing in the April 13, 2003 *Newsday* lamented "At some point soon the United States will declare a military victory in Iraq. As a patriot, I will not celebrate. I will mourn the dead—the American GIs, and also the Iraqi dead, of which there will be many, many more...As a patriot, contemplating the dead GIs, should I comfort myself (as, understandably their families do) with the thought "They died for their country?' But I would be lying to myself. Those who die in this war will not die for their country. They will die for their government."

Zinn points out that, according to the principles of the Declaration of Independence, governments are "artificial creations, established by the people." What must come first are "the people, the ideals of the sanctity of human life, and the promotion of liberty...War is almost always...a breaking of those promises. It does not enable the pursuit of happiness but brings despair and grief."

Experienced war correspondent Chris Hedges, in *War is a Force That Gives us Meaning* comments on the troubled mix of the totalitarian understanding of patriotism and the road to war: "Patriotism, often a thinly veiled form of collective self-worship, celebrates our goodness, our ideals, our mercy and bemoans the perfidiousness of those who hate us...War makes the world understandable, a black and white tableau of them and us."

The reality of war is far from the world of the "patriotic" bumper sticker. Hedges writes "There is among many who fight in a war a sense of shame, one that is made worse by the patriotic drivel used to justify the act of killing in war. Those who seek meaning in patriotism do not want to hear the truth of war, wary of bursting the bubble...The shame and alienation of combat soldiers, coupled with the indifference to the truth of war by those who were not there, reduces many societies to silence. It seems better to forget."

Pax Americana: literally, an *"American peace"* in which the world will remain at "peace," under the control of the global presence of U.S. military might. This vision of the future, held by the George W. Bush administration, likens the coming period of American world domination to the "Pax Romana"—that 200 year period during the Roman Empire beginning in 27 B.C. with the reign of Augustus Caesar.

Webster's Dictionary defines Pax Romana as "The terms of peace imposed by ancient Rome on its dominions" or "Any state of peace imposed by a stronger nation on a weaker or defeated nation." The term "Pax Americana" appears repeatedly—interchangeably with "American peace"—in the 2000 *Rebuilding America's Defenses: Strategy, Forces and Resources for a New Century"*(RAD), widely regarded as the blueprint for the White House 2002 *National Security Strategy* (NSS).

Historians often have used *"*Pax Americana" to refer to the period following World War II, in which the U.S. was the dominant military, political, and economic nation, and worked towards the rehabilitation of Europe and Japan. The current use of the term has an ominous edge that moves its proponents into a more aggressive mode.

The RAD states in its introduction "This report proceeds from the belief that America should seek to preserve and extend its position of global leadership by maintaining the preeminence of U.S. military forces...At no time in history has the international security order been as conducive to American interests and ideals.

The challenge for the coming century is to preserve and enhance this "American peace." On the same theme, the "strategic goal" of the "21st century" is to "preserve the Pax Americana."

The report repeatedly stresses, "U.S. forces have other vital roles to play in building an enduring American peace. The presence of American forces in critical regions around the world is the visible expression of the extent of America's status as a superpower and as the guarantor of liberty, peace and stability" (see *critical regions, forward-based forces*).

The RAD was the product of the *Project for the New American Century* (PNAC), a Washington, D.C.-based conservative think tank, founded in 1997. Its goal is to work towards the establishment of a worldwide "American peace" or "Pax Americana" —a "peace" marked by unilateral military aggression against any country that the U.S. government decides is not acting in America's *national interests*. The PNAC "Statement of Principles" signers included Jeb Bush, Dick Cheney, Paul Wolfowitz, and Donald Rumsfeld.

The Bush administration's 2002 *National Security Strategy* echoes the PNAC philosophy, but in somewhat more muted language. Instead of "American peace" the document says, "The U.S. National Security Strategy will be based on a strictly American internationalism that reflects the union of our values and our national interests."

The NSS may have dropped specific references to a "Pax Americana" but it is true to the concept. The document, in the words of Jay Bookman (*Atlanta Journal-Constitution*, September 29, 2002) "dismisses deterrence as a Cold War relic and instead talks of 'convincing or compelling states to accept their sovereign responsibilities...In essence, it lays out a plan for permanent U.S. military and economic domination of every region on the globe, unfettered by international treaty or concern."

Jonathan Schell, in *The Unconquerable World: Power, Violence, and the Will of the People* eloquently warns that this policy of unilateral military domination may be fatal. It "marks a decisive choice of force and coercion over cooperation and consent as the mainstay of the American response to the disorders of the time... If the wealthy and powerful use globalization to systematize and exacerbate exploitation of the poor and powerless: if the poor and powerless react with terrorism and other forms of violence; if the nuclear powers insist on holding on to and threatening to use their chosen weapons of mass destruction; if more nations then develop nuclear or biological or chemical arsenals in response and threaten to use them; if these weapons one day fall, as seems likely, into the hands of terrorists; and if the United States continues to pursue an Augustan policy, then the stage will be set for catastrophe."

pockets: small groups of the *enemy* who continue to resist. They are to be attacked and killed and wounded (see *eliminate, mopping up*). Note the following media reports:

"Sporadic U.S. shelling backed up their insistence that they will go on attacking pockets of resistance, which seem to be concentrated in the north of the town..." (Reuters, May 2, 2004)

"U.S. Marines destroy pockets of resistance in Umm Qasr. [They] waged a four-hour firefight with pockets of Iraqi troops in the southern city..." (CNN.com, March 23, 2003)

pounded: to inflict severe damage to objects, and deliver death and suffering to people. Note the following media accounts:

"U.S. troops battling insurgents in West Baghdad pounded rebel positions with artillery fire Monday night..."(foxnews.com, May 3, 2004)

"Coalition air strikes pounded Iraqi front-line positions Wednesday in...northern Iraq." (CNN.com, March 26, 2003)

"Coalition warplanes struck Iraqi positions in Northern Iraq and pounded Baghdad-controlled military targets on southern routes toward the capital..." (foxnews.com, April 7, 2003)

precision-guided munitions: *smart bombs* and missiles that are sent off to kill, directed by often highly technical guidance systems. They were introduced to great acclaim during the 1991 *Gulf War*, and later versions were used in Afghanistan in 2002 and in the 2003 *Operation Iraqi Freedom.*

About 6-7% of the 256,000 bombs dropped in the Gulf War were fitted out with small television video camera or infrared cameras. These transmit pictures to an operator, who then sends signals which adjust movable steering fins fitted to the bombs, or commands the bomb to automatically keep the target in view as the bomb falls. Videotapes from the bomb cameras were nightly TV entertainment during the *Gulf War*, as rapt viewers saw a "bomb's eye view" of the approaching target, followed by an explosion. The targets shown were typically buildings or vehicles, and their exciting demolition appeared divorced from the killing and wounding of the human occupants or those people nearby.

Of the 27,000 bombs used in the 2003 Operation Iraqi Freedom, 68% were of the precision-guided variety. Many of them employed advanced control systems (at $20,000 apiece) fitted to *dumb bombs*. These systems are guided by Global Positioning System (GPS) receivers, which collect satellite signals, informing the bomb's computers of its orientation.

Lasers lead other bombs. The operator hits a target with a laser beam, and the bomb (at $120,000 apiece) heads along the path of the reflected beam.

According to *Continuing Collateral Damage: The Health and Environment Costs of War on Iraq 2003 (working paper no.1)*, (see www.medact.org) "About 68% of the munitions used in the 2003 war on Iraq were precision-guided, compared with 6.5% in 1991. Yet the 2003 conflict resulted in more civilian casualties. The Project on Defense Alternative's report found that 'the ratio of civilian to military deaths is almost twice as high as it was in the last Gulf War in 1991.' Moreover, the number of civilian facilities hit as well as the number of friendly fire incidents proves that precision guidance is not always capable of delivering 'surgical strikes' that minimize human casualties" (see *casualties, collateral damage, friendly fire*).

Many things can go wrong with these weapons, and do. Moveable bomb fins fail, laser beams may not penetrate clouds or smoke, heavy winds may move weapons off-course, and human error may intervene. The Pentagon has admitted that ten percent of precision-guided weapons go astray (The *Guardian*/UK, April 2, 2003). Moreover, in *Operation Iraqi Freedom* many air strikes were aimed at targets nearly densely populated areas.

Precision-guided munitions in general do kill less indiscriminately than their "dumb" counterparts, with some glaring exceptions (see *launch success rate*). However, when they go astray, their guidance systems may send them even further from their targets, for example, into a crowded marketplace, or an apartment building. In any case, emphasis on the technical wizardry of these lethal weapons obscures the fact that they wound and kill men, women and children for whom the categories of civilians, collateral damage, soldiers, or enemy are ultimately irrelevant.

preemptive war: a war initiated because the aggressor claims to have certain knowledge of a specific, imminent, serious threat to its *national interests.* President George W. Bush cited such a threat as justification for invading Iraq in 2003 (see *Operation Iraqi Freedom*). However, that war was actually a *preventive war*—the application of a doctrine with even more serious consequences—which condones a war because of the assumption of a mere possibility of a serious threat sometime in the future (see *deterrence, assertive disarmament*).

The 2002 U.S. *National Security Strategy* states "America will act against...emerging threats before they are fully formed... we will not hesitate to act alone, if necessary, to exercise our right of self defense by acting preemptively." At the June, 2002 West Point commencement President Bush told the graduates "If we wait for threats to fully materialize, we will have waited too long... We must take the battle to the enemy." His audience cheered (see *Academies*).

Preemption generally is equated with the notion of self-defense. Even if one assumes a war can be justified (see *just war*) there are perils in preemption. Richard K. Betts, Director of the Institute for War and Peace Studies, Columbia University, writing in the April 1, 2003 *Ethics in International Affairs,* warns, " It is rarely possible to be sure that enemy preparations for war are definite, or are aggressively motivated, rather than precautionary reactions to rising tension and fear...If preemption becomes a regular practice...the strategy then may become self-defeating as it increases instability and insecurity."

If war is an acceptable option, killing in the name of one's *national interests* inevitably will claim legitimacy as preemptive or preventive. The global cycle of violence will continue, growing ever more lethal (see *deterrence, nuclear weapons*).

preparing the battlefield: killing the *enemy* and destroying their vehicles and equipment, in advance of a major assault, in order to intimidate the enemy and diminish their military resources. For example:

"[The U.S.] is also preparing the battlefield for future offensive actions by those [Northern Alliance] forces...United States warplanes bombed Taliban front line positions north of Kabul on Monday." (CNN.com, November 6, 2001)

"Rear Adm. John Stufflebeem...said much of the U.S. bombing is designed to soften up the Taliban for the Northern

Alliance. Stufflebeem said the bombing was 'preparing the battlefield' for future action by opposition forces." (foxnews.com, November 6, 2001)

"U.S. warplanes have struck targets in southern Iraq, preparing the battlefield ahead of a major move by U.S.-led ground forces massed in Kuwait." (ABC newsonline, March 21, 2003)

preventive war: a war initiated because the aggressor claims that its differences with the *enemy* are serious and unresolvable and, given enough time, the enemy will mobilize sufficient military strength to attack. The aggressor concludes that it is better to destroy the enemy early rather than risk a more dangerous war later (see *deterrence, assertive disarmament*).

The U.S. claims to have launched a *preemptive war* against Iraq in 2003 (see *Operation Iraqi Freedom*). A preemptive war is one initiated because the aggressor claims to have certain knowledge of a specific, imminent, serious threat to its *national interests.* Many analysts regard the 2003 U.S.-led assault on Iraq as a preventive, and not preemptive war, because the supposed threat of Iraqi *weapons of mass destruction* was a fiction. However, in the final analysis, *Operation Iraqi Freedom* was simply a blatant war of aggression in order to establish U.S. control over Iraq and its abundant oil supplies.

Project for the New American Century (PNAC): a group of political conservatives who have taken it upon themselves to declare ownership of the twenty-first century in the name of the United States.

In their own words, PNAC, established in 1997, is a "non-profit, educational organization dedicated to a few fundamental propositions: that American leadership is good both for America and for the world; that such leadership requires military strength, diplomatic energy and commitment to moral principle; and that too few political leaders today are making the case for global leadership."

The PNAC "Statement of Principles" calls for "increas(ed) defense spending," a need to "challenge regimes hostile to our interests and values," and a call to "accept America's unique role in preserving and extending an international order friendly to our security, our prosperity, and our principles" (see *national interests*).

Many of the 25 charter members of PNAC would soon go on to influential positions in the George W. Bush administration— such as Vice President Dick Cheney, Secretary of Defense Donald Rumsfeld, Deputy Secretary of Defense Paul Wolfowitz, and I. Lewis Libby, Cheney's chief of staff. Others remain notable conservative gadflies, including William J. Bennett, Gary Bauer, and Steve Forbes (see www.newamericancentury.org).

PNAC members also have played significant roles in other organizations that had set their sights on the invasion of Iraq as a critical step towards American domination in the Middle East. The *Committee for the Liberation of Iraq* was spawned by PNAC in 2002, and a number of members of the *Committee for Peace and Security in the Gulf*, the *American Enterprise Institute,* and the *Defense Policy Board* were, or still are, PNAC people. (For a guide to these Byzantine interconnections see rightweb.irc-online. org).

In 2000, PNAC produced their most influential document, *Rebuilding America's Defenses: Strategy, Forces and Resources for a New Century.* The PNAC philosophy of unilateral imposition of U.S. military might to achieve a global *American peace,* spelled out in chilling detail in that publication would evolve into George W. Bush's 2002 *National Security Strategy.*

PNAC is not simply a White House echo. In fact, some of its publications have accused the Bush administration of not being tough enough. For example, PNAC charter member Robert

Kagan— contributing editor to *The Weekly Standard* and former speechwriter during the Reagan administration—complained in the May 2, 2004 *Washington Post* " The administration is increasingly reluctant to fight the people it defines as the bad guys in Iraq...No one wants more American casualties. And no one doubts that more violence in Iraq may alienate more of the Iraqi population. But this reluctance can also appear both to Iraqis and to the American public as a sign of declining will...Among the many lessons of Vietnam is that American support for that war remained remarkably steady, despite high American casualties, until Americans began to sense that their government was no longer committed to what had been defined as victory and was looking for a way out."

That is an interesting concept, especially coming from a charter member of PNAC, a group that is an "educational organization" encouraging American "commitment to moral principles." Apparently, if only the American public had been more resolute, we might finally have achieved a *victory* in that decade-long war in which 47,378 U.S. soldiers were killed, along with 223, 748 South Vietnamese and 1,100,000 North Vietnamese soldiers. Perhaps if the military *occupation* of Iraq can garner sufficient "American support" the U.S. will be able to kill enough Iraqis to quiet even the most ardent resistance.

psychiatric casualties: wounds of war that mar the mind. Mentally debilitating disorders are a now familiar and expected result of asking *soldiers* to perform acts normally deemed reprehensible.

Symptoms can include a wide variety of problems—disturbing memories, flashbacks, hallucinations, social withdrawal, difficulty in concentrating, outbursts of anger, and other manifestations of intense psychological distress. Sometimes, through therapy and medication, there is relief. In other cases, the wounds are too deep, and the victim suffers for a lifetime.

During the Civil War, these stress-induced symptoms were poorly understood, and called "nostalgia," "irritable heart," and "soldier's heart." In World War I they became "shell-shock." Military.com (www.military.com)—a leading Web site dedicated to assisting U.S. military and veterans—outlines the evolution of the recognition that these symptoms are real, potentially disabling, and require skilled treatment. In World War II "'Psychiatric casualties' had increased by 300 percent...By then, what professionals were seeing was identified as 'combat' or 'battle fatigue'...However, the emphasis of such problems was still placed on the individual's makeup or character, or the unit's level of cohesion and discipline in combat."

They continue "In 1947, the Veterans Administration (VA) reported the number of combat veterans receiving pensions for psychiatric disabilities was 475,397...In addition to these, there were another 50,662 veterans with psychiatric disorders who were confined to VA hospitals."

In the Korean War, the favored term became "section eight." However, by that time it was clear that "the psychological trauma was caused by situational stresses related to the combat experience and had little or nothing to do with the character of the individual soldier." The Vietnam War, in which soldiers typically experienced combat for over 250 days per year—far more than their World War II counterparts—was extraordinarily damaging to their psyches.

A 1990 Congressional report revealed that 480,000 of the 3.15 million Americans who served in Vietnam were still suffering from combat-related psychological problems. Many of these were now in the category of "Post Traumatic Stress Disorder" (PTSD), a diagnosis officially recognized by the American Psychiatric Association in 1980. Dartmouth Professor Matthew J. Friedman, Executive Director of the National Center for PTSD (NCPTSD) says "For individuals with PTSD, the traumatic event remains, sometimes for a decade or lifetime, a dominating psychological experience that retains its power to evoke panic, terror, dread, grief, or despair."

Estimates of PTSD among veterans of the 1991 *Gulf War* range from 7-12 percent—in a war that only lasted for a few days—but during which thousands of *enemy* and civilians were killed. *Operation Iraqi Freedom*—with its premature announcement of *mission accomplished* and the ensuing months of deadly, relentless attacks on coalition forces—will inevitably burden thousands with PTSD.

The January 25, 2004 *Observer*/UK reported " More than 600 U.S. servicemen and women have been evacuated from the country [Iraq] for psychiatric reasons since the conflict started last March...According to Captain Jennifer Berg...whose staff sees U.S. Marines returning from Iraq, military psychiatrists have been warned to expect the disorder to occur in 20 percent of the servicemen and women in Iraq."

In July 2004 the Department of Veterans Affairs reported that 28,000 veterans of *Operation Iraqi Freedom* had had sought health care, and "one in every five was diagnosed with a mental disorder."

Full-blown PTSD is not alone in inflicting suffering on combatants. "Combat stress reaction" ranges from "disturbed sleep, forgetfulness, aggression, irrational anger, and feelings of alienation...the most pronounced cases have already ended in suicide" (see *suicide*).

The Pentagon placed "combat-stress units" throughout Iraq, where professional counselors tried to manage stress symptoms as quickly as possible. *Newsweek*, February 21, 2004 reports "Within the military, a big selling point for the combat-stress team is that they keep soldiers fighting; in military parlance, frontline psychologists are a 'force multiplier.'"

War destroys everyone—the soldiers on both sides, filled with a sense of the righteousness of their cause—as well as the civilian innocents caught in the violence of the battlefield (see *casualties, collateral damage*). Individuals may escape injuries to their bodies, but no one survives intact. Veteran Paul Fussell writes in *Wartime: Understanding and Behavior in the Second World War*: " In war it is not just the weak soldiers, or the sensitive ones, or the highly imaginative or cowardly ones, who will break down. Inevitably, all will break down if in combat long enough. As medical observers have reported 'There is no such thing as getting used to combat...Each moment of combat imposes a strain so great that men will break down in direct relation to the intensity and duration of their experience.'"

Q

"The ultimate weakness of violence is that it is a descending spiral, begetting the very thing that it seeks to destroy."

Martin Luther King, Jr.

quagmire: in nature, a boggy area whose surface appears capable of supporting one's weight, but which gives way when stepped on, trapping the intruder. As in the case of Vietnam decades earlier, Iraq was portrayed as willing to support a military assault that required killing thousands of soldiers and civilians, and would, according to the Pentagon planners, welcome the attackers as liberators.

Instead, the ground opened up, and the liberators became captive to the resistance of people who refused to be occupied.

In May 2004 Defense Secretary Donald Rumsfeld, after months of insisting that there were enough troops in Iraq to pacify the country, asked for 20,000 more to add to the 135,000 already there. General Westmoreland, commander of the U.S. forces in Vietnam had claimed he could have "won" that war with 2 million soldiers instead of the mere 1 million allotted to him. Little had changed since then in the blind faith in the escalation of violence to bring "peace."

As early as April 5, 2003—in the midst of the "official" segment of *Operation Iraqi Freedom* The (London) *Guardian*'s James Fox wrote "What took years to build up in the U.S. during the Vietnam War—skepticism and finally widespread opposition— could happen in just weeks with the help of 24-hour television. Now the actual speed and success of the war will come down to whether the Americans are prepared to kill civilians more or less indiscriminately." They were, and the fighting continued.

Columnist Michael Hill observed in the *Baltimore Sun*,

July 13, 2003, "Many in Iraq see the United States just as many Vietnamese did—not as a force bringing liberty from oppression, but as a part of a continuum of colonial powers seeking to dominate the land. The French preceded the United States in Vietnam; the British and Turks in Iraq" (see *carpet bombing)*.

Almost one year later, President George Bush, in defending his infamous May 1, 2003 *mission accomplished* speech, told reporters "We're making progress, you bet." During that year of progress, at least 10,000 Iraqi civilians had been killed, according to Iraq Body Count (www.iraqbodycount.org), and over 400 U.S. soldiers had met the same fate. Senator Edward Kennedy said in a speech on the Senate floor on April 29, 2004 "Iraq has become a quagmire...It may well go down as the worst blunder in the entire history of American foreign policy." Well-known conservative Pat Buchanan echoed Kennedy, saying, "We have gotten ourselves bogged down in what is clearly a quagmire."

By early 2005 over 1,400 U.S. soldiers had been killed and more than 10,600 had been wounded. Sixteen to eighteen thousand Iraqi civilians had been reported killed. On January 28, 2005 the newly re-elected President Bush announced, "Freedom is on the march, and the world is better for it."

A strange coincidence would link a revelation of atrocities in Vietnam with a celebrated exposure of brutality in Iraq— both incidents which eroded public support for those invasions. Seymour M. Hersh, then a young freelance reporter, revealed the gruesome slaughter of 504 civilians in the South Vietnamese village of My Lai on March 16, 1968. In The *New Yorker*, May 10, 2004 the same Hersh—by then a respected investigative journalist— broke the story of the barbarous treatment of prisoners at Abu Ghraib prison near Baghdad (see *detainees)*.

Another coincidence, perhaps even more ironic, is found in *Time* magazine, March 2, 1998. Former President George H.W. Bush and Brent Scowcroft—who had served as Bush's national security advisor—explained their decision not to push into Iraq during the 1991 *Gulf War.* They wrote, "Trying to eliminate Saddam, extending the ground war into an occupation of Iraq... would have incurred incalculable human and political costs... We would have been forced to occupy Baghdad and, in effect, rule Iraq. The coalition would instantly have collapsed, the Arabs deserting in anger and other allies pulling out as well...Going in and occupying Iraq, thus unilaterally exceeding the UN mandate, would have destroyed the precedent of international response to aggression we hoped to establish. Had we gone the invasion route, the U.S. could conceivably still be an occupying power in a bitterly hostile land."

R

"However moral the cause that initiates war...it is in the nature of war to corrupt the morality until the rule becomes 'an eye for an eye, a tooth for a tooth,' and soon it is not a matter of equivalence but indiscriminate revenge."

Howard Zinn

raghead: one of the U.S. soldiers' favorite derogatory terms for Iraqis. The insulting label is but the latest in a long list of dehumanizing slurs favored by the military—a list including "Huns," "Krauts," "Japs," and "Gooks." For many soldiers, such terms are simply part of the casual, coarse language that binds comrades together—but not always. For example, the following appeared in the April 7, 2003 Long Island, NY *Newsday*:

"It's like you're fighting a faceless enemy. They're all just ragheads to me, the same way they used to call the enemy 'gooks' in Vietnam." (Cpl Jeb Moser)

"Asked whom he considered a raghead, Atkins said, 'Anybody who actively opposes the United States of America's way...if a little kid actively opposes my way of life, I'd call him a raghead, too.'" (Lance Cpl. Christopher Atkins)

Tariq Ali, in *Bush in Babylon: The Recolonisation of Iraq* reflects on why American generals did little to protect Baghdad's cultural treasures: "Having stirred their soldiers to fight and destroy the 'ragheads,' portrayed in briefings as uncivilized barbarians responsible for 9/11, perhaps they were now fearful of admitting that the 'ragheads' were a people with a culture."

Rebuilding America's Defenses: Strategy, Forces and Resources for a New Century (RAD): a menacing document, published in 2000 by *The Project for the New American Century*, which spells out what would soon become the George W. Bush administration's belligerent and dangerous foreign policy. That policy is found in more subtle form in the White House's 2002 *National Security Strategy.*

A number of the contributors to the 40,000-word publication would become key members of the Bush government. These include Paul Wolfowitz, appointed deputy secretary of defense, I. Lewis Libby, named chief of staff for Vice President Dick Cheney, and Stephen Cambone, confirmed as undersecretary of defense for intelligence.

RAD calls for "American global leadership" to be achieved by "American military dominance"(see *hegemony, hyperpower*). The "new American century" will be a time of "Pax Americana," an "American peace" realized by spreading America's military presence around the globe (see *American peace, constabulary duties, critical regions, Defense Planning Guidance, endless war, forward-based forces, full spectrum dominance, Pax Americana, regime change*).

In order to ensure that the United States dominates the world (see *national interests*), it may have to act unilaterally and strike the *enemy* first (see *preemptive war, preventive war*). This will require increasing military spending (see *military budget*) to support major advances in military technology and weapons (see *high-tech battlefield, information dominance, nuclear weapons, Robust Nuclear Earth Penetrator*).

Jay Bookman points out in *The Atlanta Journal-Constitution*, September 29, 2002 that *Operation Iraqi Freedom* was not about *weapons of mass destruction*, terrorism, or Saddam Hussein. Fulfilling the blunt aims of RAD, it was "the official emergence of the United States as a full-fledged global empire, seizing sole responsibility and authority as planetary policeman." Concerning the lack of an *exit strategy* for the Iraq *occupation*, Bookman emphasizes, "We won't be leaving. Having conquered Iraq, the United States will create permanent bases in that country from which to dominate the Middle East, including neighboring Iran."

Donald Kagan—who served as co-chair of the RAD project— argues, according to Jay Bookman, " We will probably need a major concentration of forces in the Middle East over a long period of time. That will come at a price, but think of the price of not having it. When we have economic problems, its been caused by disruptions in our oil supply. If we have a force in Iraq, there will be no disruption in our oil supplies."

reconstruction: tear apart a country by years of *sanctions* and war and then rebuild what you have destroyed. In the process, generate enormous profits for companies with close friends in the U.S. government, and pass along much of the charge to the American taxpayer.

In late 2003 the UN and the *Coalition Provisional Authority* estimated it would take at least $55 billion to rebuild Iraq to its "pre-war" level, in what is considered to be the biggest reconstruction effort since the rebuilding of Germany and Japan after the Second World War. The U.S. Congressional Budget Office predicted that perhaps $50-$100 billion more would be necessary to finance reconstruction and security during the succeeding 3-5 years.

Before *Operation Iraqi Freedom*, Americans were reassured that Iraq's oil would fund the country's reconstruction. According to the January 16, 2004 *Financial Times/UK*, Ari Fleischer— then the White House spokesperson—said on February 16, 2003 "Iraq, unlike Afghanistan, is a rather wealthy country... Iraq has tremendous resources that belong to the Iraqi people... Iraq has to be able to shoulder much of the burden for their own reconstruction."

Paul Wolfowitz, deputy defense secretary, told the House appropriations committee on March 27, 2003 "There's a lot of money to pay for this that doesn't have to be U.S. taxpayer money, and it starts with the assets of the Iraqi people. On a rough recollection, the oil revenues of that country could bring between $50 and $100 billion over the next two to three years."

The *Times* continued: "The president's office of management and budget told Congress last week [early January, 2004] that oil revenues in 2003 were $2.9 billion and were projected to reach $13 billion this year, not enough even to cover the government's operating costs for 2004, which it forecast to reach $15.6 billion." Energy research expert James Placke, a contributor to the Council on Foreign Relations (www.cfr.org) report *Iraq: The Day After* told the *Times* "Like other aspects of Iraq, those making policy believed what they wanted to believe about oil, without reference to the facts." Placke described Paul Wolfowitz's estimates as "total fabrication...a colossal misrepresentation."

The *New York Times* (December 9, 2003) reported that the Pentagon had "barred French, German, and Russian companies from competing for...contracts for the reconstruction of Iraq." This prohibition was "necessary for the protection of the essential security of the United States." This order, issued by deputy defense secretary Paul Wolfowitz "represents perhaps the most substantive retaliation to date by the Bush administration against American allies who opposed its decision to go to war in Iraq." Only "coalition partners" would be allowed to bid on contracts (see *coalition of the willing*). The order was reversed in July 2004 at the request of the State Department.

There appeared to be other criteria for reconstruction profits, according to the October 30, 2003 report, *Windfalls of War,* from The Center for Public Integrity, a nonprofit government watchdog (www.publicintegrity.org). The report revealed that many companies that had been awarded government contracts to rebuild Iraq and Afghanistan collectively had contributed more money to President Bush's election campaigns than to any other candidate.

The report said that thirteen of the companies "employ former government officials or have other ties to various government agencies and departments...Topping the list, with more than $2.3 billion in contracts, was Kellogg, Brown & Root (KBR), a subsidiary of Halliburton, the energy services conglomerate."

Halliburton, the world's largest oil-and-gas services company, became a focal point for accusations of influence peddling in Iraq reconstruction. According to *The Progressive Populist* (June 15, 2003) the company had already signed a 10-year deal in December 2001 to supply U.S. military operations around the world with "housing, food, water, mail, and heavy equipment." The Pentagon pays Halliburton through a "cost-plus arrangement," meaning that it is "guaranteed to recover its expenses, plus receive a set profit, provided the contract terms are met."

The Progressive Populist reports that as early as November 2002, The Department of Defense recommended that the Army Corps of Engineers award a contract to KBR to repair Iraq's oil industry. KBR got that contract, worth up to $7 billion, in October 2003—without having to bid for the job. The controversy surrounding KBR centers on the fact that during the five years immediately preceding assuming the vice-presidency, Dick Cheney was chief executive at Halliburton. Cheney, who earned forty-four million dollars during his years at the company, continued to receive a hundred and fifty thousand dollars a year in delayed compensation while vice-president.

In a detailed analysis of the Cheney-Halliburton connection, the February 16 & 23, 2004 *New Yorker* reported, "The United States had concluded that Iraq, Libya, and Iran supported terrorism and had imposed strict sanctions on them. Yet during Cheney's tenure at Halliburton the company did business in all three countries. In the case of Iraq, the company legally evaded U.S. sanctions by conducting its oil-service business through foreign subsidiaries" (see *sanctions*).

Concerning Halliburton's work in post-war Iraq, Cheney has vigorously denied having any influence in the U.S. government's decisions on Iraq reconstruction contracts. Meanwhile, in addition to having to fend off accusations of favoritism, Halliburton had became embroiled in controversy surrounding allegedly overcharging the U.S. government by at least $61 million for transporting gasoline from Kuwait into Iraq and $24 million for supplying meals to troops. In May 2004 the Pentagon asked the Justice Department to assist them in an investigation of Halliburton. Meanwhile, on January 11, *The Washington Times* reported, "Iran said yesterday that U.S. oil services giant Halliburton (has) won a major contract to drill for gas (in Iran), despite U.S. sanctions against foreign investment in this country's energy industry."

Despite the rosy forecasts for reconstruction riches to be had in rebuilding Iraq, by May 2004 the escalating, violent opposition to the U.S.-led *occupation* had become so dangerous that most of the contractors working in Iraq had either left the country or had withdrawn to heavily guarded sites. Fearing for the safety of their employees, the companies were forced to hire thousands of private security forces (see *mercenaries*).

Along with its plans for rebuilding Iraq's infrastructure, the U.S. occupying powers weighed in on reconstructing the country's economy. According to the January 10, 2004 *New York Times*, "L. Paul Bremer III, who heads the Coalition Provisional Authority, wiped out longstanding Iraqi laws that restricted foreigners' ability to own property, and invest in Iraqi business. The rule, known as Order 39, allows foreign investors to own Iraqi companies fully with no requirements for reinvesting profits back into the country...Legal scholars are concerned that the United States may be violating longstanding international laws governing military occupation."

By January 2005 only $2.4 billion of the $18.4 billion marked for reconstruction had been spent. Meanwhile, the State Department asked Congress to shift $3.46 billion of the above reconstruction funds to use in part for training Iraqi security police. According to the *New York Times* (September 15, 2004) State Department officials said, "the money would come mainly from allocations to build water and sewer systems and repair and modernize the electricity system."

Author Naomi Klein, in *The Nation* (January 5, 2004), concluded "The reconstruction of Iraq has emerged as a vast protectionist racket, a neocon New Deal that transfers limitless public funds—in contracts, loans, and insurance—to private firms, and even gets rid of foreign competition to boot...Ironically, these firms are being handed this corporate welfare so they can take full advantage of CPA-imposed laws that systematically strip Iraq industry of all its protections, from import tariffs to limits of foreign ownership."

reduce: to lower the *enemy's* ability to resist by killing them in sufficient numbers. For example:

"... they have to get this situation under control. I don't think that means they have to eliminate every paramilitary guy, but they have to reduce the level of resistance. And I think the other requirement is they have to reduce the Republican Guard that's defending Baghdad." (Michael Gordon, CNN.com, March 26, 2003)

"It has become a fundamental principle of mobility doctrine to bypass major enemy formations...but this requires substantial follow-on forces to reduce the enemy formations over time." (*The Estimate,* Vol. XV, number 6, March 21, 2003)

regime change: a long-standing practice of the United States which has recently escalated into brutal, illegal, unilateral, *preemptive* military aggression. The long, dark history of bloody, sometimes covert operations aimed at bringing down political forces at odds with U.S. *national interests*—e.g. Iran, Greece, Chile, Guatemala, and Indonesia, among many others —is meticulously documented in William Blum's 2004 *Killing Hope: U.S. Military and C.I.A. Interventions Since World War II*. Of specific interest here is the culmination of the plans to attack and depose Saddam Hussein devised by a cadre of George H.W. and George W. Bush advisors and officials.

In a WABC-TV interview on June 3, 2003, Secretary of Defense Donald Rumsfeld stated "The policy of the United States Government has been regime change since the mid to late 1990s passed by the Congress and that regime has now been changed. That is a very good thing." Rumsfeld was referring to the 1998 Iraqi Liberation Act, signed by President Clinton. However, that Act simply pledged U.S. support for "democratic opposition organizations" that might encourage the overthrow of Saddam by his own people (see *Iraqi National Congress*). It also promised "humanitarian assistance" to the Iraqis once the regime had been removed from power—little consolation to the thousands of Iraqis who continued to die from the effects of the cruel *sanctions* in place since 1991.

Planning for a more violent regime change in Iraq began long before the passage of the Iraqi Liberation Act. The *Committee for Peace and Security in the Gulf* (CPSG) formed in 1990 to win support for removing Saddam Hussein by attacking Iraq. The 1991 *Gulf War* stopped short of a full-scale invasion of Iraq. The UN, with the support and encouragement of the U.S., placed strict trade *sanctions* on Iraq with the aim of creating so much suffering inside that country that Iraqi citizens would overthrow Saddam's regime. The devastating sanctions did indeed cause widespread suffering, but no coup.

In 1992, Paul Wolfowitz, then the undersecretary of defense for policy, drafted the *Defense Planning Guidance*. That first draft, which called for unilateral military action to "prevent the re-emergence of a new rival" and to assure "access to vital raw material, primarily Persian Gulf oil" was leaked to the *New York*

Times and withdrawn after widespread criticism. It was replaced by a less direct version.

In 1997 the *Project for the New American Century* (PNAC) appeared on the Washington scene. PNAC, a group of political conservatives, says in its "Statement of Principles" that the U.S. needs to "challenge regimes hostile to our interests and values." PNAC charter members included Dick Cheney, Donald Rumsfeld, and Paul Wolfowitz.

In 1998 the CPSG, by then a 39-member organization, appealed in a letter to President Clinton to "help overthrow Iraqi President Saddam Hussein and replace his regime with a provisional government." For this new government they offered the *Iraqi National Congress*, a group of handpicked Iraqi exiles. Among those signing the letter were some who would become influential members of the George W. Bush administration. Bush would appoint Donald Rumsfeld as his Secretary of Defense, and Paul Wolfowitz as his Deputy Secretary of Defense.

In 2000 PNAC produced the document *Rebuilding America's Defenses: Strategy, Forces and Resources for a New American Century*, which is a blatant call for world domination by U.S. military might (see *hegemony*). That document, which is widely regarded as the blueprint for the White House 2002 *National Security Strategy*, states that "American military preeminence" will require achieving "political goals such as removing a dangerous and hostile regime when necessary."

The tragedy of September 11, 2001 was a prime opportunity for the proponents of military action against Saddam Hussein's government. President Bush met with Cabinet members and advisors at Camp David on September 13, 2001. In a May 9, 2003 interview with *Vanity Fair*, Paul Wolfowitz recounted his discussion with President at that meeting, in which Wolfowitz had speculated about the prospects of attacking Iraq because of a "gut feeling" that Saddam Hussein was involved in the 9/11 disaster.

Wolfowitz said "On the surface of the debate it at least appeared to be about not whether but when...There seemed to be a kind of agreement that yes it should be, but the disagreement was whether it should be in the immediate response or whether you should concentrate simply on Afghanistan first."

The persistent proponents for violent regime change in Iraq, a country by then devastated by years of sanctions and practically defenseless, would finally have their day. First, however, a facade of reasons would have to be constructed to paint Iraq as an imminent threat to its neighbors and to the U.S. Only after the 'official" *end of hostilities* in *Operation Iraqi Freedom* would that facade be dismantled.

The threat of more U.S. adventurism remained. After all, in his June 1, 2002 commencement speech at West Point President Bush had said that there were "terror cells in 60 or more countries," suggesting that the latter were potential targets for regime change. The president elicited their applause when he told the young graduates "We will send diplomats where they are needed, and we will send you, our soldiers, where you're needed."

Columnist Sean Gonsalves, in Working for Change (www.workingforchange.com), December 1, 2003, asked "Given the prominence of 'regime change' in international relations today, [why] don't we have our best minds examining bloodless transfers of power...as in the case of the Mandela-led struggle against apartheid in South Africa, or the ousting of Ferdinand Marcos in the Philippines in 1986? Can't we replicate similar movements in the world's troubled spots? Why aren't U.S. diplomats submitting UN resolutions seeking the establishment of civil defense armies, who are trained in the nonviolent resistance of coercive military tyranny? Why is there no Peace Pentagon full of political scientists and war strategists well versed in nonviolent tactics?"

revisit the target: return and drop *bombs* on a target, or hit it again with *artillery* in case you did not destroy everything and kill everyone. For example:

"Artillery men want to know if they have done any damage and if they have inflicted any casualties...Live TV might do that job for them...Bomb damage assessment is an extremely useful tool in determining the effectiveness of a given raid...If the opponents can see on television what damage has been done, they can decide whether or not to revisit the target." (Barrie Dunsmore, *The Next War: Live?,* March 1996, at the Joan Shorenstein Center, Harvard University)

"The forces in theatre will be half of what they were in '91. We have more accurate bombs, so even though the unit cost is higher you generally don't need to drop as many or revisit the target." (David Gillies, January 2, 2003, reason.com)

S

"The military is acutely aware that the reason for its existence is to wage war, and war means killing people and the deaths of American soldiers as well. Because the reality of war and its consequences are so bad, the military almost instinctively tries to doublespeak when discussing war."

William Lutz

sanctions: devastating trade restrictions placed on Iraq on August 6, 1990 by the UN. The sanctions were supported and encouraged by the United States. The announced aim of the sanctions was to force Iraq—which had invaded Kuwait 4 days earlier—to follow UN resolutions and disarm. The actual goal was to make the people of Iraq suffer so much that they would overthrow Saddam Hussein's government and allow the U.S. to gain access to that country's oil reserves. The suffering reached horrendous proportions, while the oil and the country itself was finally acquired through another brutal military attack—*Operation Iraqi Freedom.*

The 1990 UN Resolution 661 blocked Iraq from any trade or financial dealings with the outside world. Iraq had been almost totally dependent on the income obtained from selling its oil. The funds were essential to not only supplying its military, but to maintaining the life support systems of the people— electricity, water and sewage treatment, transportation, and medical care. Also, Iraq imported most of its food and medicines. Despite the fact that the guidelines of the sanctions allowed the importation of "humanitarian" items, the United States blocked the full implementation of that provision until the bitter end. The chilling details of this dogged and deadly insistence on restricting the Iraqi people's access even to antibiotics are documented in Larry Everest's compelling 2004 book *Oil, Power & Empire: Iraq and the U.S. Global Agenda.*

The predictable effects of these calculated economic restrictions—widespread malnutrition, disease and death—were amplified by the destruction brought about by the 1991 *Gulf War.* The April 1991 UN Resolution 687 continued the sanctions, as Iraq's roads, bridges, industries, and electrical systems— needed for water and sewage treatment—lay in ruins. The sanctions, despite a rising chorus of outrage in the international community over the suffering of innocent civilians, continued until the U.S.-led coalition came to "liberate" Iraq in the 2003 *Operation Iraqi Freedom.*

Between 1991 and 1998, according to estimates by the United Nations Children's Fund (UNICEF) 500,000 Iraqi children under the age of five had died as a direct result of the sanctions. On October 6, 1998, Denis Halliday—who then had just resigned as the UN official in charge of the *Oil-for-Food* program in despair and disgust at the toll taken by the sanctions—observed, " There are many reasons for these tragic and unnecessary deaths, including the poor health of the mothers, the breakdown of health services, the poor nutritional intake...and the high incidence of water-borne diseases as a result of the collapse of Iraq's water and sanitation system—and, of course the lack of electric power to drive that system..."(www.accuracy.org).

Earlier that same year, on January 10, 1998, Pope John Paul II told the Vatican Diplomatic Corps "I insist on repeating clearly to all, once again, that no one may kill in God's name" recalling "our brothers and sisters in Iraq, living under a pitiless embargo... The weak and the innocent cannot pay for mistakes for which they are not responsible" (see *crusade, just war*). These kinds of appeals over the years of the sanctions never had any visible effect on President Clinton, or Presidents George H.W. and George W. Bush, all of whom share the guilt of deliberately sacrificing thousands of innocent lives for political and economic gain. The actual number of deaths and permanent disabilities wrought by the years of sanctions will never be known, nor will their names— except to their loved ones.

Denis Halliday, in a January 16, 2001 CNN.com interview remarked, "We have a United Nations today that is governed by a Charter. Articles 1 and 2 of that Charter require that the sovereignty of the member states be respected, and that the United Nations work towards the well-being of the people of the world. However, with the embargo [sanctions] in Iraq, we have a United Nations whose decisions in the Security Council have led to the deaths of possibly more than one million people in ten years. Now that is a tragedy. And that begins to meet some of the definitions of the United Nations Convention on Genocide."

secure the peace: In the case of the 2003 *Operation Iraqi Freedom*, to invade a country already ravaged by the 1991 *Gulf War* and years of lethal *sanctions*, kill thousands of Iraqi *soldiers* and civilians, brutalize prisoners, and assume that the Iraqis will welcome, at long last, this most recent occupation of their land.

President George W. Bush told his audience at the Cincinnati Museum Center on October 7, 2002: "We will meet the responsibility of defending human liberty against violence and aggression. By our resolve, we will give strength to others. By our courage, we will give hope to others. By our actions, we will secure the peace, and lead the world to a better day." In remarks to the Newspaper Association of America, April 21, 2004 Bush said, "Some people never thought they [Japan] could self-govern or be free. It dawned on me, by the way, in that conversation, someday an American President will be sitting down with a duly-elected official from Iraq, talking about how to secure the peace better in the Middle East."

Deputy Defense Secretary Paul Wolfowitz wrote in The *Wall Street Journal* (September 2, 2003), "If you'd asked Gen. Mattis and his Marines, there was no question in their minds that the battle they wage—the battle to secure peace in Iraq—is now the central battle in the war on terrorism."

Simon Tisdall, in the February 27, 2003 *Guardian*/UK comments: "Bush vows to wage war against all of America's enemies to 'secure the peace'. That this war, again in Bush's own words, will be continuous, global, and indefinite in duration is but a logical extension of a U.S. pre-eminence that came of age in the ashes of Hiroshima. That the vaguely defined 'peace' for which Bush ostensibly strives may never actually arrive is another logical deduction. America's ascendancy, if it is to be maintained and extended, requires a constant readiness to fight"(see *endless war, global war on terrorism*).

service the target: to kill people and demolish equipment and structures with *artillery* or *bombs*. For example:

"Vice Adm. Fry made a pertinent comment exemplifying the commitment of allied forces in the region: 'Now are we going to use more or less in the future?... We're going to keep, as I've said, this same kind of level of effort as we continue day by day to service the target[s]...'" (EmergencyNet News Service, March 31, 1999)

"Targets assigned by the naval or joint force commander will be allocated automatically to firing units on the fully-integrated network and precision fires executed by the air, or subsurface platform best suited to service the target[s]..." (Navy Wire Service, June 14, 2001)

Shock and Awe: according to Harlan K. Ullman, principal author of the 1996 *Shock & Awe: Achieving Rapid Dominance*, this is a battle plan "to destroy or so confound the will to resist that an adversary will have no alternative except to accept our strategic aims and military objectives...Shutting the country down would entail both the physical destruction of appropriate infrastructure and the shutdown and control of all vital information and associated commerce so rapidly as to achieve a level of national shock akin to the effect that dropping nuclear weapons on Hiroshima and Nagasaki had on the Japanese."

Air Force Magazine, November 2003 reported that Ullman, responding to a query by CBS News correspondent David Martin in January, 2003, described this potential scenario: "You're sitting in Baghdad, and all of a sudden you're the general, and 30 of your division headquarters have been wiped out. You also take the city down. By that, I mean you get rid of their power, water. In two, three, four, five days they are physically, emotionally, and psychologically exhausted."

"Shock and Awe" became the media mantra for the entertaining fireworks that would initiate *Operation Iraqi Freedom*. The Pentagon, while not admitting to any official acceptance of Ullman's philosophy, allowed the term to remain viable. For example, Gen. Tommy Franks, commander of U.S. Central Command promised in a March 22, 2003 press briefing "This will be a campaign unlike any other in history, a campaign characterized by shock...and the application of overwhelming force." (On May 25th, 2004, in a little-publicized ceremony, the title of honorary Knight Commander of the Order of the British Empire was conferred on the then retired General Franks.)

The assumption that "Shock and Awe" was coming was reinforced by Ullman's close relationship with Bush administration officials. For example, Secretary of State Colin Powell had written in his 1995 autobiography *My American Journey*: "A teacher who raised my vision several levels was Harlan Ullman...possessed of one of the best, most provocative minds I have ever encountered." Also, in October, 1999 Donald Rumsfeld, along with three former secretaries of defense recommended the concept of Rapid Dominance to the then Defense Secretary William Cohen.

Despite media predictions that the U.S.-led coalition would rain down 3,000 *precision-guided munitions* in the first 24 hours of the war, after four days of bombing they had delivered a total of about 2,000. Hundreds of military and government buildings were destroyed and uncounted *soldiers* and civilians had been killed. However, on April 1, 2003 Harlan Ullman, in an article titled "'Shock and Awe' Lite" complained that "Unlike in 1991's Desert Storm, Iraq's land forces were not unmercifully pounded before the ground attack...the focus and fixation on continuing to attack strategic targets around Baghdad raises questions. Had the air campaign destroyed a substantial chunk of Iraq's ground forces, it's possible that Iraqi resistance might have been softened" (see *air campaign, soften*).

Media reports took the lack of a Hiroshima-like effect to heart. For example a *Los Angeles Times*, March 30, 2003 headline remarked "Too Little Shock, Not Enough Awe." WorldNetDaily. com, April 3, 2003 commented "No Shock, No Awe, It Never Happened." Meanwhile, the Pentagon began distancing itself from the fray. Deputy Secretary of Defense Paul Wolfowitz told CBS on April 1, 2003, when asked about "Shock and Awe" replied, "I don't care for that phrase" (see *Project for the New American Century*). Air Force General T. Michael Moseley said in an April 5, 2003 press briefing "The term Shock and Awe has never been a term I've used. I'm not sure where that came from."

According to Reuters, October 24, 2003, by that time the U.S. Patent Office had received 29 applications for products using the label "Shock and Awe." These included pesticides, dietary supplements, video games, energy drinks, lingerie, and "infant action crib toys."

smart bomb: a *bomb* sent off to kill directed by sometimes highly technical guidance systems. In comparison to the *Gulf War*, in which most of the bombs were the unguided *dumb* variety,

68 percent of the bombs used in *Operation Iraqi Freedom* were "smart." These are designed to hit specific targets rather than simply explode in the general area, thus theoretically limiting *collateral damage*. However, when the guidance systems fail, these deadly weapons may stray far from their intended path, for example, into a crowded city street or apartment complex (see *precision-guided munitions*).

soft target: the object of violence. It may be a particularly vulnerable area, e.g. "They concentrate on 'soft' targets, unprotected areas, such as quiet Kuta Beach." (*Hawaii Business Magazine,* May, 2003), or "Insurgents chose a 'soft' target impossible to defend against when they bombed a Baghdad hotel Wednesday." (CNN.com, March 18, 2004)

Sometimes a hard object can be a soft target, as " A Stinger [missile] will do 300 points of damage to a soft target such as a helicopter." (www.razorworks.com). People are soft in several ways—as objects of attack, e.g. "...a few tips to help ensure your safety and keep you from becoming a 'soft' target" (www.usembassyjakarta.gov), or in battle "A hard target is a military person and a soft target is a civilian." (*Comeford's Art and it's Development*, librarythinkquest.org) (see *hard target*).

"Soft targeting" refers to the propaganda practice of dropping leaflets or broadcasting on radio or television stations.

soften: to kill, injure and demoralize the *enemy.* For example:

"Much of that speculation, fueled by Pentagon officials, centred on 'shock and awe', the lengthy and intense bombing campaign that was supposed to begin the war, softening up Iraqi resistance before ground forces moved in." (www.theage.com.au, April 19, 2003)

"Even with the bad weather, the U.S. continued to use

satellite-guided bombs to soften up Republican Guard positions."
(CNN.com, March 25, 2003)

"'The preponderance of the Republican Guard positions
that were outside of Baghdad are now dead,' [Air Force Lt. Gen.
Michael Moseley] said. I find it interesting that folks say we're
softening them up. We're not softening them up. We're killing
them." (Associated Press, April 5, 2003)

soldier: In the U.S., typically a young man, often a teenager,
who has entered military service voluntarily (see *military
recruitment).* Young soldiers are needed because their youth offers
physical strength and agility, and it generally assures that they
lack the experience of older individuals that might tempt them to
question the wisdom of their actions. Unquestioning obedience
is a requirement on the part of soldiers in battle (see *cowardice,
desertion).*

The young volunteers enter *military training*, where whatever
ideals of *patriotism* and *glory* that they may nurture are fortified
with the essential understanding that, in the final analysis, they
will be fighting to survive and protect their comrades at the risk
of disgrace.

The soldiers who are ordered into combat, convinced that they
are fulfilling a duty, are often remarkably brave and self-sacrificing.
Many are killed, and at least five times as many wounded, often
remaining permanently disabled. Many who endure bloody
battles suffer psychological damage that may destroy their lives
(see *psychiatric casualties*). After a war ends, it continues in the
bodies and minds of the soldiers. Eventually, as veterans age, the
call goes out to others to fight again. Another generation of young
men, flush with the strength and reckless enthusiasm of youth,
are asked to offer themselves to fight whoever the government
decides is the latest *enemy.*

In 1973, after the Vietnam War, President Richard Nixon

ended the military draft. Nixon explained that there would no longer be any conventional wars requiring large armies—only small armies requiring special skills would be needed. The military now advertised itself as a means of furthering one's education, learning new skills, and exciting travel. Many young men and some young women, who may not have been as easily able to achieve those ends as their more affluent peers, answered the appeal. Some acted at war during times of relative peace, while others were given new opportunities—for example in Panama, Grenada, Afghanistan or Iraq—to kill and be killed.

Henry David Thoreau, in his essay "Civil Disobedience," says because most citizens have an unquestioning respect for law, "By means of their respect for it, even the well disposed are daily made the agents of injustice. A common and natural result of an undue respect for law is, that you may see a file of soldiers... marching in admirable order over hill and dale to the wars, ay, against their common sense and consciences, which makes it very steep marching indeed...They have no doubt that it is a damnable business in which they are concerned; they are all peaceably inclined...The mass of men serve the state thus, not as men mainly, but as machines, with their bodies."

suicide: self-inflicted death, which the Pentagon categorizes as a "non-hostile casualty." After five U.S. soldiers killed themselves in Iraq during July 2003, the Army surgeon general sent a 12-member Mental Health Advisory Team there to "assess and provide recommendations on Operation Iraqi Freedom—related mental health services...and [on] effective suicide prevention measures for soldiers in active combat."

By the end of 2003 there had been 23 suicides within the military in Iraq and Kuwait, including two women. One more suicide occurred in early 2004. By that time seven other suicides had been reported among returning veterans. The Pentagon finally released their report (available at www.armymedicine.army.mil) on March 25, 2004. It concluded "Compared to the average Army suicide rate of 11.9 [per 100,000] Soldiers, the rates for *Operation Iraqi Freedom* Soldiers assigned in Iraq...was 21.2."The Advisory team recommended that the existing Army Suicide Prevention Program be applied to soldiers in combat areas (see *psychiatric casualties*). They were unable to compare the suicide rates among soldiers serving in Iraq with those in previous wars because "The Army does not calculate suicide rates for specific deployments. A review of the professional literature found few references to suicide rates during combat or other military operations."

By March 1, 2005 the Department of Defense had reported 32 suicides in the military during service in Iraq, and 10 in Afghanistan. At least 29 others had occurred among returning veterans.

support the troops: advice so vague as to be virtually meaningless, yet so emotionally laden that the admonition is a powerful political tool. As the troops (see *soldiers*) began to mobilize in early 2003, preparing to attack an already debilitated and suffering Iraq (see *sanctions*), the Republican National Committee distributed yard signs across America proclaiming "I support President Bush and the troops."

Concern for the well-being of the young men and women in the U.S. military, shared by all Americans, was cleverly conflated with approval for *Operation Iraqi Freedom*—a war justified by the Bush administration by outright lies and deception. Even the Democratic presidential candidates fell into the trap. Howard Dean, an outspoken opponent of the plans to attack Iraq, pledged that once the war was underway "Of course I'll support the troops." John Kerry said, "I support the troops, and I support the United States of America winning as rapidly as possible" (see *victory*).

Valid meanings of "support the troops" are almost as

numerous as the seventeen definitions for "support" in Webster's Unabridged Dictionary. On one end of the spectrum it can mean encouraging soldiers to put themselves in *harm's way* to kill whoever the government decides is the *enemy*. At the other, it can be interpreted as vigorously opposing the immoral, illegal war, and demanding that the troops be sent home immediately, ensuring both their safety and that of the designated enemy.

The query "Do you support the troops?" is a rhetorical trap, but it offers an opportunity to make distinctions usually lacking in the public discourse on war. Perhaps the best answer is "Let's get to the point."

T

"There is a huge silver lining in this cloud...War is a tremendous focus...Now we have this focusing opportunity, and we have the fact that [terrorists] have actually attacked our homeland, which gives it some oomph."

General Peter Schoomaker

take out: to kill. For example:
"Now, are there orders not to contact the enemy, or do they take them out when they see them?" (Bill O'Reilly, foxnews.com, February 19, 2003)

Asked whether he favored any policy changes in Iraq, Sen. Trent Lott (R-Miss.) answered, " Honestly, it's a little tougher than I thought it was going to be...If we have to, we just mow the whole place down, see what happens. You're dealing with insane suicide bombers who are killing our people, and we need to be very aggressive in taking them out." (*The Hill*, October 29, 2003) (see *assassination, collateral damage, degrade, dispatch, kill, mopping up, neutralize, pound, reduce, take out*)

Total Information Awareness (TIA): a Pentagon data-gathering program initiated in 2002 that would have been the largest surveillance system ever devised—and would have made possible unprecedented government access to U.S. citizens' personal information.

The Total Information Awareness (TIA) program came out of the Information Awareness Office (IAO) within the Defense Advanced Research Projects Agency (DARPA), the major research and development organization for the Defense Department (see *high-tech battlefield*). In January 2002, John Poindexter was appointed to be the director of the IAO.

Poindexter had served as the national security advisor under

President Ronald Reagan. *Washington Post* columnist Robert O'Harrow summarized Poindexter's background on November 12, 2003: "[He] was convicted in 1990 of five felony counts of lying to Congress, destroying official documents and obstructing official inquiries into the Iran-contra affair, which involved the secret sale of arms to Iran in the mid-1980s and diversion of profits to help the contra rebels in Nicaragua. He was sentenced to six months in jail." The U.S. Court of Appeals would later overturn that conviction on the grounds that he had been granted immunity before testifying.

Poindexter—labeled by *New York Times* columnist William Safire as a "master of deceit"—had resurfaced as the man in charge of a $200 million budget to develop new computer technologies that could sift through mountains of U.S. citizens' personal data, seeking telltale patterns that might signal terrorist plots. Ordinarily private transactions—including passport applications, car rentals, airline ticket purchases, medical and educational records, bank accounts—even Web sites visited, would be noted, stored and sifted for signs of suspicious patterns.

The implementation of this blatant proposal to violate traditional privacy safeguards would need new legislation to get underway, including amending the Privacy Act of 1974, which put limits on the government's use of personal information. Civil liberties activists rallied opposition to the proposal. Marc Rotenberg, director of the Electronic Privacy Information Center in Washington, D.C., called it the "'Perfect Storm' for civil liberties in America."

In February 2003 Congress demanded a report from Poindexter's Information Awareness Office on all aspects of TIA program. The report came back with assurances that the Defense Department had no intention of snooping on innocent citizens— and as a gesture of good faith DARPA had changed the title Total Information Awareness to Terrorist Information Awareness.

Soon, an even more outlandish DARPA plan led to John Poindexter's resignation—the Policy Analysis Market. The *New York Times*, July 29, 2003 described this as "an online futures trading market, in which anonymous speculators would bet on forecasting terrorist attacks, assassinations, and coups...The Pentagon called its latest ideas a new way of predicting events and part of its search for the 'broadest possible set of new ways to prevent terrorist attacks.'" Traders could deposit money and win or lose based on their prediction on events. These events would include "economic, civil and military futures of Egypt, Jordan, Iran, Iraq, Israel, Saudi Arabia, Syria and Turkey and the consequences of United States involvement with those nations."

Somehow, monitoring the fluctuations of this market supposedly would send useful signals to the Defense Department—but the public outrage over the proposal quickly convinced them to shut down the program—for which President Bush had requested $8 million.

John Poindexter resigned as director of the Information Awareness Office in August 2003. In September, a conference committee of the House and Senate deleted funding for the TIA program. The committee said it was "concerned about the activities of the Information Awareness Office" and directed that the office be "terminated immediately."

turkey shoot: On Tuesday, February 26, after Iraq's offer to withdraw from Kuwait under international supervision and accept UN Resolution 660 had been rejected, thousands of Iraqi troops streamed out of Kuwait. They were laden with loot, in an irregular convoy of tanks, armored vehicles, trucks, buses, motorcycles, and whatever other vehicles they could muster. As they fled north towards home along the Basra road, near Mutlaa, U.S. aircraft attacked. They bombed both ends of the convoy and then, in the words of Christopher Hitchens in *The Nation,* 8 April 1991, "returned to shred and dismember the resulting traffic jam again and again." Conservative columnist Michael Kelly, reporting on the war (without Pentagon sanction), described this as the "highway to hell."

A U.S. officer described the carnage as a "turkey shoot" after the popular marksmanship contest, usually held, according to Webster's Dictionary, "at a festive gathering, in which rifles are fired at moving targets..." Others described it as "shooting fish in a barrel." Estimates of the number of dead, ranging into the thousands, were sketchy, because, as John Taylor points out in *Body Horror: Photojournalism, Catastrophe and War*, "modern weapons, such as fuel-air bombs or...uranium shells, leave little evidence of human remains."

The May 1991 *Bulletin of the Atomic Scientists* reported that Gen. Merrill "Tony" McPeak, air force chief of staff had explained "When enemy armies are defeated, they retreat, often in disorder, and we have what is known in the business as the exploitation phase. It's during this phase that the true fruits of victory are achieved from combat...It's a tough business...It often causes us to do very brutal things—that's the nature of war."

U

*"They (the Americans) called on us from the tanks to
stay at home because they were going to hit targets and they
also said: 'If you want to watch our show you can go to the
rooftops."*

Hamziya Ali

uniforms: unique, often colorful outfits worn by all members
of the military. Uniforms are especially useful for convincing
young men to enlist (see *military recruiting*). The 17th century
Swedish king Gustavus Adolphus is generally cited as the first
to require all of his soldiers to wear highly visible uniforms. The
king's commanders on the battlefield could monitor and control
their large armies fighting in the Thirty Years' War much more
efficiently when their men wore recognizable outfits.

The modern military uniform serves other important purposes
beyond the original intent. Military service requires a unity of
purpose fostered by carefully crafted training-intensive, repetitive
drill and discipline, specialized jargon, and the molding of discrete
units of comrades with shared experiences and challenges. The
uniform is a symbol of that unity.

The various branches of the military design uniforms for
functional as well as psychological roles. The battle uniform
is highly practical while helping the combatant to distinguish
comrades from the *enemy.* However, this often does not apply to
modern air warfare in which the victims are too far away to be
seen. In the war against Afghanistan (see *Operation Enduring
Freedom*) the Taliban forces did not wear uniforms, as required by
the *Geneva Conventions.* The punishment of the captives for their
non-conformity was to be denied prisoner of war (POW) status as
defined by the Geneva Conventions. Nevertheless, U.S. Defense
Secretary Donald Rumsfeld did reassure the world in his February

8, 2002 press conference that "The United States government will continue to treat them humanely" (see *detainees, extraordinary rendition*).

The formal dress uniform instills pride in the unit and identifies it with the larger group. The various medals and decorations displayed on the dress uniform reinforce the understanding that the acts of war that the decorations represent are not only condoned but praised by society.

Military recruitment would be even more difficult without the seduction of the attractive uniform. Rather than suggesting the invitation to a life of uniformity, uniforms are displayed as symbols of adventure, excitement, athleticism, and an invitation to camaraderie and brotherhood.

The military is careful to regulate how and where the uniform is to be worn. For example, the April 4, 2003 *Northwest Guardian*—official newspaper of the Army's Fort Lewis, Washington—warned that "Soldiers must be careful at [anti-war] rallies...The anti-war activity going on around America seems to be getting more aggressive and more threatening...Soldiers cannot wear their uniforms [at an anti-war demonstration]." According to Captain John Merriam, Staff Judge Advocates Office, while individual soldiers can speak about their opinions "We are war fighters, we're not decision makers. We (the Army) have no position on the war."

unit: in war, a specific group of *soldiers*. When they are attacked many of the people in the unit are killed, injured, and mutilated (see *camps*, *barracks, garrisons, enemy positions*). For example:

"Lieutenant Colonel Chris Holden [said], 'the target is to destroy Fedayeen units or anyone else trying to disrupt our lines of communication...We are going to destroy them.'" (*Guardian Unlimited*, April 2, 2003)

"America-led forces dropped 1,000 pound bombs on Iraqi Republican Guard units ringing Baghdad today..." (Associated Press, March 28, 2003)

V

*"We'll win this war, but we'll win it only by fighting
and by showing the Germans that we've got more guts than
they have; or ever will have. We're not just going to shoot the
sons of bitches, we're going to rip out their living Goddamned
guts and use them to grease the treads of our tanks."*

General George S. Patton, Jr.

Viceroy: one of the fanciful titles applied by the media to
Lt. Gen. Jay Garner (ret.) after the Bush administration chose
him in January 2003 to take charge of civilian reconstruction in
"post-war" Iraq. Other appellations included viceroy-designate,
president-in-waiting, proconsul, king, and sheriff of Baghdad.

Garner's official title was Director of the Office of
Reconstruction and Humanitarian Assistance (ORHA). His
appointment, on the recommendation of Defense Secretary
Donald Rumsfeld, was immediately controversial. Among the
questions raised about Garner's past were his staunch defense of
the failed *Patriot Missile*, his ties with SY Coleman, a missile
defense contractor, and his public support for Israel. In 2000
Garner signed a statement praising Israel's "remarkable restraint"
in its treatment of Palestinians—a position hardly likely to inspire
Arab confidence in his leadership.

After the "official" *end of hostilities* in Iraq, Garner and a staff
of 200 arrived in Baghdad on April 21, 2003. They were charged
with stabilizing and rebuilding the country. Garner, appearing on
Iraqi television, pointed into the camera and assured the viewers
in his affable Texas accent "I'm here to help you rebuild your
country...most of you now have the electricity back on...over the
next few weeks you will all see these services restored." He went
on "You must return to work...you will be paid for your work,"
adding, "I'll be here for a short time."

He was right about the last point. On May 6, 2003 the Bush administration, professing disappointment with the slow pace of Garner's momentous task, replaced him with L. Paul Bremer III. Garner, according to the April 23, 2004 *New York Times*, had "told the BBC that he was sacked in part because he wanted to hold quick elections (see *occupation*).

Newsday Washington Bureau Chief Knut Royce commented (May 2, 2003), "The White House plans to name a politically astute career diplomat to replace Jay Garner...another former senior State Department official who worked with Bremer said that Bremer is a 'voracious opportunist with voracious ambitions...what he knows about Iraq could not quite fill a thimble.'" Garner's ORHA was replaced by Bremer's *Coalition Provisional Authority*, which would attempt to oversee the stabilization of Iraq from deep inside Baghdad's fortified *Green Zone.*

Jay Garner had been dubbed only half-in-jest as "Viceroy." The British had long used that label for the governor of a country or a province who ruled as a representative of the King. However, as book critic Simon Schama pointed out in the June 6,2003 *New Yorker*, there was little similarity between the rhetoric of Britain's most famous Viceroy—George Nathaniel, Viscount Curzon— and that of "Viceroy" Garner. Curzon, speaking of the British imperial mission, intoned "The message is carved in granite; it is hewn out of the rock of doom—that our work is righteous and it shall endure." Jay Garner, musing on the American role in Iraq concluded, "If we make headway on a lot of major things, we will put ourselves in a marvelous up-ramp where things can begin happening. If we don't do that we are on a negative ramp."

victory: in war, creating sufficient numbers of widows, orphans, and dead, blinded, burned or otherwise mutilated *enemy* so that the opponent finds it necessary to submit to your will. Sometimes these victories are described as *brilliant* and are said to bring *glory* to the victors.

Revered leaders send armies forth to seek victories. For example, in 1863 Abraham Lincoln exhorted Major Gen. Joseph Hooker, leader of the Army of the Potomac, "Beware of rashness, but with energy, and sleepless vigilance, bring us victories." When Hooker's men were defeated at the battle of Chancellorsville, he was demoted. Less fortunate were the 3,255 soldiers killed, the 18,868 who were wounded, and the 7,267 who were "captured/ missing" (see *war buff*).

Sometimes victory is declared prematurely. The April 8, 2003 Mirror.co.uk announced, "Allied forces have already won the war on Iraq. Colonel Chris Vernon...said at his field HQ "Militarily we've won the war. The British control Basra and U.S. forces will control Baghdad in days. Resistance is sporadic and incoherent."

W

"But in the long run, I always believe through transformation of heart, that's the ultimate real method to the elimination of terrorism. So in that case, compassion and friendship, dialogue and understanding, that's the only way to transform the emotion of [the] human heart. Force cannot change the human mind, the human heart."

the Dalai Lama

war buff: an individual who enjoys studying the tactics, maneuvers, and historical details of past wars. Such people often gather in groups to re-create famous battles, which to them appear to have been quite exciting, colorful events, particularly those occurring in the Civil War. They dress in detailed replicas of the uniforms of the period, carry the weapons of those days, and try to replay the drama of the long-ago conflicts on bloodless battlefields. After a day of glorious play, they and their families retire for refreshments. The ghosts of the maimed dead are not invited to the feast.

weapons of mass destruction (WMD): a collective term for *biological, chemical,* and *nuclear weapons.* The Bush administration's announced principal justification for attacking Iraq in 2003 was their claim that Saddam Hussein had these weapons in his arsenal, and that he was prepared to use them (see *Operation Iraqi Freedom*).

Vice President Dick Cheney told the Veterans of Foreign Wars 103rd National Convention on August 26, 2002 "Simply stated, there is no doubt that Saddam Hussein now has weapons of mass destruction. There is no doubt that he is amassing them to use against our friends, our allies, and against us." In his January 28, 2003 State of the Union address, President Bush warned "Saddam

Hussein has gone to elaborate lengths...to build and keep weapons of mass destruction—but why? The only possible explanation... is to dominate, intimidate, or attack." Among a series of "proofs" of his assertions, the president revealed, "The British government has learned that Saddam Hussein recently sought significant quantities of uranium from Africa" (see *yellowcake*).

These and many similar warnings proved to be false and misleading, but only after Operation Iraqi Freedom— a war which had long been sought by Bush's advisers (see *Committee for the Liberation of Iraq, Defense Planning Guidance, Project for the New American Century*).

In early January 2004 the Washington, D.C.-based Carnegie Endowment for International Peace—a non-partisan think tank— published a scathing assessment of the Bush administration's systematic misrepresentation that Iraq had posed a serious threat. Among the conclusions in the 107-page report, *Evidence and Implications* was "Administration officials systematically misrepresented the threat from Iraq's WMD and ballistic missile programs...The National Security Strategy's new doctrine of preemptive military action is actually a loose standard for preventive war under the cloak of legitimate preemption" (see *National Security Strategy, preemptive war, preventive war*).

In his January 20, 2004 State of the Union address, President Bush assured his listeners "the Kay Report identified dozens of weapons of mass destruction-related program activities." David Kay, chief U.S. weapons inspector, resigned one week later, having concluded that Saddam Hussein did not have stockpiles of WMD.

After years of searching, no evidence of WMD were found in Iraq. On February 24, 2004, the Associated Press reported Hans Blix, the former chief of weapons inspector as concluding "The justification for the war—the existence of weapons of mass destruction—was without foundation...Saddam was dangerous to his own people but not a great, and certainly not an immediate, danger to his neighbors and to the world."

The Carnegie Report urged the creation of a "non-partisan, independent commission" to look at the prewar intelligence claims that Iraq had WMD. On February 6, 2004 President Bush responded, under pressure from many members of Congress, by appointing a nine-member panel to examine intelligence information compiled not only on Iraq, but on North Korea, Iran, Libya, and Afghanistan as well. Haven given them such a wide-ranging task, the president gave them until March, 2005 to submit their conclusions—four months after the 2004 presidential elections.

On February 8, 2004 President Bush appeared on NBC's "Meet the Press With Tim Russert." In response to Russert's reminder that before *Operation Iraqi Freedom* the President, Vice President Dick Cheney, Secretary of State Colin Powell, and Defense Secretary Donald Rumsfeld had all said there was "no doubt" about Saddam Hussein's stockpiles of WMD, President Bush replied "...I don't want to get into word contests."

On October 6, 2004 U.S. arms inspector Charles A. Duelfer presented Congress with the conclusions of the Iraq Survey Group, a 1,200-member team charged with making the definitive search for WMD in Iraq. His report concluded, according to that day's *New York Times* " At the time of the American invasion...Iraq had not possessed military-scale stockpiles of illicit weapons for a dozen years and was not actively seeking to produce them."

President Bush's February 2, 2005 State of the Union address dropped the subject of WMD in Iraq. He referred vaguely to "regimes" still "seeking weapons of mass destruction" but added that "Iran" was "pursuing nuclear weapons" (see *axis of evil*).

win the peace: after attacking the *enemy,* devastating their land, and killing and injuring sufficient numbers of them to cause them to surrender, convince them that all the terrible destruction, death, and suffering was for their ultimate benefit. If any object to this largesse and become aggressive, they are to be terrified into submission, or if necessary, killed. Eventually all survivors are expected to be content with their lot.

Richard Nixon first made the phrase popular when he was a presidential candidate in 1968. Nixon promised that his "new leadership will end the war and win the peace." He did, in fact, end the war—five years later. Despite its dubious history, the phrase has become familiar rhetoric. For example, Defense Secretary Donald Rumsfeld wrote in a September 25, 2003 *Washington Post* editorial, "Then coalition forces took Baghdad in 21 days. Today Gen. Tom Franks's innovative and flexible war plan, which so many dismissed as a failure, is being studied by military historians and taught in war colleges. Today in Iraq, an innovative plan is also being implemented to win the peace." In then presidential candidate John Kerry's April 15, 2004 weekly radio address he said, "We have a duty to look ahead so that once victory on the battlefield is won, we have a plan to win the peace." (see *victory*).

Michele Fluornoy of the Center for Strategic and International Studies in Washington, D.C. was more specific in her recommendations. The August 20, 2003 *Baltimore Sun* reports Fluornoy, an "expert in post-conflict policy," as lamenting "When major combat ended, the coalition did not send an overwhelming force into Iraq to win the peace...If you compare the density of troops in Iraq to Kosovo or Bosnia, there is no comparison per capita, or by territory—so from the beginning, we never provided the manpower to overwhelm opponents and external threats."

Y

"Of all the enemies to public liberty, war is, perhaps, the most to be dreaded because it compromises and develops the germ of every other. In war, too, the discretionary power of the executive is extended...and all the means of seducing the minds are added to those of subduing the force of the people."

James Madison

yellowcake: lightly processed uranium ore useful for making nuclear weapons and for manufacturing reasons to justify waging war against Iraq.

In his January 2003 State of the Union speech, President George W. Bush said, "The British government has learned that Saddam Hussein recently sought significant quantities of uranium from Africa." This allegation would be a central argument in the Bush administration's insistence that the Saddam Hussein regime was an imminent threat and had to be destroyed.

The International Atomic Energy Agency (IAEA) had long since concluded that Iraq had no nuclear weapons or facilities for their production. However, in the late 1990s Iraqi defectors were telling Ahmad Chalabi and other members of the *Iraqi National Congress* elaborate tales about Saddam Hussein's active nuclear, biological and chemical weapons programs. None of this information could be corroborated by the CIA or the State Department (see *democratization, Defense Policy Board, Iraqi National Congress*).

Investigative reporter Seymour M. Hersh revealed in the October 27, 2003 *New Yorker* that "some senior [Bush] administration people, soon after coming into power, had bypassed the government's customary procedures for vetting [screening] intelligence." This gave them, according to Kenneth

Pollack, a former National Security Council expert on Iraq "information to back up their public claims, but it was often very bad information."

In this case, the information was very bad indeed. In the fall of 2001, soon after the attacks on September 11, a discredited intelligence report from Italy's Military Intelligence Service (SISMI) suggesting that Iraq's ambassador to the Vatican had traveled to the African country of Niger in 1999 to purchase uranium ore (yellowcake) for Iraq caught the attention of Vice-President Dick Cheney. Already eager to build a case for attacking Iraq, Cheney pursued the report relentlessly in spite of repeated denials of its accuracy. In early 2002, Secretary of State Colin Powell would tell the House International Relations Committee, "With respect to the nuclear program there is no doubt that the Iraqi are pursuing it."

In February 2002 the CIA sent retired Ambassador Joseph Wilson to Niger to get to the bottom of the story. Wilson reported that there was no substance to the allegations. The White House preferred to remain unconvinced of such denials. On August 7, 2002 Vice-President Cheney said of Saddam Hussein, "What we know now, from various sources, is that he...continues to pursue a nuclear weapon." British Prime Minister Tony Blair weighed in with a September 27, 2002 dossier in which he stated "The assessed intelligence has established beyond doubt that Saddam... continues in his efforts to develop nuclear weapons."

In October 2002 an Italian businessman offered to sell a photocopy of an intriguing twenty-two-page document to an Italian newspaper. The documents appeared to contain evidence that Iraq's Vatican ambassador had in fact tried to purchase yellowcake from Niger—but the story was soon shown to be pure fiction. However, the document—which earlier would never have made its way to higher levels—arrived at the Pentagon. Hersh comments "Everybody at every step along the way knew they were false—until they got to the Pentagon, where they were believed."

On January 26, 2003 Secretary of State Powell, in a speech before the World Economic Forum asked, "Why is Iraq still trying to procure uranium?" Two days later, in his 2003 State of the Union speech, President Bush kept the fable alive, attributing the discovery of the attempted uranium deal to "The British government."

The IAEA finally got to see the Niger documents in February 2003, a few days after the President's speech. Their investigation quickly showed that the documents were crude forgeries. In fact, the still-anonymous fabricator(s) got the name of the foreign minister and of the government itself wrong. However, Seymour M. Hersh recounted, "On March 16th, Cheney, appearing on 'Meet the Press'...[said] 'I don't have any reason to believe they (the IAEA) are any more valid this time than they have been in the past.' Three days later, the war in Iraq got under way, and the tale of the African-uranium-forgery sank from view."

In a July 6, 2003 op-ed article in *The New York Times* Joseph Wilson wrote: "Based on my experience with the administration in the months leading up to the war, I have little choice but to conclude that some of the intelligence related to Iraq's nuclear weapons program was twisted to exaggerate the Iraqi threat...If... information was ignored because it did not fit certain preconceptions about Iraq, then a legitimate argument can be made that we went to war under false pretenses."

Joseph Wilson soon was rewarded for his candor. According to Wilson, I. Lewis "Scooter" Libby, the vice president's chief of staff, along with one other White House "official" leaked the story that Wilson's wife Valerie was a CIA analyst and had urged that the C.I.A. send him on the investigative trip to Niger. Columnist Robert Novak published the story on July 14, 2003 in the *Washington Post*. Wilson stated in the May 2, 2004 *Miami Herald*, "...revealing the name of a CIA operative is not only dangerous—

to her and her sources—it can also be against the law."

On July 9, 2003 White House Press Secretary Ari Fleischer admitted to reporters "We now know that the yellowcake ties to Niger were not accurate." He added that although the specific reference to Niger yellowcake was incorrect "That does not change the fundamental case from being right...Saddam Hussein had biological and chemical weapons that were unaccounted for that we're still confident that we'll find. It will take as long as it takes until they (WMD) are discovered."

On July 15,2003 President Bush told reporters "I think the intelligence I get is darn good intelligence." Nevertheless, the President's Foreign Intelligence Advisory Board concluded in December 2003 that the White House had been so "anxious to grab onto something affirmative" that it had disregarded criticisms of the yellowcake-related reports. In his January 28, 2004 State of the Union Speech the President could only offer the tortuous excuse that recent investigations had uncovered "dozens of weapons of mass destruction-related program activities." He offered no details.

V

W

About the Author

Thomas F. Lee, Ph.D. has been a biologist, professor, researcher, and social activist for over thirty-five years. He is a frequent contributor to *Encyclopedia Americana* and is the author of five books. These include *The Human Genome Project: Cracking the Genetic Code of Life* and *Gene Future: The Promises and Perils of the New Biology* in which he explains the science as well as the ethical controversies surrounding modern biotechnology. In *Battlebabble* the author shares his conviction that war is not the final solution to political conflicts, but a totally unacceptable alternative, ravaging its perpetrators as well as its intended victims. The language surrounding war softens its brutal realities, and serves as a vehicle to engender public support and encourage participation under the guise of patriotism. The author offers realistic, honest definitions of this language so often used by government and media.

The author lives with his wife Eileen in Goffstown, New Hampshire. They have six children.

dirklee45@hotmail.com